Tourist Behaviour

ASPECTS OF TOURISM
Series Editors: Professor Chris Cooper, *University of Queensland, Australia*
Dr C. Michael Hall, *University of Otago, Dunedin, New Zealand*
Dr Dallen Timothy, *Arizona State University, Tempe, USA*

Aspects of Tourism is an innovative, multifaceted series which will comprise authoritative reference handbooks on global tourism regions, research volumes, texts and monographs. It is designed to provide readers with the latest thinking on tourism world-wide and in so doing will push back the frontiers of tourism knowledge. The series will also introduce a new generation of international tourism authors, writing on leading edge topics. The volumes will be readable and user-friendly, providing accessible sources for further research. The list will be underpinned by an annual authoritative tourism research volume. Books in the series will be commissioned that probe the relationship between tourism and cognate subject areas such as strategy, development, retailing, sport and environmental studies. The publisher and series editors welcome proposals from writers with projects on these topics.

Other Books in the Series
Tourism, Mobility and Second Homes
  C. Michael Hall and Dieter Müller
Strategic Management for Tourism Communities: Bridging the Gaps
  Peter E. Murphy and Ann E. Murphy
Oceania: A Tourism Handbook
  Chris Cooper and C. Michael Hall (eds)
Tourism Marketing: A Collaborative Approach
  Alan Fyall and Brian Garrod
Music and Tourism: On the Road Again
  Chris Gibson and John Connell
Tourism Development: Issues for a Vulnerable Industry
  Julio Aramberri and Richard Butler (eds)
Nature-based Tourism in Peripheral Areas: Development or Disaster?
  C. Michael Hall and Stephen Boyd (eds)
Tourism, Recreation and Climate Change
  C. Michael Hall and James Higham (eds)
Shopping Tourism, Retailing and Leisure
  Dallen J. Timothy
Wildlife Tourism
  David Newsome, Ross Dowling and Susan Moore
Film-Induced Tourism
  Sue Beeton
Rural Tourism and Sustainable Business
  Derek Hall, Irene Kirkpatrick and Morag Mitchell (eds)
The Tourism Area Life Cycle, Vol.1: Applications and Modifications
  Richard W. Butler (ed.)
The Tourism Area Life Cycle, Vol.2: Conceptual and Theoretical Issues
  Richard W. Butler (ed.)

For more details of these or any other of our publications, please contact:
Channel View Publications, Frankfurt Lodge, Clevedon Hall,
Victoria Road, Clevedon, BS21 7HH, England
http://www.channelviewpublications.com

ASPECTS OF TOURISM 27
Series Editors: Chris Cooper (*University of Queensland, Australia*),
C. Michael Hall (*University of Otago, New Zealand*)
and Dallen Timothy (*Arizona State University, USA*)

Tourist Behaviour
Themes and Conceptual Schemes

Philip L. Pearce

CHANNEL VIEW PUBLICATIONS
Clevedon • Buffalo • Toronto

Special thanks to Anne Sharp
in recognition of our sustained professional partnership

Library of Congress Cataloging in Publication Data
Pearce, Philip L.
Tourist Behaviour: Themes and Conceptual Schemes/Philip L. Pearce.
Aspects of Tourism: 27
Includes bibliographical references and index.
1. Travelers–Psychology. 2. Tourism–Psychological aspects. 3. Tourism–Social aspects.
I. Title. II. Series.
G155.A1P3622 2005
910'.01'9–dc22   2005003806

British Library Cataloguing in Publication Data
A catalogue entry for this book is available from the British Library.

ISBN 1-84541-023-8 /EAN 978-1-84541-023-0 (hbk)
ISBN 1-84541-022-X / EAN 978-1-84541-022-3 (pbk)
ISBN 1-84541-024-6 / EAN 978-1-84541-024-7 (electronic)

Channel View Publications
An imprint of Multilingual Matters Ltd

UK: Frankfurt Lodge, Clevedon Hall, Victoria Road, Clevedon BS21 7HH.
USA: 2250 Military Road, Tonawanda, NY 14150, USA.
Canada: 5201 Dufferin Street, North York, Ontario, Canada M3H 5T8.

Typeset by Wordworks Ltd.
Printed and bound in Great Britain by the Cromwell Press.

Contents

Preface

What tourists do, and why they do it has fascinated a lot of people. What tourists think, how they feel and what influences their thoughts and feelings is especially fascinating to tourists themselves, to the people who manage their behaviour and to analysts studying contemporary life.

This volume tackles in a fresh way many of the core topics in tourist behaviour. While it is no way a second edition to one of the author's earliest books - The Social Psychology of Tourist Behaviour, Oxford: Pergamon, 1982 - it does follow in part the structure of that volume, and covers parallel territory. The benefit of nearly 25 years of research, and the changing face of tourism and global travel are reflected in many ways in the present work. There are now a variety of promising schemes and mini theories, 'conceptual schemes' as they will be referred to in this book, which help illuminate long standing tourist behaviour topics.

The author has been fortunate to work with talented colleagues in a stable academic environment. These efforts and forces have fostered a productive publication stream from the James Cook University tourism group, some of which is reported in relevant sections of this volume. In particular, several key individuals have assisted the author's thinking and working environment and deserve special credit. Key colleagues include Gianna Moscardo, Laurie Murphy, Lui Lee, Chiemi Yagi, Aram Son, Pierre Benckendorff, Glenn Ross and Robyn Yesberg.

While it is appropriate to record the special efforts of local colleagues there are also wider influences contributing to the enthusiasm for writing about this area. Colleagues in the Unites States, notably Joe O'Leary and Alastair Morrison, have been good friends, interested observers and at times partners in the author's work. A set of colleagues in Asia, the United Kingdom, Europe and Africa have helped the author maintain an interest in the usefulness and diverse applicability of tourist behaviour across cultures.

The volume is intended to be both a resource and an integrating force for the analysis of an important part of tourism. It seeks to be educational rather than prescriptive, probing new ways of tackling topics. It is eclectic in its methodological tolerance rather than narrowly defined. Like tourism itself, it is hoped that it will fulfil multiple needs in diverse settings.

Philip L. Pearce
Australia, 2005

Chapter 1
Studying Tourist Behaviour

Beyond the Personal Perspective

The noted adventurer and travel writer Redmond O'Hara argues that you write well about a topic only if you have experienced it and, at times, have been traumatised by it (O'Hara, 2003). Does the author, a Professor of Tourism, have just such a range of traumatic experiences to help him write about tourist behaviour? Fortunately the answer is, yes. Some incidents include being petrified in Panama City, being propositioned in Phuket, and being mugged in Marseille. On other occasions the experiences have included enduring all-day airline delays in China. In one such delay in X'ian, the one available plastic seat in the airport lounge was not made any more comfortable by the public announcer's frequent call – 'The flight to Shanghai is not leaving because the plane is somewhere else'. There is indeed much personal material upon which to draw. Undoubtedly readers too have varied and sometimes traumatic personal experiences to recount: effectively titillating tales to tell about their travels.

Nevertheless this is a research-based account of tourist behaviour and, while it might have been stimulated and enriched by personal experiences, it relies much more on the empirical work of an immediate research circle, on the efforts of leading scholars in tourist behaviour and on a diverse array of insights from occasional contributors to this field of study. It draws on the disciplines of psychology, sociology and anthropology but is most dependent on the emerging specialism of tourism studies, itself now a productive global research field (Jafari, 2000; Pearce, 1993a). The term behaviour will be interpreted in its widest psychological sense in this volume as a summary for the observable activities as well as the mental processes guiding and resulting from social life (Harré & Secord, 1972).

One particular advantage of adhering to a title with behaviour as the leading description of the area of interest is that it provides a focused reminder of the physical nature of human existence. Since much of the writing about tourists' views of their travels is sociological, and hence is often concerned with abstract systems and social structures, there is an emerging argument that demands that researchers recognise the limits, needs and characteristics of the human body in tourist study (Selanniemi, 2003). This may be as simple as recognising motion sickness and the effects of sleep deprivation on mood, or it may generate new conceptual

1

appraisals such as in augmenting conventional ideas about destination images with a fuller recognition of the sensory responses that humans have to environments (Ashcroft, 2001; Veijola & Jokinen, 1994).

Additionally the term tourist behaviour is useful to both link and differentiate the material from the broader yet distinctively different literature describing consumer behaviour. The nature of these differences will be explored later in this chapter.

A further dimension of interest in the present volume that extends the study beyond a personal perspective lies in the geographical reach and scope of the material considered. A partial focus of this volume will be on emerging studies of tourist behaviour in Asia but these additional contributions will be viewed against a backdrop of several decades of work conducted predominantly in North America, Australia, New Zealand and the United Kingdom. Some insights from European scholars will also be considered in select chapters.

A final and definitive extension of the present work beyond the personal perspective is the planned and systematic use of conceptual schemes and mini-theories to explain and interpret the topics pursued.

The Sin of Homogenisation

Tourists are not all alike. In fact, they are staggeringly diverse in age, motivation, level of affluence and preferred activities. Galani-Moutafi (1999) and Nash (2001) warn would-be analysts of tourist behaviour to avoid the sin of homogenisation, of treating all travellers as the same. They recommend that researchers should specify, wherever possible, which types of tourists are being discussed. The warning is appropriate at the start of a book on tourist behaviour. There will be few easy generalisations about tourists in the following pages. An important aim of the volume will be to provide multi-faceted accounts of the complexity of tourist behaviour while still recognising that it is convenient for both analysis and practice to work at the level of meaningful groups or market segments rather than purely individual experience. The importance of avoiding the sin of homogenisation will be re-emphasised in Chapter 2, where some of the key demographic factors frequently used to describe tourists are considered.

A Professional Approach: The Etic–Emic Distinction

An important step in moving towards a professional appraisal of tourist behaviour lies in recognising that there are multiple perspectives on behaviour. In particular one important approach arising out of research in linguistics and anthropology is the etic–emic distinction (Pike, 1966; Triandis, 1972). An *emic* approach is one that takes the perspective of the participant – the person engaging in the behaviour. The topic of interest may be the experiences of a young budget traveller, a senior tourist or an ardent birdwatcher, for example. The emic approach to their behaviour involves finding out from them how they see the world, how they look at the setting, the other people in it and the value of their experience. This can be contrasted with an *etic* approach where the researcher, as an observer and outsider, classifies and describes the tourist's behaviour. An example might be studying a young European budget traveller sun-tanning on an Australian beach. If the researcher asks the traveller to describe his or her experience (i.e. works at obtaining an emic perspective), the response may be 'Actually I'm worshipping the sun god. This is a deep cosmic experience for me to lie in the sun in wintertime because I come from Finland and fundamentally there is so little sun that this is absolutely marvellous for me'. The outside observer may simply have interpreted the behaviour as everyday relaxation. The core distinction is that, when researchers ask people to describe their experiences in their own words and not according to pre-judged categories, they are adopting an emic perspective and beginning to see the socially-constructed world from the participants' point of view (Gergen, 1978).

It can be suggested that both new students of tourist behaviour and senior scholars sometimes struggle with the multiple realities and challenges inherent in identifying emic and etic perspectives. For the new scholar it is sometimes difficult to see that a travel experience that he or she would never undertake could be fulfilling and rewarding for someone else. For example, a not-very-affluent student might find the expenditure on a luxurious hotel room at several hundred dollars a night to be an incomprehensible choice when the same amount of money might buy a camping trip with a white-water-rafting experience and a skydiving thrill. Equally, the cautious quieter tourist with a deep interest in wildlife experiences might find large expenditure on nightclubs, drinks and a party lifestyle in such Mediterranean resorts as Ibiza and the Greek Islands to be socially unattractive. The issues here extend beyond understanding to personal identity and deeply held social values.

Senior scholars too sometimes fail to grasp the range of meanings that certain subgroups of travellers bring to a setting. Thus de Albuquerque (1998) effectively scoffs at the notions of romantic tourism proposed by Pruitt and La Font (1995). He discounts the perspective that indirect payment by women for their companionship experiences with Caribbean beach boys constitutes romantic and meaningful relationships, and argues that it is simply prostitution. The fact that he failed to interview the women themselves and obtain an emic perspective somewhat compromises his argument.

In the arena of research into visitor conflict and crowding, Jacob and Shreyer (1980) have argued that disagreements sometimes arise because participants have a low tolerance of lifestyle diversity. Such a concept may partially explain the lack of insights described in the examples above, but there is more involved than simple tolerance. It is about recognising the full appreciation and value that other people experience from a different style of travel behaviours. The understanding and empathy for other people's behaviour that can be developed by emphasising an academic emic perspective is of considerable relevance in the tourism educational sphere. Young managers and junior executives assisting tourists, and designing and marketing experiences for them, have to be able to know empathically how their target group of visitors view the world. It can be argued here that a professional and workplace understanding of tourist perspectives can be built from researcher insights generated by building and distinguishing emic and etic perspectives.

Expressions within the Field

Rojek and Urry (1997: 1) report that tourism studies are beset with definitional problems, and comment that tourism 'embraces so many different notions that it is hardly useful as a term of social science'. Pearce, Morrison and Rutledge (1998) suggest that the emphasis placed on defining tourism depends on the goal of the analyst or practitioner. In this view what is emphasised in a definition of tourism will depend on the commentator, with planners, forecasters, academics and managers attending to different processes, connections and hierarchies of interest. For most tourism researchers, a working pathway through this definitional maze has been to subscribe to a basic or *core systems* model of tourism (c.f. Leiper, 1989; Mill & Morrison, 1985). The need to update and expand the reach of this core systems model is a topic of contemporary concern (Farrell & Twining-Ward, 2004). An additional difficulty is that tourism researchers frequently use words and expressions that are in everyday use. It is then difficult at times to impose more formal, tighter and more specific meanings on top of the existing language use. The very word 'tourist' is its own definitional problem child. Its first use and origins lie in the 17th century as a descriptor of the travellers undertaking the Grand Tour (Hibbert, 1969). It is used pejoratively by some to describe a superficial appraisal or experience of phenomenon and by others as a marker of affluence and freedom (Dann, 1996a). The word is used to describe both international and domestic travellers. The World Tourism Organisation definition of a tourist relates exclusively to international tourists. In this statistics-collecting framework, tourists are overnight visitors who cross international boundaries for periods of up to a year. Some travellers who are not included in the World Tourism Organisation statistics are diplomats, military personnel, refugees, people in transit, nomads and migrants (Pearce *et al.*, 1998). More than 170 countries around the world have now agreed to conform to these definitional conventions in recording international arrivals. Nevertheless, for a study of tourist behaviour, particularly where there is an interest in the management of tourists, this definition is perhaps not as complex or complete as might be required. In particular it provides no guidance on how domestic tourists should be classified.

A study conducted by Masberg (1998) reflects the slippery and shifting definition of domestic tourists by regional authorities. Masberg interviewed managers and executives of convention and visitor bureaux (CVBs) in the United States. These organisations are often involved in lobbying for the expansion of tourism in the region and offer quite all-inclusive definitions of tourists. Some of the respondents defined their domestic tourists as 'people who travel 50 miles (80 kilometres) to come here', others said 'it's people who stay overnight in our region', while a third group suggested 'it's people who are here for pleasure'. These tourism organisation perspectives from the United States would probably be replicated in many other parts of the world, as an indication of growing visitor numbers is often an important argument when such CVBs seek funding from allied businesses and governments. The critical issue here is to be explicit in the definitions of the term 'tourist' when communicating research findings and in interpreting community perspectives on tourism. Clearly, not all researchers and analysts hold and work with exactly the same definition of the tourist as do their audiences. In the present volume, 'domestic tourists' will usually refer to visitors from outside the region of interest who stay for at least one night. The broader term of 'visitor' will be used to embrace international tourists, domestic tourists and tourist-facility users from the local region or home town.

'Consumer' is also a term used widely in literature that is relevant to this volume. It refers to people in both the public and private sector who are involved in the purchasing and experiencing of products. There are often specialist courses in consumer behaviour in universities and there are many parallels between consumer and tourist behaviour. Regrettably, the term 'consumer' has some negative connotations. Studies of consumer behaviour and the general use of the term 'consumption' have traditionally not addressed good environmental practices, good community links, and socially responsible actions. Overall there has been a tendency for studies in the mainstream consumer behaviour literature to pay limited attention to sustainability issues (Gee & Fayos-Sola, 1997). An awareness of this connotation is necessary in tourist behaviour studies where sustainability issues are a dominant focus (Moscardo, 1999).

The word 'customer' tends to have a business focus, and is used less in public settings, but is frequently employed in business or private sector settings. The term will be used from time to time in this volume, particularly when exploring and reflecting on the large topic of customer satisfaction.

There are some other useful terms that focus on the individual and his or her behaviour in relation to tourism settings. Sometimes the word 'user' is employed. This is a term that is useful in certain public facility contexts. Just as 'customer' is useful in a business context, the term 'user' is valuable when discussing individuals or groups who may be travelling along a highway and using open access public facilities such as a rest area. Both in everyday life and in the existing literature, commentators refer to a highway user or a beach user, rather than to a customer in such contexts.

'Client' is another expression that is occasionally useful. The term is usually reserved for professional services, so there are legal clients and clients for financial services. Travel agents often refer to their customers as clients. It is apparent that the term client connotes a serious professional service and may be used to upgrade the status of an industry sector. Indeed, it is quite common for the word client to be used in the sex trade (Ryan & Kinder, 1996).

'Participants' and 'stakeholders' are further terms of broad relevance to this discussion. They both refer to settings where the person is involved in a partnership, or acts in an advisory capacity. Many natural environment management agencies have stakeholder groups – people who help the agency staff make decisions about the settings that they caretake.

To complete the framework of relevant terms there are other circumstances where a person might be labelled a patient, a player, a spectator, an audience or a crowd member and some of these studies will be relevant to the interest in tourism. Nevertheless the focus of the volume will be specifically on tourists and tourist behaviour.

Tourist Behaviour: To Whom Does It Matter?

First, tourist behaviour tends to matter to tourists. People are concerned with their life experience – what they do – and they like to understand it. So, one answer to the question is that tourists themselves are very concerned with their own experiences and how to maximise each one, whether it be a short regional visit or an extended international holiday.

A second answer to the question is that tourist behaviour matters to people who are making decisions about tourists. There is a whole array of such decision-makers. They may be people in the public sector who provide permits for tour operators; they may be managers who let others go to the Great Barrier Reef or white-water rafting, or canoe down one of the scenic rivers in North America. All sorts of people are concerned with tourist behaviour because their job involves making an enabling decision or policy choice about tourist activities.

A subdivision in the types of decision making clarifies the kinds of people involved. There are public decision-makers who make either policy or management decisions about on-site behaviour. There are marketers in joint public–private cooperative endeavours whose interests include such factors as what will influence travellers to come to place A, B or C. There are also business decision makers concerned with the design and financial success of tourism products. These kinds of interests focus on what tourists will prefer and how they make their travel choices and purchases. Tourism industry lobby groups may also be interested in select tourist behaviour issues, particularly topics such as user-pays fees and taxes on activities.

There are further groups who are less frequently interested in tourist behaviour. For example, if tourists are creating certain kinds of impacts (maybe positive ones such as economic impacts, or even negative socio-cultural and environmental impacts), the local community and then the media may find tourist behaviour noteworthy. In turn political comment

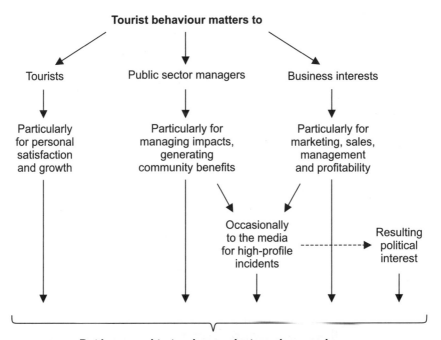

Figure 1.1 To whom does tourist behaviour matter?

on tourist behaviour can quickly follow. In an overarching generic sense, the individuals with the most enduring and consistent interest in studying tourist behaviour are business analysts and academic researchers. Their work influences and considers the needs of the decision-makers as well as addressing the interests of the tourists themselves. It is their work that is the basis of this volume. A summary of these interested parties is presented in Figure 1.1.

Approaching Tourist Behaviour

Links to other study topics in tourism

The topic of tourist behaviour depends upon, interacts with, and occasionally determines other components of tourism. Tourist behaviour is powerfully connected to and often contingent upon marketing activities: it strongly shapes the wellbeing of many small businesses, and it can generate considerable socio-cultural and environmental impacts. These influences should not, however, be extended too far. Tourist behaviour is indirectly connected to tourism issues such as globalisation and localisation; it influences only peripherally major financial decisions on infrastructure investment and as a specific topic it attracts relatively little attention in governmental policies.

It is widely recognised in the tourism literature that the phenomenon of tourism is built on interconnected elements that are variously represented in systems-type diagrams (Farrell & Twining-Ward, 2004; Gunn, 1994a; Leiper, 1979; Mathieson & Wall, 1982; Mill & Morrison, 1992; Murphy, 1985; Pearce, Moscardo & Ross, 1996). The emphasis given to tourists and, implicitly, their behaviour in these global descriptive and summary models is quite varied.

An important feature of these systems models and descriptions of tourism is the way in which change is conceptualised. In some of the early approaches, the systems were implicitly linked to a linear view of change with incremental improvement or growth in one part of the system (such as airport access) generating neatly corresponding growth in other systems elements (such as visitor attendance at attractions) (e.g. Mill & Morrison, 1992; Murphy, 1985). In the last decade a number of tourism scholars, as well as analysts with tourism interests from allied disciplines such as ecology, sociology and biology, have challenged the linear model of change and suggested that a more dynamic, constantly-evolving non-linear and chaos-theory driven approach to the evolution of tourism places is also appropriate (Farrell & Twining-Ward, 2004; Faulkner & Russell, 1997; McKercher, 1999; Walker *et al.*, 1999).

As Gould (2004) observes, it is sometimes too easy in the world of academic discourse to be drawn into tidy dichotomies where the views of one group are seen as entirely incompatible with the perspectives of the other. In biology the expression 'consilience' is employed to depict the desire to respect knowledge systems and approaches by identifying those realms of convenience where each approach operates with most insight (Wilson, 1998). It can be proposed that what is needed here in outlining tourism systems and change is intelligent eclecticism where there is 'a patchwork of independent affirmations' (Gould, 2004) rather than a simple victory for one view or a false union of ideas.

The study of tourist behaviour as a consequential and contributing element in tourism systems is rarely treated in a specific way in tourism systems diagrams (c.f. Farrell & Twining-Ward, 2004). Nevertheless some of the themes concerning tourist behaviour that are dealt with in this volume (specifically tourist motivation, tourist destination choice, tourist satisfaction and learning) deal with change, growth and development. The conceptual schemes that inform these themes, consistent with the larger perspectives on tourism systems as a whole, will not always be simple linear growth models, but will also consider discontinuous, episodic and chaotic change mechanisms and incidents.

The need not to overstate the role of tourist behaviour is also brought out by the systems-style diagrams. For Gunn, and Farrell and Twining-Ward in particular, there is a range of forces operating outside the core tourism system that are described as salient overarching contexts for the operation of tourism. Tourist behaviour matters, but it is a link and a force in understanding tourism; it is not always going to be what matters most in solving tourism problems or developing tourism in a region.

Tourist Behaviour and Consumer Behaviour

There are several critical dimensions that create differences between tourist behaviour and consumer behaviour. One such major difference lies in the extended phases that surround tourist activities. Clawson and Knetsch (1966) identified five such phases. They noted: (1) an anticipation or pre-purchase (2) a travel to the site segment, (3) an on-site experience, (4) a return travel component, and (5) an extended recall and recollection stage.

Consumer behaviour, as a field of inquiry with its own journals, textbooks and courses, is centrally focused on the choices of products and the satisfaction with products (Bagozzi *et al.*, 2002; Schutte & Carlante, 1998). In each phase of tourist behaviour outlined by Clawson and Knetsch, some differences from the standard consumer behaviour studies can be noted. In the first anticipation phase, many tourists plan for and fantasise about their forthcoming travel for months, sometimes years ahead. While this might be similar for the purchase of a motor vehicle, it is somewhat absurd when applied, for example, to the purchase of hair shampoo or groceries. Models of behaviour built on the latter examples are unlikely to be relevant to tourist behaviour.

For both the travel to the site and the return travel phases of tourist behaviour there is no sensible analogy in the consumer behaviour literature. Yet, the anticipatory elements of tourist experiences are heightened by the need to access the visited location and such travel is often an integral part of the total experience. Further, and from a business perspective, the pre- and post-travel phases are important subcomponents of the total expenditure that travellers must make to access the on-site experience.

The central phase of Clawson and Knetsch's typology is about being somewhere. Typically this is an intangible experience, an opportunity to view, absorb, feel, hear and sense the place visited. McCarthy describes it as:

> The magic that some places hold, that special feeling that embraces landscape and history and our personal associations, but somehow goes beyond the sum of them. Energy. Spirit ... call it what you like. It's just words to describe a real experience we can't explain when we get that shiver or the hairs stand up. (McCarthy, 2000: 370)

The peak and flow experiences of travellers occupy much attention in the tourism and leisure literature (Bammel & Bammel, 1992; Mannell & Kleiber, 1997). While there are clearly other services and intangible products studied in the consumer behaviour literature (education, for example, can be cast in this framework), the deeply personal reactions and sometimes the socio-environmental consequences of the tourists' on-site behaviour are distinctive.

Finally, but not insignificantly, the reflection phase of tourist experience is often long lasting. People think about their tourist experiences a month, two months, sometimes years after they have been to the site. In this sense the experienced product does not decay or wear out and may indeed be augmented by ongoing information about the site or by repeat visits. The centrality of experience as the product in tourism is consistent with the wider treatment of what has been termed the experience economy (Pine & Gilmour, 1999). Certainly individuals frequently tell travel stories, re-examine photographs, have group reunions and write long travelogues about their past adventures (Pearce, 1991a; Yagi, 2001). Consumer behaviour research is concerned with and has produced some distinguished contributions to understanding satisfaction but with many products purchased there is a limited and over time waning enthusiasm to reflect on their lasting contribution to one's life.

The distinctive phases of tourist behaviour study have stimulated a number of conceptual approaches and concerns in the literature. For example, an emphasis on the meanings of time, on thresholds and change, on place and identity are all partly driven by the distinctive phases of the tourist experience (c.f. Ryan, 2002a).

Another marked difference between much consumer behaviour and tourist behaviour is that the latter is a part of a very social business. Tourism is a people-to-people business in both its consumption and its production. Tourists are frequently with others, and often jointly decide upon and frequently share their tourist experience. The businesses that serve tourists (the hotels, the airlines, the tour operators, the attractions) and the larger visited community (who are sometimes passive extras in the total tourism production) are inherently performers on a social stage (Crang, 1997). It is therefore important to treat models of consumer behaviour built on non-social modes of production and consumption with some caution if attempts to extrapolate them to tourist choice and satisfaction are attempted.

A particular instance of this difficulty of extrapolating a consumer behaviour model to tourist behaviour lies in the treatment of expectations and their role in satisfaction. The topic will be pursued in more detail in Chapter 7 but it is sufficient to note here that the match is inexact. As de Botton observed when writing about arriving in Barbados:

> Nothing was as I had imagined – surprising only if one considers what I had imagined ... a beach with a palm tree against the setting sun ...a hotel bungalow with a view through French doors .. an azure sky .. But on arrival a range of things insisted that they too deserved to be included within the fold of the word Barbados.. a large petrol storage facility ...an immigration official ...in an immaculate brown suit ...an advertisement for rum ..a picture of the Prime Minister ..a confusion of taxi drivers and tour guides outside the terminal building ...we are inclined to forget how much there is in the world beside that which we anticipate. (De Botton, 2002: 13)

De Botton reminds the researcher and tourism analyst that the expectations for even a large and expensive purchase item such as an automobile are likely to be much clearer than for the multi-faceted holiday destination.

There is a further non-trivial distinction between consumer products and the opportunities that arise from travel purchases. Most consumer products of some complexity come with an owner's manual. These kinds of documents provide operational instructions, safety hints, advice on replacement parts or persons to whom one can direct service inquiries. Perhaps the closest parallel in the world of tourist behaviour is the guide-book. Even here, however, there is a range of guide books for any one place. The holiday consumer is free to consult multiple owner manuals, to redesign and further refine his or her experience. Tourists interact with their destination and this mutual influence process is sometimes assisted by interpretation, which is itself a process of presenting places for tourist use. The ability of tourists to refine and reshape their experiences as they are participating in them is a distinctively tourist behaviour dimension.

A case study illustrates the power of this issue in tourist settings. In the Kimberleys in Western Australia there is a local setting described by one tourist officer as 'the best tourist site in the Kimberleys'. To reach the site is in itself an experience, demanding travel on rough roads and through dry landscapes sprinkled with a few spectacular Boab or 'bottle' trees. On arrival the visitor is confronted with a long stock trough and acres of barren cattle paddocks. By itself the attraction and the setting are at best not compelling, less kindly, it is a depressing wasteland. But an enthusiastic presentation that identifies the site as the conclusion of the longest stock drives in the world and relates it to the pioneering history of the Kimberleys rich in social drama, transforms the ordinary into the notable. In the language of some tourism analysts, it transforms the profane into the sacred (Graburn, 1989). Tourists, both with assistance and (sometimes) by themselves can transform their ongoing product experiences.

There is also a view that the study of tourist behaviour is really market research. There is a considerable interest in tourism studies in the analysis of markets. Nevertheless much of the published tourism work is reflective and contains more ideas to understand both the segments identified and the marketing implications than studies done within the commercial consultancy world. For example academic research studies in tourism markets have incorporated such ideas as convergence and divergence of segments (Pizam, 1999a), cross-cultural market variability (Richards & Richards, 1998), and the discriminatory power of different segmentation approaches (Moscardo, Pearce & Morrison, 1996). The further elaboration of how commercial market research differs from academic studies in tourist behaviour can be achieved by understanding the importance of conceptual schemes in the construction and interpretation of market related research in this field.

Conceptual Schemes, Theories and Tourism Study

The subtitle of this book employs the expression 'conceptual schemes'. The expression stresses the value of using some level of abstraction and academic organisation to understand tourist behaviour. For the purposes of this book the term conceptual schemes refers to the use of well-defined and interconnected concepts as summary and explanatory tools in eluci-dating how tourist behaviour arises and functions. Conceptual schemes go beyond both description and mere re-statements or re-labelling of the observed world. They are not, however, fully functioning theories (Blalock, 1969; Greene, 1994).

One important distinction between conceptual schemes and theories lies in the greater formality and organisation of a theory. The component parts of a theory include axioms or assumptions, proposed linked concepts (i.e. conceptual schemes) and propositions that formally interrelate two or more concepts at a time (Baron & Byrne, 1997; Gross, 2001). In this sense conceptual schemes are partial or pre-theories, they tend not to be cast as predictive sets of propositions for further testing, especially statistical testing, but they could be used to develop theory.

Conceptual schemes are more abstract and organised than empirical generalisations. Even a lengthy list of what is known about a specific topic does not constitute a conceptual scheme. The format in which conceptual schemes can be expressed is variable. They may simply be verbal statements specifying relationships. They can include typologies and taxonomies that are either categorical or ordinal systems. They may also be models that are non-semantic devices to portray relationships amongst factors and variables (Pors, 2000).

Models are a particularly important subcategory of conceptual schemes since diagrammatic and spatially-portrayed links between variables and forces tend to have considerable power as a mechanism for the communication of ideas (Blalock, 1969). In addition, conceptual schemes can include stage or sequence approaches that define steps in an ordered process.

The fact that the author selects and employs the concept of conceptual schemes in this volume, may lead readers to deduce that the author believes there are few true theories of tourist behaviour. Such a deduction is correct. It is not, however, a corollary of this view that the lack of theory makes the study of tourist behaviour less interesting, less sophisticated or less useful. Nor should researchers approach the study of tourist behaviour with less confidence because the theoretical garden has not been well cultivated. A brief detour into the analysis of scientific knowledge and the nature of disciplines, including tourism as an emerging topic of study is necessary to justify such confidence.

The literature on studying the nature of knowledge and the characteristics of fields of inquiry is voluminous (Becher, 1989; Biglan, 1973; Calhoun, 2000; Fuchs, 1992; Gergen, 1983; Glaser, 1992; Glaser & Strauss, 1967; Knorr-Cetina, 1983; Kuhn, 1970).

One perspective to emerge from these extensive discussions is the development of a research-based understanding of the world is not well described by a linear relationship where some disciplines are at the bottom of the pile and others are impressively advanced (Becher, 1989). This kind of linear thinking derives from the now deeply questioned view, advanced by Kuhn (1970), that a field of study could be legitimately considered as a science only if the majority of its workers subscribed to a common global perspective or paradigm. In this approach the term paradigm referred to an agreement and consensus among scientists on how to work. It was often equated with the operation of a single theory or at least a small cohort of theories and methods. Pre-paradigmatic areas of inquiry were seen as lesser beasts, at the bottom of the scientific totem pole, characterised by little agreement on theory and on how to approach topics. In earlier analyses, Pearce (1993a) argued the case that tourism as an emerging specialism of study was in this pre-paradigmatic category, not only because of a lack of theory but also because of topic variability, training issues and the spread of researchers.

Both Becher (1989) and Gould (1997) warn against seeing trends in phenomena (in this case disciplines), as hierarchically directed, with one state ultimately on the way to somewhere else. Gould explains:

> The common error lies in failing to recognise that apparent trends can be generated as by-products or side consequences, of expansions and contractions in the amount of variation within a system, and not by anything directly moving anywhere. (Gould, 1997: 33)

Tourism study, it can be argued, is not on the way to 'growing up' into a science with theories and tight paradigms of operation. It is the study of a phenomenon with a range of diverse contributions and some conceptual schemes. It may develop some theories but, given the rich contextual changing nature of the core phenomenon under analysis, it is more likely to retain a strong interplay between observations, data and tightly-fashioned and sometimes localised conceptual schemes and explanatory systems (cf. Tribe, 2004). This view is very closely allied to the practice and philosophy of grounded theory and its developments (Glaser, 1992; Kushner & Morrow, 2003).

Another notable force in tourism that stimulates the value of localised conceptual schemes is the role of practitioners and management personnel. Fuchs argues that:

Fields with low levels of disciplinary professionalism, weak formal and informal entry restrictions and loose organisational boundaries are often influenced by lay audiences (who become) an important source of recognition and they may also influence the general standards and directions of research (Fuchs, 1992: 183)

Tourism is one such field and its practitioners have had and continue to have an influence on its development. It is particularly notable that tourism managers and operators have typically not undertaken university education or been exposed to research cultures. Unlike teachers or doctors, for example, a lack of experience with the value of scholarly and research activity may predispose tourism practitioners to maintain an anti-intellectual and pragmatic business outlook. This orientation can further restrict the growth of theoretical activity in tourism studies, especially where the outside group shapes research funding.

Nevertheless an opportunity is being lost by this disavowal of the more abstract elements of research activity. Kurt Lewin (1951: 169) is often cited for his line 'There is nothing so practical as a good theory (or conceptual scheme)' and Gergen (1983: 105) observes that by pointing the way to hidden or relevant factors 'theory thus stands available to expand the scope and sophistication of the practitioner's program'.

Some tourism researchers and commentators have expressed their discomfort, and dissatisfaction, with the level of theoretical and conceptual analysis in tourism (Aramberri, 2001; Cooper, 2003; Seaton, 1996; Tribe, 1997). Following the distinctions outlined earlier the source of that discomfort should be labelled a lack of conceptual schemes rather than a lack of theory, but the point remains that some scholars want to see researchers generate more powerful emancipatory perspectives on social life. Gergen (1983) notes the need to distinguish between two kinds of academic effort – activities internal to the discipline and theoretical work beyond the discipline. In both cases, Gergen argues that the value of conceptual schemes or theoretical formulations lies in the ability to sharpen the language of the relevant community of interest – to have the new approach function as a rhetorical instrument that re-shapes the existing way of thinking. A particular emphasis here lies in the distinction between providing insights within the field of study and beyond it. It is notable that the concept of how a discipline or study area should function may drive how the researcher sees the adequacy of conceptual schemes and theoretical work. Gergen notes that those with an instrumental orientation might be well served by approaches that please clients and make money, while others with the goals of contributing to academic discourse generally may be concerned with the broader consequences of theoretical viewpoints (Calhoun, 2000). In this context it is notable that researchers writing about tourism as a field but working from sociological and anthropological traditions in tourism (Aramberri, 2001; Dann & Cohen, 1996; Hollinshead, 1999; Selanniemi, 2003) as opposed to those from within business schools and marketing programmes (Gunn, 1994b; Morrison, 1996; Pizam, 1994; Ritchie, 1994) seem to be more prominent in seeking an expanded role for tourism theory. Additional consideration of these perspectives and their relevance for the future of tourist behaviour research will be explored in the final chapter of this book.

The guiding approach in this book will be to use conceptual schemes as systems of insight to summarise empirical work, to suggest new insights into the work and to offer the promise of generalising studies for practical action.

Information Anxiety and a Road Map

Information anxiety is a term coined by Saul Wurman (1989), who argued that people need to distinguish between being stupid and being ignorant and on occasions there is a tendency to blur the distinction. A healthy perspective, Wurman argues, is to willingly state one's ignorance and seek clarification and information to overcome it. Individuals should not cast this ignorance as an enduring state since ignorance, but not stupidity, can be altered with effort. Wurman's further idea is that we should not be anxious about all the information in an area such as tourist behaviour, we should follow our own interests and try and get a number of systems or mental structures – plans or road maps – of areas of knowledge to organise the information. The concept map that forms Figure 1.2 is a guide to information and to the subsequent sections of this book.

Figure 1.2 plots a pathway to understanding some of the main destinations in analysing tourist behaviour, beginning with a consideration of the characteristics of the individual tourist. This material will be reviewed in Chapter 2, and one view of the motives for travel behaviour that arise from these individual characteristics will be considered in Chapter 3. In Chapter 4 the perception of the destination will be reviewed and the decision-making processes resulting from the images of the destination will be considered. Tourists' on-site experiences will be the subject of Chapters 5 (the social dimension) and 6 (the environmental dimension) and the outcomes of visitors' travels as expressed in such topics as satisfaction and learning will be reviewed in Chapter 7. Although not indicated in Figure 1. 2, the final chapter will consider some of the pressing forces that shape future studies of tourist behaviour. The map featured in Figure 1.2 is not a conceptual scheme, as discussed in the previous section, but instead is an organiser for the systematic treatment of the fascinating topic of tourist behaviour.

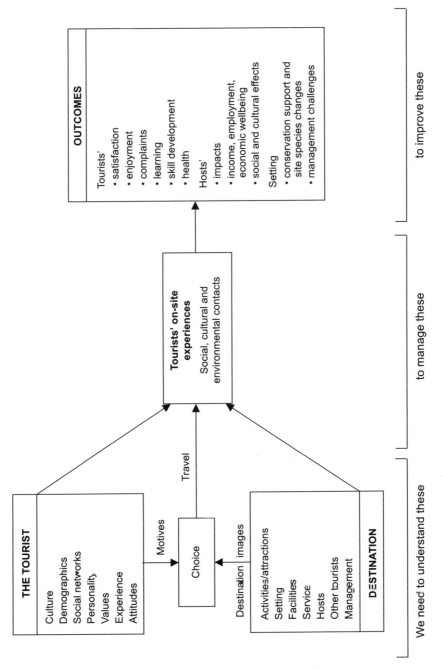

Figure 1.2 Concept map for understanding tourist behaviour

Chapter 2

Social Roles and Individual Characteristics

It has already been established that the sin of homogenisation lurks within the field of tourist behaviour research (Galani-Moutafi, 1999). Tourists are not all the same, but it is usually inefficient when building the systematic study of a phenomenon to consider numerous individual cases in detail. It would, for example, be difficult if analysts endeavoured to document all of the variables of age, gender, nationality, economic well being, travel style, marital and family status, sexual preference, previous travel experience, attitudinal profiles and personality characteristics whenever they attempted to characterise a market.

It is convenient to see some broad commonalities across some tourist behaviour variables, for the immediacy of site-based management, for effective marketing action and for social analysis exploring cross-situational and future trends. In particular, there is often an appropriate level of analysis and detail for each specific purpose. For example, an association of Turkish hotels might be broadly interested in affluent European heritage tourists (Dinçer & Ertugral, 2003). Yet again, a more precise specification of individual variables could be required by tour operators in Hong Kong who are seeking to connect with British tourists interested in colonial architecture and affluent enough to join a seven day Oriental tour (Hong Kong Tourist Association, 1995). For the tourism researcher interested in exploring cultural changes it might be necessary to assess previous travel experience as well as social groupings and age in studying how older Japanese are changing their heritage-related travel activities (You & O'Leary, 2000).

In this chapter, the role of the tourist and the individual characteristics of the tourist are central concerns. Undoubtedly the sin of homogenisation, the problem of being simplistic or overgeneralising about tourists, is difficult to avoid in sampling the key dimensions used to characterise tourists. The warning is important because this section of the book provides a snapshot of key visitor characteristics and product-related visitor profiles, not a full-length feature on each segment. The aim is to provide a blueprint or an outline of key defining characteristics for such dimensions as age, gender, nationality and the kinds of tourists drawn to specific products. There are more comprehensive treatments of these topics in individual monographs and reviews, so the intention here is to build a framework with which readers and analysts of tourist behaviour can assimilate other related (and even future) research findings.

In order to document the key characteristics of the tourist, a number of themes will be explored here. First, the existence and nature of tourist stereotypes will be considered. Then, the role of the tourist as a social position in society will be pursued. This treatment, together with some important conceptual schemes that help organise the stereotypes and role-related studies, will be followed by a consideration of the rich range of univariate approaches frequently used to classify tourists.

Stereotypes of Tourists

Negative views of tourists prevail in literature and in historical and popular writing. Strictly, stereotypes are agreed images of entities, in this case a group of people (Secord & Backman, 1964). In the early work on the topic of stereotypes, specific attempts were made to suggest that 15% or more of the sampled viewing group had to agree with the characteristic before the label could be considered as a stereotype (Berry, 1969; Katz & Brady, 1933; Pearce *et al.*, 1981). In this system of stereotype determination both positive and negative characteristics were commonly reported. The looser and less precise use of the term implies that any striking image or colourful statement demonstrates the existence of a stereotype (c.f. Ryan, 1997a). In this usage negative portrayals are common. Tourists are seen as indulgent and exploitative, lacking civility and having a restricted appreciation of cultures and places (Crick, 1989). They are also often described as overweight, badly dressed and less than attractive. For some, it is the arrogant American who epitomises the term: for others, groups of travellers from Japan are typical, and for a few more it is the British or the Germans in the Spanish coastal resorts (Rosenow & Pulsipher, 1978).

A number of tourism analysts flaunt these descriptions as if they were novel and, additionally, insightful. They are certainly not novel. From the earliest days of the use of the word tourist, returning young aristocrats were lampooned by 17th century savants. There is nothing 'more conceited, more unprincipled, more dissipated and more incapable of any serious application to study or to business' than a returning tourist lamented Adam Smith in 1775 (Hibbert, 1969: 224).

Is the citing of such sharply-turned phrases insightful? It is partly, but not so much for its overgeneralised account of tourists as for its appraisal of the commentators. It is the perceiver rather than the perceived who reveals something of psychological interest in these comments. In so far as the tourism authors and analysts express sympathy with these perceived views, they too may be showing more of themselves than intended. Thus, passages railing against permissive tourists exposing too much flesh may reflect conservative, even repressed viewers; an emphasis on older and ugly tourist images sets up the observer as judgemental and possibly narcissistic while those who consider tourists as unutterably vulgar and uncouth do so at the risk of exposing their own social and intellectual pretensions.

There is often passion and anger in the denouncement of tourists, including one's fellow tourists. This theme is exemplified by *Homesickness* Bail's (1980) sustained satirical account of an Australian package tour group travelling through a world of exaggerated tourist attractions. One of the groups complains

> God, I hate tourists ... they've made a mess of everything. Nothing is real any more. They obscure anything that was there. They stand around droves of them clicking with their blasted cameras. Most of them don't know what they are gawking at. (Bail, 1980: 81)

The irony here is that the character complaining about others is the most ignorant, boorish and easily bored in the whole travel party.

Two conceptual schemes are insightful in furthering an understanding of the topic of stereotyping and the negative portrayal of tourists in general. The concepts are *social representations* and *role distance*. The social represen- tations perspective was developed by Moscovici (1984, 1988) and elabo- rated by Farr (1987, 1990, 1993) and others. Its application to tourism the phenomenon was explored in an account of how communities see tourism (Pearce *et al.*, 1996). Social representations are the shared, publicly-commu- nicated, everyday belief systems about large-scale topics such as sex, health, madness and the present interest area, tourists. Social representa- tions are more than attitudes and values: they are driven by large-scale themes and images, they derive their meaning from multiple sources and they organise areas of people's everyday understanding and behaviour. Social representations are our everyday theories and knowledge networks about sizeable chunks of the social world. In the analysis of tourism in Hawaii, Pearce *et al.* (1996) report that one community segment saw tourism as 'an engine of growth' while another group viewed it as a 'vul- ture destroying cultures'. An extension of the social representations research applied to tourists (rather than to tourism) is possible from the earlier studies and yields macro-organising images of tourist such as those already discussed – the loud exploitative ugly visitor or, more kindly, the people from afar who are like us, but here (Pearce *et al.*, 1996: 177). The value of the social representations framework in illuminating the tourist stereo- types lies in two directions. First, it directs attention to who shares the particular macro views of tourists, and asks how this group comes to have this view. The second advantage of the social representation framework is the focus on the consequences of holding such stereotypes. In this contribution the important point is that likely behaviours towards tourists, and towards associated tourism developments, are a part of a connected system of people's everyday understanding and a guide to how they will respond. In this view tourist stereotypes are not just amusing, not just socially driven attempts to gain status and identity, but powerful shapers of action and interaction.

The second conceptual scheme that relates to understanding stereotypes is that of tourist roles and the notion of role distance. This is a major topic in tourist behaviour analysis and warrants special attention.

Social Roles and the Tourist

A role is a formal sociological term for the position that a person occupies in society. Typically roles are to be found in work, leisure and domestic life. The terminology 'social role' adds to this basic concept by extending the non technical and interpersonal nature of the term (Argyle *et al.*, 1981; Bales & Slater, 1955; Parsons, 1951). Social roles can be tightly or loosely defined, with the roles of tourist and student being in the latter category while prisoner and priest are in the former group of tightly circumscribed roles with a limited range of permissible behaviours. Deviation from expected role behaviours are viewed tolerantly for some roles, such as students and pop stars, but judged more harshly for others such as doctors and soldiers (Garfinkel, 1967). The term 'role theory' was used for a while in the 1960s and 1970s (Biddle & Thomas, 1966) but as Argyle *et al.* (1981: 165) report 'it has been objected that role theory isn't a theory, and we are inclined to agree'. So does the present author. In this view role theory fails as a theory because it lacks cumulative and predictive power. Nevertheless there are a number of useful elaborations of the concept of role that assist in the explanation of tourist behaviours, and these extended terms constitute at least a useful lexicon for generating insights. Some of the relevant extensions of the term role include: role conflict (where two or more positions that the person occupies actually clash), role ambiguity (where it is not clear what is expected), role bargaining (where individuals renegotiate with others the way to perform the role) and role distance (where individuals express their individuality by flaunting conventional role behaviour). Additionally a term of interest for tourism studies is 'altercasting' where the strong presence and behaviour of another manoeuvres an individual into a complementary role.

The early work of Bales (1950) and Bales and Slater (1955) on roles in small groups led researchers to the position that many social organisations, including tourist parties, tend to develop group-facilitating social roles such as comic, organiser, problem solver and go-between (cf. Goffman, 1959, 1971; Marsh *et al.*, 1978).

Not surprisingly, the early work in tourism research used and applied the work on social roles that was being conducted in psychology, sociology and anthropology. Smith (1978) devised a model of how tourist roles changed over time for any given destination. In this approach the early tourists to an area were explorers, next were the adventurers, and these in turn were followed by the drifters. With expanding numbers the roles were then those of the mass and charter tourists. Cohen (1974) employed similar ideas characterising an array of tourist roles including the explorer, the drifter, the individual mass tourist and the organised mass tourist.

Pearce (1982) added some specific behavioural characteristics to the tourist stereotypes, as judged by a sample of Australian students. In this work the five clearest role-related behaviours for tourists were: takes photos, buys souvenirs, goes to famous places, stays briefly in one place, and does not understand the local people. By way of contrast, the five clearest role-related behaviours for a traveller were: stays briefly in one place, experiments with local food, goes to famous places, takes photos, and explores places privately. With these distinctions in roles and employing Goffman's (1971) concept of role distance, it is possible to view some of the stereotypes of tourists reported earlier as being generated by travellers wishing to distance themselves from their tourist cousins.

More contemporary work on tourist roles has included an attempt to develop role schemes as a kind of indirect access to tourist motivation (Foo *et al.*, 2004; Yiannakis & Gibson, 1992). This research direction again gauges public responses to pre-labelled or etically-derived tourist roles (Gibson & Yiannakis, 2002). In these studies, tourist roles are seen as the vehicles through which travellers achieve their goals and motives, but the current studies in this tradition only point to the dramaturgical possibilities of these roles rather than illuminate how visitors act them out. The further value of this line of work will be described more fully in Chapter 3, which is explicitly concerned with developing an approach to motivation.

Horne (1992) has argued for the development of the tourist role in terms of there being a new style of intelligent tourist – one who appreciates the culture and history of the places visited. Similarly, and working within the tradition of sustainable tourism studies, Swarbrooke (1999a) has outlined the basic role responsibilities of the tourist and the extra role responsibilities of the sustainable tourist. The role prescriptions are presented in Table 2.1.

Swarbrooke's analysis is akin to prescriptions for desirable tourist behaviour found in codes of conduct developed by tourist bodies and committed value-oriented organisations (Malloy & Fennell, 1998; Mason & Mowforth, 1996). Two kinds of difficulties exist with this tight specification

Table 2.1 Role responsibilities of tourists

Tourists in general	Sustainable tourists
• to obey local laws • not to participate in widely condemned, albeit legal, activities • not to offend religious beliefs • not to damage the physical environment • not to overuse resources	And additionally • not to visit a place with a poor human rights record • be responsible to learn about the visited place including some language • meet and form friendships with local people • boycott local businesses which pay staff poor wages • not to spread disease • contribute to the local economy

of desirable tourist role conduct. First, it is not clear from an evidence-based perspective that all of the suggested behaviours will produce sustainable outcomes. One can, for example, call into question the appropriateness of encouraging tourists to boycott places with a poor human rights record. It can be suggested instead that tourists and the governments who represent them may be forces for social change in such communities. Meeting and forming friendships with local people may seem a desirable ideal and a positive role behaviour, but it needs to be managed so that issues of privacy invasion and the pressure of sustained visitor–local contact are equitably distributed.

The second kind of problem with some of the prescribed roles is that it is difficult to make the necessary judgements. Consider, for example, the proposed practice of boycotting businesses. It is difficult to determine if a Vietnamese hotel or a Filipino attraction is exploiting its workers or indeed its subcontractors or the local community. Amounts of money that may seem trivial in the United States may be substantial in Indonesia, and jobs that look menial and almost pointless in populated destinations such as India and China may provide dignity and some income of value to poverty-stricken regions. The assessment and comparative judgement problem is also strikingly complex for the human rights issue. Few countries have a totally clean bill of health in the way ethnic, indigenous and migrant subcultures are treated, and Western ethnocentrism appears to underpin some of the codes of conduct for global travellers.

In reviewing the attempt by an array of organisations to prescribe ideal tourist roles, several of the earlier terms from the lexicon of role-related issues are applicable. *Altercasting* is a common tourist role experience, particularly for Westerners in Asian destinations, and refers to the structuring of roles by the strong presence and organisation of others. It occurs, for example, when a tour operator structures the itinerary of an all-day coach tour so that the sites, shops and scenes to be experienced are all tightly pre-determined. The tourist's role in these structured settings is therefore closely defined; it is expressed as standardised stops for taking photos, access to certain types of shops selling a limited array of products, specific culinary experiences and almost full insulation from any prolonged contact with local community members. If an observer identifies the resulting behaviour as fitting a tourist stereotype then arguably this is a correct assertion, but it is a role that is prescribed through altercasting rather than negotiated. It is also likely to lead, in some cases, to outbursts of role-distancing behaviour. In a different tourism context Murphy (2001) describes a role-related breakout amongst young budget travellers in Australia and Asia. She observes that in this highly social environment where such travellers are constantly meeting others, the tourist role involves repeatedly presenting oneself and one's life with a high degree of self-disclosure. This aspect of the backpacker or youth budget traveller role is repetitive and Murphy notes that some tourists in this setting respond by fabricating new life stories, thus finding a way to renegotiate the role and distance themselves from the earnest truthfulness required in multiple self-disclosing and open encounters.

The notion that one can distance oneself from the role of the tourist, that is to be an outsider or onlooker, introduces another major theme in describing the tourist's social position.

The Outsider

While a number of earlier writers had commented on the peculiar role of the visitor or outsider moving through communities, it was Simmel in 1906 who first identified unique dimensions of the outsider that are pertinent to tourism (Outhwaite, 2000). Simmel's analysis partly concentrated on the stranger who stays in a community and who is able to offer unique insights on that location and its culture. In addition, Simmel identified the stranger who moves on as another distinctive role that is distinguished by its own behavioural attributes. Tourists may fit both of these outsider roles. Since tourists typically move on, there is a clear link to Simmel's second category, the mobile stranger. In this role tourists can receive 'the most surprising revelations and confidences, at times reminiscent of a confessional about matters which are kept carefully hidden from everybody' (Simmel, 1971: 145). When exploring the social relationships of tourists and local people, as well as tourists and other tourists, this spontaneous intimacy will be considered more fully.

Taken as a social category rather than as individuals, tourists can also be seen to fulfil Simmel's outsider role of the stranger who stays. Many communities have tourists in them all the time, clearly not the same tourists but a continuous juxtaposition in time, space and activities of similar individuals and groups. According to Simmel, it is a distinguishing feature of this recurring stranger role that the stranger's views are heard because of a special kind of objectivity they bring to the situation. Tourists come from other places and have been to other places and yet, by being present in the visited community, they are likely to be sympathetic rather than harsh critics. In the larger picture of the influence of tourist behaviour on local destinations and societies, the views of tourists can count when determining how destinations and their constituents view their own identity and envision their future. The theme of strangers, outsiders and the related term of the familiar stranger will be discussed further in Chapter 5, which looks at social relationships of tourists.

Thresholds and Liminality

Liminality is a concept that has been employed with increasing frequency to understand the role of the tourist (Graburn, 1989; Ryan, 1997a; Turner & Turner, 1978). The work is connected to earlier anthropological writing on thresholds, rituals and transition zones (van Gennep, 1906/1960), in which there are three zones or states of interest.

First there is the regular or *normal* state, sometimes referred to as the profane state of being, such as the individual's life and experiences at home. Next there is a *liminoid* phase, literally a threshold phase, where the tourist is in a state of transition and life is abnormal, not always comprehensible and often puzzling. This is sometimes seen as a sacred or spiritual phase where the possibilities of life and existence are expanded. More specifically, a distinction is made in this conceptual scheme between the terms 'liminoid' and 'liminal'. The latter refers to imbuing the transition phase, such as a marriage ceremony, with spiritual or cosmic significance whereas the term liminoid is more prosaic and is restricted to the acts and action of people participating in the transitions.

To complete the sequence of terms and phases there is a third phase, labelled a *post-liminoid* phase, which describes a return to the ordinary, everyday or profane state. Graburn (1989) depicts the tourists' return to their everyday world and lives as the post-liminoid experience for the tourist role.

This conceptual scheme, rooted in the works of anthropologists, has particularly strong appeal when tourist behaviour involves cross-cultural encounters which are challenging and which occur in novel settings. The threshold approach appears to be less applicable (but is potentially still of some value), when describing tourists taking short breaks in familiar and neighbouring communities.

Some connections between the liminal–liminoid thresholds approach to understanding the tourist role and other ideas describing phases and consequences of tourist contact can be identified. In their early work on recreation and tourism and as reported in Chapter 1, Clawson and Knetsch (1966) suggested five phases of interest – a planning phase, a travel to the site, an on-site experience, a return travel phase and a recollection or recall stage. The links between the liminoid-threshold approach and this earlier work are not straightforward as their juxtaposition raises questions about when the tourist role really begins and ends. Is it only the on-site experience that is sacred or liminoid or are other parts of the tourist-travel sequence also perplexing, challenging and out of the ordinary? The possibility of using each system to better explore the accuracy and substantive meaning of the other is a potentially interesting research direction.

One of the frequent and well-established consequences of the tourist role is that of culture shock (Oberg, 1960). In the context of thresholds and liminal-liminoid approaches it can be argued that culture shock is a clear consequence of having entered the liminoid zone and its resolution may well be complete only when returning to the post-liminoid phase. Interestingly, cross-cultural researchers refer to the readjustment problem in culture shock (Ward *et al.*, 2001). This enduring dimension or consequence of the tourist role is not well accounted for in the post-liminoid approach and again the meshing of concepts might be mutually useful for understanding post-tourism malaise and restlessness.

The discussion on thresholds and the tourist role which to date has been largely in terms of sociological and anthropological perspectives can also be developed by considering the physical parameters that shape tourist behaviour and experience (Ashcroft, 2001). A significant part of the threshold experience in some tourism settings may be the tourists' struggle with their own physical adaptation to the location. The tourist role can be influenced by issues of acclimatisation, altitude, changing pressure gradients, dehydration, motion sickness, physical responses to new foods, lengths of daylight, new allergens, and of course viruses and infections. Additionally one of the reasons tourists are the butt of jokes is that it is sometimes difficult to find the right style and combination of clothes to deal with the physical demands of a challenging new setting. An ineffective and unusual wardrobe makes the tourist highly visible as well as uncomfortable both physically and psychologically (Hatt, 1982). It may be something as simple as an inadequate hat or burdensome shoes, but the wrong clothes combined with the multiple contributions of environment shock forces can be a contributor to fluctuating daily moods and a considerable contributor to the tourists' discomfort (Pearce, 1981a). An additional psychological rather than physical adjustment issue also looms large for most tourists. Wurman (1989) reports that managing information is a growing problem in all walks of life. For the tourist, the problems of information management are particularly acute, and retrieving the right data for finding where to go, how to get there, how to pay and how to behave are challenges central to Wurman's concept of information anxiety. The link here is so clear that Wurman, a notable business researcher, has also published thematically-organised and colour-coded information guides to a number of cities (Wurman, 1991, 1992).

In summary, the broadly-conceived stereotypes of tourists and the social roles they occupy have raised a number of recurring themes. It is not easy to fulfil the tourist role. It is ambiguous, it may be organised by others, lampooned by some and require physical adjustment as the individual

Table 2.2 Individual variables describing tourist groupings

Demographic factors	*Travelling style distinctions*	*Product and activity classifications*
Age	Accommodation used	Cultural tourists:
Gender	Activity participation	• heritage tourists
Nationality	Destination patterns	• ethnic tourists
Additional demographic factors:	Length of stay	Nature oriented tourists:
	Trip purpose	• wildlife tourists
• expenditure	Distance travelled	• ecotourists
• occupation	Travel party composition	Adventure tourists
• education	Seasonality/travel time	Educational tourists:
	Travel arrangements:	• science tourists
	• independent	• volunteers
	• package	Theme park tourists
	• mixed	Casino tourists
	Transport mode	Urban tourists
		Agricultural tourists:
		• wine tourists
		• farm tourists
		Sex tourists:
		• romance tourists
		• companionship tourists
		Business tourists:
		• conference tourists
		• events tourists

moves across thresholds of experience. The discussion in this section has not only raised the topic of stereotyping and roles, but introduced some concepts and schemes which will be employed further in this volume to comment on groups of tourists and their behaviour. Attention will now be directed towards some of the prominent demographic labels used to characterise tourists. Table 2.2 provides a preview of the specific individual variables that will be included in the portrayal of the tourist in the following sections.

Age

Age is both an observable and a universal demographic descriptor. It is frequently a substitute or proxy variable for physical fitness, activity levels, interests and previous travel experiences.

In contemporary Western societies it is conventional to think of such age descriptions as teenagers, baby-boomers and seniors but simply counting in terms of a number of years or birth decades gives prominence to one definition of age – that of chronological time. Waugh (1999) has observed that the way time and hence age is measured reflects the triumph of just one of many possible counting systems. As Pearce and Singh (1999) suggest, individual reactions to one's age measured in years and socio-cultural treatment of people of a certain age are potentially major modifiers of the 'years since birth' measure of age. In this expanded approach to assessing age it has been suggested that in addition to aging 'chronologically' (Bonder & Wagner, 2001), people can age biographically, socially, psychologically and spiritually (MacNeil, 1987; Minichiello *et al.*, 1992; Moschis, 1996).

This recognition of the complexity of aging has resulted in two trends in the tourist behaviour literature. One set of researchers uses a broad stage or sequence approach to aging, and describes the tourist motives, decisions and experiences of a particular cohort (cf. Cleaver *et al.*, 1999, and their study of 'baby boomers'). In this kind of approach other factors associated with the age of the observed group are measured and included in the analysis, but the defining point of the segmentation is the chronological measure of age. A second and less common approach is represented by the work of Moschis (1996), who uses multiple definitions of aging for the initial selection of the market segments. In this approach the biophysical, psychological and social states in life that determine the aging process are used in the initial sorting procedure as well as actual chronological age. Such a multiple-factor approach to aging is closely allied to the integrative concept of life stage and life-cycle, which will be discussed in more detail in Chapter 3.

The more common approach to aging as measured simply in years will be pursued here. Nevertheless it remains important to reflect on the view that what it means to be a child, a teenager or a senior in the present is different from what was meant a generation ago or what it will mean for a generation in the future.

Children, conventionally classified as 12 years and under, are an emerging group of interest to travel researchers. Meikle (2003) reports that for day trips to tourist attractions and for family holidays, children in Australia and Singapore are important contributors to a number of decisions. While adults, either separately or jointly, decide where to go, in such attractions as zoos and theme parks it is often children who determine what to do and which sequence of activities to follow. These findings confirm indications from the literature a decade earlier, where Ryan (1992) noted that children are often the most willing participants in activities at heritage sites. Importantly the participation of children in demonstrations, games, events and rides may galvanise adult interest, extend the time of the visit and have commercial implications in terms of souvenir and food purchases.

A particular consequence in the realm of tourist behaviour for the growing importance of the child consumer as a participating decision maker relates to the whole of the family or whole of the group's satisfaction. Thornton *et al.* (1997) suggest that adults' satisfaction may largely depend on the satisfaction of their children in some tourism settings. There is not yet a detailed understanding of how this total party satisfaction system or appraisal works, but the creation of children's clubs in such settings as cruise ships, resorts and even gambling destinations is one solution to meeting multiple travel party needs. An alternative solution, which may be better for some family groups, is the design of more whole-family joint participatory activities.

Studies of the tourism experiences of teenagers are limited, and mostly come under the umbrella of educational tourism such as school study tours or are investigated as a part of the lower bounds of the independent youth market (Ritchie, 2003). The literature on leisure has contributed some important insights relevant to tourism studies on adolescent travel behaviour by noting marked sex differences and the central importance of social relationships and status for this age cohort (Mannell & Kleiber, 1997). Importantly, there is evidence that patterns of leisure activity begun in adolescence are quite likely to continue into adult life (Csikszentmihalyi, 1990; Stebbins, 1992). Further studies of the continuity of travel behaviour from teenage years to adult life could identify new patterns of transition in tourist behaviour research.

Some literature exists on late adolescent youth travel and there are studies of break-out or party style episodes in youth tourism such as Spring Break in the United States and schoolies week in Australia (Josiam *et al.*, 1998). These hedonistic and indulgent encounters sometimes raise important management challenges for the communities visited, including protection of the participants and the control of drug use, aggression and the consequences of sexual promiscuity.

An important classification of tourists in the Asia Pacific region that is strongly dependent on age is the backpacker phenomenon (Murphy, 1997; Pearce, 1990a). The age range of key interest here is the 18–35 segment. The label 'backpackers' to connote a certain age-dependent travel style is largely concentrated in South Asia, South-East Asia and Australasia. A short history of the origins of backpackers can help us to understand this phenomenon. Three traditions coalesce to form the background to this market, which accounts for around 12% of international visitors to Australia (Buchanan & Rossetto, 1997). The first tradition is an educational one; since the days of the Grand Tour there has been a sense of young people travelling to round out their education. The second theme is the tradition of travelling for work or new work experiences. It has its origins in 17th and 18th century Europe when individuals learning their trades and crafts travelled across national borders to develop their skills. A third style of travel behaviour influencing contemporary backpacking is the German youth movement linked to the formation of Youth Hostels (McCulloch, 1992). Youth Hostels were essentially a way for people to travel on a budget, using such facilities as old school houses and civic buildings. This German movement in particular had a health-conscious, ascetic character.

These core forces underlying backpacker travel were augmented in the 1960s and 70s with the style of travellers who were labelled drifters, wanderers and hippies (Riley, 1988). In contemporary Thailand there are still airport arrival signs announcing 'No hippies welcome'. Such signs also encourage youth visitors to be neat in appearance and modest in their dress. Backpackers, however, are not hippies. They are the next generation, the next youth travel movement evolving from the hippie/drifter syndrome. The term backpacker specifically refers to individuals, typically those aged in their 20s with a preference for a budget accommodation style, but willing to purchase quite expensive travel experiences (Pearce, 1990a). As well as being defined by age and the preference for budget accommodation, backpackers are identifiable by independently organised and flexible travel schedules, a social orientation, long (from four weeks to a year) rather than brief holidays, and a preference for participatory activities. Many of them work for some portion of their time while travelling (Buchanan & Rossetto, 1997). As a regionally-distinctive, age-related traveller cohort, backpackers are a specific market who illustrate many of the conceptual schemes used to understand tourists as a whole. Backpackers express a clear role distance in relation to other tourists; they display behaviours consistent with being in a liminal or threshold phase of their life; and they constitute a subculture with their own strong social representations of the purpose of travelling (Foster, 2003; Murphy, 1997, 2001).

Another age-based segment is that referred to as the 'baby boomers'. The term refers specifically to the cohort of people born between 1945 and 1966 (Muller & Cleaver, 2000). The expression baby boomers applies best to the countries of Canada, the United States of America, Australia and New Zealand where economic conditions after the Second World War were sound and families were encouraged. By way of contrast, war-affected countries in Europe and Asia and developing countries in other continents did not produce the same conditions for family life and did not experience such high birth rates. Nevertheless European and Japanese travellers, in particular, share some of the characteristics outlined in North American and Australian studies (You & O'Leary, 1999).

It is notable that the baby boomers in the countries specified have benefited from growing up in affluent and opportunity rich societies. Muller and Cleaver (2000) and Cleaver *et al.* (1999) observe that baby boomers are now settled and mostly comfortable with their place in the world. They see themselves as competent, and as recognising the complexities of life, but they do have clear ideas about what makes them happy. As baby boomers are on the cusp of entering the senior-travellers category, they do so with the richest array of previous travel experiences and the highest expectations of any cohort in human history. It can be predicted that, even though the stereotypes of senior travellers have been changing (Moscardo & Green, 1999), further revision of the stereotype will be inevitable when baby boomers become seniors.

The label 'senior' in general, and 'senior tourists' in particular, has been evolving in the last two decades. Two statistics will serve to document the extension of the human lifespan that underlies the scale and hence the growing market importance of seniors. By the year 2050, for the first time, the world will contain more people over the age of 60 than under the age of 15. This will mean 2 billion people over 60 as compared to 600 million in the year 2000. The trend for greater numbers of older people will be global, and the Asia Pacific region will be heavily affected by this shift in demographic structure. Notwithstanding some Asian predilections for cosmetic attention to one's hair colour, the 'grey' army of travellers will be increasingly visible within and throughout Asia–Pacific tourism in the next 50 years.

Existing studies of senior travellers note a balance of forces influencing their tourist behaviour. On the one hand there is the view that contemporary seniors are becoming more active, more adventurous and remain healthier for longer (Moscardo & Green, 1999). Nevertheless physical and health conditions do impose some limits and shifts in activity patterns have been repeatedly noted. For example, Javalgi *et al.* (1992) found that an over-55 group was more likely to undertake cruises, go touring and visit relatives or friends but less likely to visit cities, theme parks and resorts. Blazey

(1992) reported that older travellers stay away from home longer. This finding is reinforced by those studies of long-distance car touring by seniors – the so-called grey nomads – both in North America and Australia (Black & Clark, 1998; McHugh & Mings, 1991, 1992).

It is a recurring theme in the seniors-based studies that there are fine-grained subdivisions within this age group and some researchers opt for further age-based groupings such as younger seniors (less than 65) and older seniors (over 65), while others tie their classifications to retirement or to expansive versus disengaging attitudes (Powers, 1997; Wearing, 1995). Moscardo and Green (1999) in their detailed study of older tourists on Australia's Great Barrier Reef report that those in the oldest senior market segment were the most satisfied with their experience – a finding which indicates that the promise of travel, as a purposeful and rewarding activity in the senior citizen's life, can be fulfilled. The growing needs and the expanding number of seniors will undoubtedly become high profile topics in tourist behaviour studies in the near future.

Nationality

Nationality is a widely used demographic descriptor in tourism studies. It is sometimes an observable characteristic with physical appearance, clothing styles, and tour party characteristics providing identifiable markers of nationality. Like age, nationality is often used by tourism researchers as a proxy or substitute variable. In particular, it is often used as an indicator of the cultural allegiance or roots of the tourist. Nationality is sometimes measured, although not very accurately, by establishing the tourists' country of residence.

Dann (1993) raised some objections to the continued use and usefulness of nationality as a demographic descriptor in tourism studies. He noted that people often hold dual passports, which give them bi-national allegiances. He further noted that countries and nationalities are changing with new divisions and amalgamations making the contemporary meaning of nationality more problematic. Further, inside any one country there are multiple ethnic identities such as Tibetan Chinese, Vietnamese Australians or Hispanic Americans. Some of these ethnic identities are politically volatile, others are the outcome of successful blending and still others are emerging as potentially dominant regional forces reshaping cities and regions. While such ethnic identities are prevalent in most countries, it is perhaps noteworthy that this is less the case for Korea and Japan which, in the Asian context, consist of relatively homogeneous populations (Sheridan, 1999). For Indonesia, Malaysia, India and China there are minorities and ethnic groups who number in the millions making such groups substantially larger in size than the populations of some other countries in the region.

There are, however, pragmatic arguments for continuing to use the construct of nationality to describe tourist behaviour. The argument stems from so-called indirect studies which demonstrate that those interacting with tourists frequently employ nationality-based interpretations in their dealings with the relevant groups (Pizam, 1999a). Additionally, a set of direct studies using the nationality construct explores differences in the behaviour and satisfaction levels of tourists themselves (Kozak, 2001).

Pizam and colleagues have conducted a number of studies using the indirect approach with a particular focus on how tour guides perceive differences between tourists from a range of countries (Pizam, 1999a, 1999b; Pizam & Jeong, 1966; Pizam & Reichel, 1996; Pizam & Sussman, 1995; Pizam *et al.*, 1997). Strong differences in the perception of the tourist role behaviours of the nationality groups were common. As an illustration of this approach the study by Pizam and Sussman (1995) is typical. Japanese, French, Italian and American visitors were assessed by London-based British tour guides. Japanese were seen to be the least social, highly interested in shopping and more satisfied with staged or set-up tourist experiences. The Americans and Italians were the most social and, despite some communication difficulties, the Italians were the most adept at and enthusiastic about bargaining. The French and Italians shared the designation of being the most adventurous, but were less interested in London-based shopping than the Americans or Japanese.

It is clear from the work of Pizam and colleagues that these kinds of detailed judgements and appraisals exist across a number of countries and contexts. As a further example, de Albuquerque and McElroy (2001) report that the harassment of tourists in the Caribbean is directed towards targeted nationality groups, while du Cros and du Cros (2003) note that in Crete certain kinds of romantic approaches are made towards Scandinavian tourists rather than towards all female travellers. Nationality, it appears, matters in the treatment of tourists.

A complementary style of nationality-based tourism studies involves the direct assessment of what motivates travellers, how they behave and what they derive from their experiences. Several of these studies are comparative, while others focus on just one nationality group. The comparative studies include work that compares groups on destination image and attitudes, on motivation, on travel patterns, in communication style and on satisfaction levels (Chadee & Mattson, 1996; Kozak, 2001; Kozak & Neild, 1998; Reisinger & Turner, 1999; Richardson & Crompton, 1998; Yuan & MacDonald, 1990). The nationalities compared are varied and reflect convenience samples rather than systematic research programs. They include Japanese and Americans, British and German, Korean and

Table 2.3 Factors affecting Japanese tourist behaviour

Key factor	*Description*
Belongingness	Travelling in groups and seeking comfort in togetherness
Family influence	Purchasing gifts for close friends and family members and reciprocating
Empathy	Projecting the feelings of others and not expressing true personal feelings, including displeasure
Dependency	Being loyal and devoted in exchange for security and protection
Hierarchical acknowledgement	Behaving in accordance with social status
Propensity to save	Accumulating funds for an emergency and saving to overcome feelings of insecurity
Concept of *kinen*	Collecting evidence of travel to prestigious tourist destinations
Tourist photography	Importance of photography
Passivity	Avoiding participating in physical activities
Risk avoidance	Avoiding adventurous leisure pursuits
Concept of *omiyage*	Purchasing souvenirs to strengthen networks
Concept of *akogare*	Respect for fashionable Western products and lifestyle

Australian, French and English Canadian and a number of European comparisons.

Further, for almost any one individual nationality, there are detailed assessments of characteristics and behaviours. For example, in relation to Japanese tourists there are studies of life-cycle, age effects, buyer behaviour, reactions to package tours, facilities and environments (Ahmed & Kron, 1992; Kim & Lee, 2000a, 2000b; March, 2000; Nishiyama, 1996; Park, 2000; Yagi, 2001; Yamamoto & Gill, 1999; You & O'Leary, 2000). Ahmed and Kron (1992) and Yagi (2003) suggest some defining distinctive elements for the Japanese that influence their behaviour as tourists. These factors are identified in Table 2.3.

For many researchers, including tourist researchers, nationality acts as a proxy or substitute construct for other fundamental concepts. In particular cultural differences interest a vast array of researchers (Ward *et al.*, 2001). The traditions of interest here include work by sociologists, anthropologists, linguists and cross-cultural psychologists (Gudykunst *et al.*, 1992;

Kagitcibasi & Berry, 1989). In this literature concepts such as individualism–collectivism are seen as potentially important organising dimensions, but these constructs are debated and contested (Hofstede, 1984; Triandis, 1994). A full treatment of the topic of cultural classifications and systems for understanding differences in culture represents a separate and major topic beyond that of nationality. In this book the varied approaches to characterising cultures will be explored specifically in Chapter 5, where the social relations between tourists and the people they encounter are considered. As a preliminary observation, however, it can be noted that individuals from markedly different cultures may not react in highly predictable ways in a tourism context. A special feature of tourist behaviour studies lies in recognising that the process and principles devised to assess the behaviour of diplomats, business persons and migrants in contact with the host community might not apply to tourists with short-term goals and experiencing the excitement and euphoria of novel settings.

Jafari (1987) notes that tourists exist in multiple cultures and his view may be characterised as a tripartite approach to nationalities and cultural groups in contact. He suggests there is a 'tourist culture', the world of airports and hotels, of attractions and international restaurants that have a broad commonality across cultures and borders. Further, there is the 'local culture', the way things are done in the visited setting. Local culture may embrace an array of relevant influences on interaction, from the management of time to food styles and the expression of relationships. Tourists too bring with them some of their home culture, Jafari refers to this as 'residual culture', and uses the term to describe the cultural baggage or bubble which travellers deploy to manage a novel experience. In this tripartite view of cultural interaction amongst nationalities, the liminoid nature of tourist behaviour can be emphasised and special attention needs to be given as to how well cultural classifications describing other people in contact settings actually apply.

Gender

Gender is another ubiquitous demographic descriptor in tourism studies. Even more than age and nationality, it is an immediately observable and relatively unambiguous characteristic. There is, however, a need to differentiate gender studies from those pertaining to sexual orientation and sex tourism. Gender roles are concerned with the consequences of being male or female and the societal expectations and opportunities affecting these positions, in this case in tourism settings (Swain & Momsen, 2002). Sexual orientation, by way of contrast, is one of a number of demographic descriptors that may or may not influence much tourist behaviour (Clift *et al.*, 2002). Further sexual orientation is not necessarily connected to sex tourism which in turn focuses on sexually-related activities as a defining feature of the tourists' product choice (Bauer & McKercher, 2003).

The distinctions are not trivial, and they are confused and juxtaposed in some of the existing literature. For example, Clift *et al.* (2002) discuss gay sex tourism in South-East England, but sample only tourists participating in openly gay events or subscribing to gay publications. Here sexual orientation and sex tourism are interwoven. Such approaches may miss the point that many homosexual couples and individuals take their holidays in non-specialist locations and choose the same products as other community members. A more extensive analysis of the contributions and limitations of tourist studies concerned with sexual orientation and sex tourism will be developed later in this volume.

Gergen (1983) cites gender studies as one of the major heuristics that researchers can use to explore the adequacy of their discipline. He argues that by focusing on previously hidden or neglected dimensions of a topic fresh perspectives can be generated. Such an effort at eliciting the muted voices of female travellers is underway in tourism (Small, 2002; Swain, 2002). Currently three perspectives can be identified in this literature: what female travellers want from their travel experiences, the concern they have with how they are treated by staff and strangers, and the physical layout of tourist settings and places. As Burman (2002) argues, perhaps these three directions are not yet fulfilling the role of transforming tourism studies by fully exploring societal power structures, but there have been some achievements in the registering and cataloguing of women's perspectives.

Research by Westwood *et al.* (2000) and Clift and Forrest (1999) is representative of some of the achievements. The studies begin with the perspective that, perhaps unwittingly, perhaps by design, many tourist settings have a covertly masculine bias. For example, some hotel rooms have modest grooming facilities, some bars and restaurants force people to share tables and spaces and many airline business lounges have traditionally cultivated the atmosphere of a gentleman's club. The reactions of female business travellers in particular to these kinds of settings has led to some evolution in product design. Women travellers have sought and in many places have effected changes in décor, better facilities for managing their appearance, and more flexible spaces for working and for being alone.

A particular gender role issue identified by Westwood *et al.* (2000) relates to the clumsy and inept treatment of professional women by some service providers. As one female business traveller reported, 'It is always assumed that I am the secretary, wife or mistress of the male next to me, not an independent business traveller in my own right' (Westwood *et al.*, 2000). The attitude of staff and the need for expanding professionalism in the treatment of all customers is highlighted by this example.

Security issues also concern female travellers. Security at check-in was identified as an issue, with a desire for the woman's name and room number to be managed discreetly. Further, hotel staff were seen as needing to be more attentive to security issues such as women using carparks and being in the lobby at night time. The difficulties of arriving in foreign destinations at challenging times was also seen as requiring some more customer care by airline staff. Respondents in Westwood and Pritchard's study also raised the topics of personal space and hygiene. Women reported some embarrassment and concern about sleeping next to total strangers on long overnight flights. Preferences for aisle seats for easy access to toilets, rather than having to climb over and around strange males, were noted. For toilet and bathroom facilities, there were suggestions for women-only toilets as well as larger spaces for changing clothes and reconstructing one's public appearance.

Many of these concerns apply to both genders. Men, too, need their privacy to be treated with respect, and security issues are not unimportant – particularly in known tourism trouble spots. Many men also want to be well groomed, both as business travellers and in leisure settings. Such a perspective does not negate or diminish the needs of women and their concerns, but recognises that changes made for women may be beneficial to all travellers.

These kinds of setting and service delivery requirements take place within the larger framework of what women seek from their holiday experiences. Before undertaking such a discussion, some fundamental points about the integration of demographic and psychographic factors in this book are timely. It is a part of the structure of the present chapter to highlight individual demographic variables and their influence on tourist behaviour. Nevertheless there is an enduring recognition that, while this approach is organisationally convenient, sophisticated studies of the influences on tourist behaviour necessarily adopt a multivariate approach: a multiplicity of demographic and psychographic factors shape what tourists want and do and how they respond. In dealing further with gender studies in tourism, it is necessary to at least foreshadow the importance of some integrative concepts influencing tourist behaviour (such as motivation, life-cycle and personality) which will be explored more fully in subsequent chapters.

It is possible, for example, to explore existing studies within the framework of what women seek from travel at certain stages in their life-cycle. Madrigal *et al.* (1992) established that married men and women who thought of their relationship as egalitarian both tended to express greater enthusiasm for holidays than couples with more clearly and traditionally-defined gender roles. McGehee *et al.* (1996) report that an ethic of care characterises women's roles in many Western relationships, and this ethic may both limit and shape women's holiday motivations. In a detailed empirical study of outbound Australian male and female travellers, McGehee *et al.* report that 'push' factors of cultural experience, family and kinship and prestige factors are significantly more important for women. The Australian male travellers rated sports and adventure significantly higher than did the women in the sample. Importantly both genders rated the culture and heritage factor as the most important, but women simply rated it more highly. In a linked part of the analysis, the researchers reported that both genders assessed the destination features of the budgetary environment and the opportunity to be in comfortable and relaxing settings as key 'pull' characteristics.

In a qualitative study of young Australian girls and 40 year old Australian women, Small (2002) reports that for older women the break from traditional roles was a primary determinant of a good holiday experience. It is notable that this was not construed as a break from work (many of the women studied did work), but a freedom from the mental and physical load of family organising. The findings for the 12 year old girls reinforced the centrality of freedom, and for both groups the best holidays were those where the sense of escaping duties was maximised. The difficulty of 'letting go' of domestic responsibilities was also identified and is consistent with earlier studies of women on holiday (Crawford *et al.*, 1992).

Ryan (2002b) reports some further quantitative results from both male and female samples describing holiday motivations. In a sample of over 1000 people and using 14 motivation items from the Ragheb and Beard Leisure Motivation Scale, several significant differences were recorded. Females were significantly more likely to report a higher score for relaxing physically, relaxing mentally and being with others. These results are highly consistent with those of Small (2002) and McGehee *et al.* (1996). In the Ryan study women also reported an additional two higher scores for gaining a feeling of belonging and discovering new places and things (Ryan, 2002b). Men, by way of contrast, did not record significantly higher scores for any of the motivation variables. A closer examination of this data identifies two fairly typical problems in existing research into tourist behaviour. The comprehensiveness or range of attributes measured by many tourist behaviour studies is not always adequate. One is forced to ask if all of the potential motives that men and women might want to record are adequately covered on a 14-point scale. Would an expanded range of motives reveal some areas where men might indicate that holidays were especially important to them as compared with women travellers? The more complete study reported by McGehee *et al.* (1996), which did establish gender differences, suggestd that this could be the case. A second and equally serious challenge to the integration and cumulative power of tourist behaviour research is the way in which significant findings are summarised and interpreted. The original researcher Ryan seems to appreciate the problem here by stating only that the evidence is 'mixed' for gender being a factor that influences holiday motivation (Ryan, 2002b: 45). In fact if the emphasis on the substantive meaning of the findings (i.e. the direction of the evaluations and their relative difference on the 7-point scale) is considered, then the evidence is indeed less than impressive. The mean differences between the men and the women are as follows: relax physically (0.45), gain a feeling of belonging (0.61), discover new places and things (0.21), relax mentally (0.32) and be with others (0.33). For both the relaxation items and the discovery items, the scores of both genders hover around 6 on the 7-point scale. In brief, statistical inference and significance testing establish the likelihood of that difference occurring again in another sample, but the difference is slight and the constructs were of considerable importance to both genders (Oakes, 1986).

The main reason to be concerned about this kind of finding on gender difference is how it is taken up and reported further by other researchers. For example, when evaluating the importance of relaxation, a small difference at the upper end of the importance scale for both groups can be erroneously interpreted in subsequent literature as relaxation both physical and mental being more important to females than to males on holiday (cf. Oakes, 1986). This summary leads rather too frequently to the transmitted view that it unimportant to men. The shift is subtle but inaccurate, and such reporting distortions bear close scrutiny in assessing gender-based tourism studies.

There is considerable scope for further novel and varied studies in the area of gender roles and tourist behaviour. Using the three kinds of emphasis reported earlier, further analyses of the ways in which women perceive built tourism settings and tourist environments are warranted. These kinds of pre-construction and post-occupancy evaluations could build a repertoire of results that better establish how women see such settings as suiting their needs. There are important studies to be carried out of how women could contribute to the training of tourism personnel, including the advantages and disadvantages of cross-sex and same-sex service personnel. In terms of travel motivation and the meaning of travel experience for women, a rich mix of creative qualitative and quantitative accounts can be envisaged. In all of these studies tourist behaviour researchers should maintain a particular kind of vigilance. It may be that much of what has been achieved in tourist behaviour studies lacks a fully developed conceptualisation of gender politics and power. On the other hand, the possibility must also be entertained that tourism space is only weakly infused with generic gender bias and the relevance of gender lies largely in its integration with other powerful demographic and psychographic constructs.

Additional Demographic Factors

There are a number of other widely used demographic descriptors, including education, occupation, household composition and income. Such demographic descriptions are often employed in larger-scale assessments of tourist markets (Morrison, 1996; Smith, 1995). On occasions these variables are linked together to form an index appraising or estimating disposable household income or to make estimates of likely household expenditure (Hong *et al.*, 1999). The point of constructing such indices is to define light, medium and heavy actual or potential spenders (Spotts & Mahoney, 1991). In more familiar terms, such measures enable tourist behaviour researchers to link with business interests in budget, mid-range and luxury tourist markets.

The separate treatment of many of the individual variables that are built into expenditure pattern studies have been somewhat neglected in tourism. For example, apart from historical accounts largely undertaken in Britain, there are few studies of how people from different occupational groups travel (Pimlott, 1947; Ryan, 2002b; Urry, 1990). An array of potentially interesting and quite market-relevant studies can be envisaged, for example by exploring the travel behaviour of professionals such as doctors, lawyers, teachers and accountants. One can suggest that there might be consistent within-profession similarities and between-profession differences partly due to the vestigial traces of taste and status even in a postmodern world. Additionally such status and self-esteem distinctions might be reinforced by similarities in income, education, values, and the time available for holidays. Interesting work remains to be done on such topics as doctors and their destinations, teachers travelling, and accountants abroad.

A set of studies reporting the travel behaviour of professional and work groups is implicitly connected to two other frequently measured demographic descriptors: previous travel experience and membership of special associations, interest groups or clubs. In particular measures of club membership as well as personal investment in products help define involvement and specialisation in many market segments (Woods, 2003). This specialisation topic will also be explored in the following section on tourist markets pertaining to particular tourist products.

Distance travelled to the destination is often used as a demographic descriptor. It addresses the effort of the tourist, is often allied to the expense involved and serves also to indicate familiarity with the product for first-time visitors versus repeat visitors. Local, regional, intrastate and interstate visitors are frequently contrasted in tourist behaviour studies. The differences in visitors' use of facilities such as visitor centres and their participation in activities is often markedly different for travellers arriving from near and far sources (Fesenmaier *et al.*, 1993; Moscardo, Pearce & Morrison, 2001).

A final but complex defining variable is that of ethnicity. In colloquial terms and within sectors of the tourism world, this expression equates to that of race. As Sykes (2001) suggests there is mounting genetic and molecular evidence that the old Asian/Caucasian/Negroid racial distinctions are no longer clear cut and indeed are anything but neat or comprehensive categories. There is nevertheless some sensitivity and contradictory academic reactions to dealing with race and ethnicity as social science variables. In particular one view is that to use race as a variable is to emphasise it in an a priori fashion when attention might be directed towards other more powerful variables of poverty, educational opportunity and health. To study gender differences is seen as liberating, to profile the needs of people of different ages is valuable but researchers need to be aware that to raise the relevance of race and ethnicity can be viewed as discriminatory. Certainly there is not a marked tourist behaviour tradition exploring the travel of Black Americans, indigenous Taiwanese or Tamil Sri Lankans. There are exceptions such as the work of Fan (1994) exploring US-Hispanic and US-Asian household expenditure on travel, that of Stephenson and Hughes (1995) on the UK Afro-Caribbean community and holidays, and that of Teye and Leclerc (2003) on the appeal of cruise operations for ethnic minorities. Again the opportunity for sensitive and novel tourism work potentially following some of the traditions in leisure on ethnic preferences would seem to be an important opportunity both for researchers and for business interests.

Travelling Styles

The individual demographic variables considered so far have not been peculiar to tourism. They are basic descriptors widely employed throughout behavioural and social science research. In tourism study there are some distinctive variables that apply to travel behaviour. These variables are sometimes labelled 'tripographics' and represent an array of dimensions describing tourist roles and choices (Hu & Morrison, 2002). Some of the suggested tripographic or travelling style variables are type of accommodation used, activity participation, multiple or single destination, length of stay, expenditure pattern, trip purpose (e.g. business or pleasure as distinct from traveller motivation), transportation mode, travel arrangements (such as package tour or independent travel or a combination of the two), travel distance, travel party and the season of travel. The list is extensive and has been used in part in many tourist behaviour studies.

Several existing typologies of tourist markets and roles use travelling style variables as the basic dimensions to construct organising systems. For example, the study of the visiting friends and relatives market has used travel distance (short or long-haul), multiple or single destination visit pattern, accommodation (with friends or relatives, or commercial accommodation) and trip purpose (to be with friends or relatives, or both) to formulate a 16-cell or 32-cell model of the market. The growing body of work in this area (a sharp contrast to the lack of work in the early 1990s), has been building increasingly varied typologies using these trip variables, and further, demonstrating that they matter in characterising different behavioural profiles (Hu & Morrison, 2002; Jackson, 1990; Lehto *et al.*, 2001; Moscardo *et al.*, 2000; Seaton, 1994; Seaton & Tagg, 1995).

Another illustration of the use of trip style variables comes from the study of self-drive travellers. In this literature important trip-related variables are party size, nights away from home, distance travelled and accommodation usage (Pennington-Gray, 2003). Further specialist studies of the senior self-drive travel market add the further trip style variables of the season of travel and a preference for multiple destinations (Hardy, 2003; Mings & McHugh, 1996; Pearce, 1999a; Prideaux & Carson, 2003).

The use of travel style variables, like the demographic variables already discussed, is usually not considered in isolation but forms a part of the explanatory framework for studies of tourists experiencing particular kinds of products. A product-based approach to classifying tourists will now be considered.

Tourists and Tourism Products

A substantial and frequent mode of describing tourists is to refer to their choice of a tourism product and to define their characteristics and behaviours in relation to that product. The range of tourism categories and hence tourist classifications that can be considered in this way is considerable. Ashworth (1992: 3) noted that the conjunction of terms such as heritage and tourism, cities and tourism, farms and tourism and so forth produces a set of '(nouns) and adjectival tourisms that splatter the literature'. Further, many of the designated areas of tourism described with this compound labelling approach have their own subdivisions and additional distinctions. Rural tourism, for example, can be subdivided into agricultural tourism, rural touring and farm tourism (Cox & Fox, 1991). Farm tourism in turn can be studied in more detail as farm tours, farm stays and specialist animal attractions such as horse farms (Pearce, 1990b). It is almost as if the phenomenon of interest disappears in infinitely receding steps towards individual businesses.

There is, however, a value in reviewing in an integrative and cross-situational style the product-based tourism categories and the tourists who are interested in them.

One of the wider purposes of tourist behaviour research, which was discussed in Chapter 1, is to establish some cross situational-generality and cumulative power as a part of understanding tourism.

In this section individual product categories will not be reviewed in full but common themes in the description of tourists accessing those products will be developed. The principle product categories to be considered, together with some of the key references used to develop this analysis are heritage tourism, including culture tourism and ethnic tourism (Dann & Seaton, 2001; Moscardo & Pearce, 1999; Prentice, 2003), nature-based tourism including ecotourism and wildlife-based tourism (Duffus & Dearden, 1990; Moscardo, 2002, 2003; Newsome *et al.*, 2002; Orams, 2002; Shackley, 1996; Wight, 1996; Woods, 2003) and cruise tourism (Dickinson & Vladimir, 1997; Miller & Grazer, 2002; Morrison *et al.*, 1996). In addition, some consideration will be given to wine tourism (Beames, 2003; Charters & Ali-Knight, 2002; Getz, 2000), urban tourism (G.J. Ashworth, 1992, 2003; Law, 2002; Page, 1995; D. Pearce, 1998, 2001), educational tourism including scientific tourism and volunteer tourism (Ritchie, 2003; Wearing, 2001; Weiler & Richins, 1995), sex tourism including romance tourism (Bauer & McKercher, 2003; Swain & Momsen, 2002) and theme park tourism (Pearce, 1998; Swarbrooke, 1999b).

Like any sample drawn from a large population, there is always the possibility that some omissions from this list contain distinctive new meanings and variables. Nevertheless the broad spectrum detailed in the above selection samples tourism products from many countries and from large-scale and successful product areas to smaller emerging and topical phenomenon. It considers types of tourism with a long history and those that have arisen in the last decade. It includes tourism that is visible, even obtrusive, and tourism that is partly hidden within other social forms and institutions.

Five considerations will be reviewed in detailing tourist characteristics associated with particular kinds of tourism products. First, the considerably daunting issue of assessing the markets will be outlined. Next, the variability in each of these product categories will be noted with an emphasis on illustrating the existence of a distinctive product–place interaction for all of the 'adjectival/noun tourism' types considered. As a third step, an integrative model built on the main themes in tourism product marked analyses and drawn from across these areas of interest will then be presented. This model represents a kind of meta-analysis of the tourist studies in the product areas and helps to establish cross-situational commonalities in understanding tourist markets. As a fourth step, the model will then be explained and illustrated by studies drawn from some of the constituent areas of interest. Further, the role of the model in assisting future tourist product profiles will be noted as a fifth and final consideration.

The juxtaposition of studies that assess scope, size and growth rates of the number of tourists interested in that tourism topic produces some potentially contradictory outcomes. For nearly all of the interest areas there are frequent claims that the area is growing rapidly or indeed is one of the fastest growing tourist markets. For example, Davis and colleagues (1997: 261) claim that 'the demand for tourism activities based on interacting with wildlife has increased rapidly in recent years', Beames (2003: 207) suggests 'the wine tourism industry has the potential to grow at a much faster rate than most parts of the tourism industry', thus adding to Getz's (2000) view that 'a golden age for wine and wine tourism' was on the horizon. Morrison *et al.* (1996) suggest that the rate of growth of cruise tourism is far greater than that of any other North American vacationer category, and this perspective is reinforced by Miller and Grazer (2002) who observe that the cruise industry is growing at 8.4% per year – approximately twice as fast as other global tourism markets. Can all of these claims be correct? Logically not every market can grow faster than all others. At least two possibilities exist. Potentially, there is just one area of tourism that is indeed growing very rapidly while others are losing their proportional importance. It is difficult to identify with empirical evidence any one such area, which raises the second possibility that the data on which these growth claims are made are at best suggestive and at times indeterminate or distorted.

The point about data distortion can be illustrated by reference to sex tourism. Unlike the other product areas of tourism, it seems that no one wants to claim that sex tourism is one of the fastest growing sectors with a very bright future. The example illustrates the point that it might well be that it is researcher enthusiasm (or lack of it) that is driving the claims for market importance and growth. Comments made by Ashworth (1992) in relation to urban tourism are applicable across many of the product-based interest areas. Ashworth (1992: 6) notes that 'most studies are based on very global estimates of quantities and very vague descriptions of the nature of visitors ... Usable information is just much more difficult to obtain about the tourist than the facility'.

Moscardo (2000) notes that, where evidence is provided to support growth claims, it is usually a selective example from the product range (e.g. whale watching or bird watching for wildlife tourism, museum visiting for cultural tourism, dance performances for ethnic tourism or theatre going for urban tourism) (Daniel, 1996; Findlay, 1997; Hughes, 1998; Jansen-Verbeke & van Rekom, 1996; McFarlane, 1994). Moscardo also notes that participation may be a result of a mixed itinerary on a package tour, which would overestimate serious independent interest in the phenomenon. These cautions are more than concerns of academic definition. Overestimating markets can lead to the rapid development of facilities to serve markets, a result reported by Dickinson and Vladimir (1997) for cruise tourism, where they note declining occupancy rates but rising capacity, and by Moscardo (2000) for wildlife tourism products in Southern Australia where she records despondency among operators because of low visitor numbers. Boxall and McFarlane (1993: 391) summarise the problem by noting that the 'extrapolation of results from a special event or site-specific sample to a larger constituency may be inaccurate'.

The second generic issue that follows from the problem of market size estimates is that of the variability within product categories. Many researchers recognise this issue. Sex tourism, wildlife tourism and cultural tourism, to cite just three examples, come in many different forms with marked regional and site-specific variability. Wildlife tourism in any marine setting is markedly different from wildlife tourism in rural England or the savannahs of Botswana and Zimbabwe (Shackley, 1996). Sex tourism in Thailand is unlike that in the Caribbean, Sydney or Taiwan (Bauer & McKercher, 2003). Heritage tourism may include Lenin's tomb and Xi'an's Terracotta Warriors but is equally applicable to Niagara Falls and the Great Barrier Reef (Howard, 2003). The important implication of this diversity and the theme of place specificity is that individual market segmentation studies of tourists will inevitably be closely tied to the idiosyncratic characteristics of that place. It is thus unlikely that any simple transfer of classifications of tourists for tourist products will take place from Bulawayo to Bristol or from Taipei to Trinidad. Instead there needs to be a structural linking mechanism that serves to integrate tourist appraisal studies across locations and across subdivisions of tourism interest areas. The following model attempts to develop one such systematic appraisal.

The constituent parts of Figure 2.1 are underpinned by a diverse literature. The work on serious leisure infuses all categories in the figure. Here, the emphasis is on strong commitment to the activity, potentially a career in the activity, durable benefits from participating, plus strong identification with the sub-culture and a willingness to talk about the experience (Parker, 1992; Stebbins, 1982; Wearing, 2001).

The notion of cultural capital is reflected in the post-experience outcomes and recognises the work of Holt (1995) and the experience economy emphasis of Pine and Gilmour (1999). The model pays attention to mindfulness (Langer, 1989; Moscardo, 1999) and considers quality interpretation as a form of involvement likely to promote mindfulness. It employs the passive notion of gaze in contrast to multisensory involvement (Selannameni, 2003; Urry, 1990). The ideas are influenced by the teleological implications of the North American benefits model (Driver *et al.*, 1991; Mannell & Kleiber, 1997). The approach adopted is also consistent with the specialist market segmentation studies conducted in all of the tourism content areas of interest and locates the frequently-used specialists–generalists approach in a wider context of tourism concerns.

The model is organised by considering the previous experience and commitment of the tourist, which could vary along interrelated involvement dimensions but is expressed here simply as a high and low contrast. The on-site style category may be active and involved. It is influenced by interpretation, embraces multisensory experiences and possibly results in mindfulness and active mental processing. By way of contrast, some on-site tourist behaviour styles are restricted to passive observation with limited involvement where the tourist receives rather than processes information.

In the section of the figure reporting post-experience outcomes, varied levels of the range of benefits and psychological states are portrayed. These outcomes include appreciation, achievement, knowledge, skills, social capital, rejuvenation, satiation and even boredom. These three phases of the experience lead to an array of product classifications of tourists. Although the labels are flexible and synonyms may be equally appropriate for some of the terms, the system identifies specialists, the serious and the involved, the determined, generalists, accidental and incidental visitors, dabblers and amateurs, and the disinterested.

Two examples drawn from different areas of tourist product classifications will illustrate how the conceptual framework illustrated above can heighten the appreciation of existing schemes and build new cross-situational comparisons.

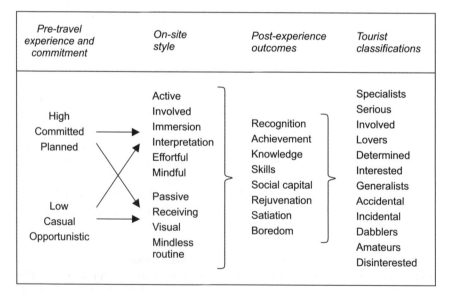

Figure 2.1 Classifying tourists involved in tourism products

One example of a tourist classification for the product area of wine tourism is reported by Charters and Ali-Knight (2002), who use the dual concepts of wine interest and wine knowledge as self-rated items from the pre-travel experience and commitment phase. They then proceed to use this a priori classification to identify four groups of wine tourists who visit the Margaret River area in Western Australia. The identified tourist classifications fit closely with the generic labels identified in Figure 2.1. Charters and Ali-Knight identify a wine lover group (with a sub-group labelled connoisseur), a 'wine-interested' group and a 'wine novice' cluster (with a subgroup labelled 'hangers on'). The on-site style and post-experience outcomes reported for the groups are also consistent with Figure 2.1. For example, the members of the wine-interested group are keen to have an on-site experience that involves learning how to taste, a mentally active and physically involving option. Some 70% of the wine-interested group reported the desire to develop these skills which identifies a post-experience outcome of knowledge and skill building.

Charters and Ali-Knight (2002) observe that there may not always be a tight relationship between the pre-travel level of commitment and the on-site experience. They comment:

> It is important to distinguish their general role as a [type of] wine tourist from their specific purpose in making any one visit ... the most dedicated connoisseur may pop into a cellar door outlet for 2 minutes just to buy a bottle ... the most uncertain wine novice may succumb to the offer of a guided tour of the winery followed by a tasting of older vintages. (Charters & Ali-Knight, 2002: 317)

Tourist classifications, the researchers remind us, are overviews and subtle motivational and specific visit intentions need to supplement the general view in understanding single behavioural incidents.

Moscardo (2000), also working in Australia, reports a classification of tourists from the wildlife tourism field. The classification is based on surveys of over 2000 tourists in the Whitsunday region in Queensland, the opposite side of the continent from the Margaret River wine area. The initial assessment of the sample was undertaken by considering responses to a survey question on the importance of seeing wildlife while in the region. More than one-third of the sample reported that opportunities to view wildlife/birds that they do not normally see were very important, just over one-third reported such chances were somewhat important and a quarter considered the opportunities to be not at all or not very important. A factor analysis of 22 destination experience features was also undertaken and the relationships among the interest groups and these on-site experiences established. The 'high wildlife importance' group assigned significantly greater importance to experiencing nature, to culture, to being physically active and to learning opportunities than did the other two groups. The group for whom wildlife viewing was moderately important provided mean scores for the on-site experience variables that lay midway between those of the other two groups. In the full reporting of the study Moscardo, established further links to visitors' appreciation of the setting, interest in specific animals and other tourist activities. Based on these desired experiences and preferred outcomes she concluded:

> The pattern of results suggest that the sample could be divided into a Wildlife Not important group and two groups which appear to be at different stages of specialization, a Generalist and a Specialist group. (Moscardo, 2000: 48)

Moscardo recognises, however, that a full appraisal of specialisation documenting interest levels, club membership, previous wildlife experiences and personal economic investment was not undertaken. It is apparent from associated data in the researcher's tables that the intensely-interested specialists with a sole wildlife focus on bird species or other animals was consistently less than 10%.

This identification of a small elite specialist group in tourist product profiles is consistent with other work on ethnic tourists and cultural tourists (Moscardo & Pearce, 1999; Prentice *et al.*, 1998). Thomas (1989, cited in Cooper, 2003) reporting on heritage attractions in Wales provides a similar theme by reporting that castles and abbeys in South Wales are popular because of a general interest in sightseeing rather than a specific or specialist interest. In the same part of the world, the Wales Tourist Board (1984, cited in Cooper, 2003) notes that 14% listed a specific interest in industrial archaeology in visiting the Big Pit. Prentice (2003) suggests that casual rather than serious or specialist consumers dominate cultural tourism, and that post-experience outcomes such as relaxation, amusement and socialisation prevail rather than cultural capital, education and knowledge.

The classification reported in Figure 2.1 draws attention to important features of the total tourist behaviour framework for researchers to measure and managers to consider in tourist product classifications. Studies, whether they be academic or consultancy based, that neglect to assess all of the key columns in Figure 2.1 are likely to be inadequate, and provide only a partial picture of product-based tourist interests. A particular caution emanating from Figure 2.1 and reflected in diverse international work is that researchers should not overestimate the percentage of the tourist market who are specialists. This caution derives from two sources: first the prevailing percentages from multiple studies suggest that only small numbers are truly single-mindedly focused on product areas; then there is the capacity for even specialists to have interests in more than one product category. One can, for example, be a dedicated specialist bird watcher and also a wine lover. This insight partly helps to explain why tourist product areas are frequently claimed to be growing rapidly – interests in tourism products are not mutually exclusive and specialist experience in one area may build generalist and later even specialist experience in another field. The topic of how people build an interest in a tourism product area, what drives that interest and what changes occur in interest levels over time requires a detailed consideration of two further integrating concepts in tourist behaviour research, motivation and life-cycles. A synthesis of these driving forces shaping tourist interests in products is the next fundamental analysis in this volume.

Chapter 3

Motivation: The Travel Career Pattern Approach

The previous chapter presented an organising model that classified tourist interest, experience, outcomes and segments. It suggested that two large scale and as yet briefly cited organising forces in tourist behaviour research (specifically motivation and life-cycle) needed to be integrated into this classification. The two topics will be treated in this chapter in a novel and integrated fashion. In the first two chapters of this book, a wide canvas of existing research was used to explore fundamental issues in studying tourism and defining tourist roles. The present chapter presents original research linking tourist motivation and life-cycle studies. In terms of Figure 2.1, the diagram which classified tourists involved in tourism products, the relevance of motivation and life-cycle studies lie in expanding the understanding of pre-travel experience and commitments.

The approach taken in this chapter develops one specific travel motivation research effort – the travel career approach. More explicitly it proposes a connection between this motivational framework, life-cycles and previous experience measures. Two linked studies of motivation are presented and a third more general and descriptive research analysis is added to illustrate the directions implied in this approach.

The first study assesses travel motivation amongst Western travellers, the second assesses travel motivation amongst travellers from Korea, and the applied study illustrates the applicability of the integrated travel-motivation/life-cycle scheme to self-drive tourists. As a precursor to the empirical work, a background to motivation research in tourism is provided.

Motivation Studies: A Background

From the outset, motivation has been an important topic of leisure and tourism study (Crompton, 1979; Dann, 1981; Galloway, 1998; Veal, 1997). Wahab (1975) suggested that the area of travel motivation is fundamental in tourism studies and basic to tourism development. Crompton (1979) observed that it is possible to describe tourist behaviour and to classify tourists but it is more difficult to answer the question 'why' – the key factor underlying all tourist behaviour. Several researchers have seen motivation as the driving force behind all actions (Crompton, 1979; Fodness, 1994; Iso-

Ahola, 1982). Motivation is then an initial point in studying tourist behaviour and beyond that for understanding systems of tourism (Gunn, 1988; Mill & Morrison, 1985). Although commentators have agreed on the fundamental importance of motivation, in 1987 Jafari noted that no common theoretical understanding had emerged at that time (Jafari, 1987). There has been research attention and commentary since then, but Jafari's view still seems appropriate since, despite multiple efforts, no widely agreed conceptual framework has emerged (World Tourism Organisation, 1999).

The difficulties in studying motivation are considerable. Unlike the frequently measured purpose of travel (e.g. 'for business' or 'for pleasure'), which is considered to be public and self-explanatory, the motivations or underlying reasons for travel are covert in that they reflect an individual's private needs and wants (Gee *et al.*, 1984). The wide range of human needs and the methodological difficulties in measuring them also make travel motivation research challenging (French *et al.*, 1995). Additionally the universality of the topic potentially poses problems in constructing theories that apply across cultures (Smith, 1995). Nevertheless, despite the difficulties, the value of pursuing travel motivation studies can be described as extensive.

Motivation studies are of interest to business and commercial analysts because sound market appraisals can be built on such appraisals (c.f. Tribe, 2004). Further, it has been widely suggested that various tourist visit patterns are the result of a destination-choice process which, in turn, is influenced powerfully by tourists' motives and backgrounds (Lue *et al.*, 1993; Um & Crompton, 1990). Moscardo *et al.* (1996) proposed that motivation could be linked to activities and, in turn, to destination choice. In this kind of scheme, travel motivation becomes a topic of central interest to those who market and manage tourism. Similarly Mansfeld (1992) suggested that improved travel motivation theory would benefit the study of both travel behaviour and travel choice. There is also an interest in motivational studies from researchers working within a sociological tradition who may not seek to employ motivation scales or measures but who do seek to understand the meaning and experience of travel (Ryan, 2002b).

Although there has been an awareness of the need to develop motivation theories, existing approaches only partially meet all the requirements of a good theory (Pearce, 1993b). Seven elements that have been identified as important for tourist motivational theory are presented in Table 3.1.

This chapter concentrates on the modification of one of the existing theories of tourist motivation – the *travel career ladder* (Pearce, 1988, 1991b, 1993b). Much potential exists for other research on travel motivation to advance parallel conceptual endeavours such as Plog's allocentric–psychocentric theory (Plog, 1974, 1987, 1991), Iso-Ahola's optimal arousal theory (Iso-Ahola, 1982) and Beard and Ragheb's leisure motivation

Table 3.1 Key elements for a sound theory of tourist motivation

	Element	*Explanation*
1	The role of the theory	Must be able to integrate existing tourist needs, reorganise the needs and provide a new orientation for future research
2	The ownership and appeal of the theory.	Must appeal to specialist researchers, be useful in tourism industry settings and credible to marketers and consumers
3	Ease of communication	Must be relatively easy to explain to potential users and be universal (not country specific) in its application
4	Ability to measure travel motivation	Must be amenable to empirical study. The ideas can be translated into questions and responses for assessment purposes
5	A multi-motive versus single-trait approach	Must consider the view that travellers may seek to satisfy several needs at once. Must be able to model the pattern of traveller needs, not just consider one need
6	A dynamic versus snapshot approach	Must recognise that both individuals and societies change over time. Must be able to consider or model the changes that are taking place continuously in tourism
7	The roles of extrinsic and intrinsic motivation	Must be able to consider that travellers are variously motivated by intrinsic, self-satisfying goals and at other times motivated by extrinsic, socially controlled rewards (e.g. others' opinions)

approach (Beard & Ragheb, 1983). The value of pursuing the travel career approach resides in continuing to develop a line of work sustained over a period of time, particularly as it has been used in both academic and applied studies and has attracted some detailed commentary suggesting the need to improve the approach (Blamey & Hatch, 1998; Ryan, 1998; Todd, 1999). The kind of attention and effort advanced in this chapter is consistent with the needs to understand motivation and travel goals in future survey work. Nevertheless it is anticipated that some of the ideas advanced in the final model proposed will be of interest to some tourism researchers in the sociological tradition.

The travel career ladder approach was developed by Pearce (1988, 1991b, 1993b), Pearce and Caltabiano (1983) and Moscardo and Pearce (1986a) and was based in part on Maslow's (1970) needs-hierarchy theory of motivation. The travel career ladder (TCL) describes tourist motivation as consisting of five different levels: relaxation needs, safety/security needs, relationship needs, self-esteem and development needs, and self-actualisation/fulfilment needs. Following Maslow, the needs of travellers were seen as organised into a hierarchy or ladder with the relaxation needs at the lowest level, followed in order by safety/security needs, relationships needs, self-esteem and development needs and finally, at the highest level, fulfilment needs. Travellers were considered to have more than one level of travel motivation, thought it was suggested that one set of needs in the ladder levels might be dominant.

As Rowan (1998) reports, popular undergraduate texts often oversimplify and misrepresent Maslow's work. In particular reports of Maslow's work that depict these needs as a simple five-part triangle with some marvellous end-point of personal growth oversimplify the complex layering of two kinds of self-esteem needs and several variants of self-actualisation and competence. In revising the TCL into a more complex patterning of motives, the full complexity of motivational possibilities in the tourism context needs to be explored (cf. Ryan, 2002b).

The ideas of Maslow were only one contributor to the construction of the TCL. The career concept in leisure or tourism was equally important in shaping the TCL approach (Goffman, 1961; Hughes, 1937). In this line of inquiry, it is argued that people's motivation changes with their travel experience. People may be said to have a travel career, reflected in a pattern of travel motives, which changes according to their lifespan and/or accumulated travel experiences.

The usefulness of the career concept in tourist motivation research has received little sustained attention. In the leisure research field the idea of a career has been recognised particularly as it has been developed around the concept of specialisation. Bryan (1977) originally developed the specialisation notion, and suggested that there are distinct classes of participants who exhibit unique styles of involvement for a given recreational activity. Participants in any given activity exhibit a continuum of behaviour from general interest to a very focused involvement. Chapter 2 discussed the applicability of the notion of specialisation, for example, in relation to wine tourism activities and wildlife viewing. Previous experience, knowledge about the activity, and the level of investment in the activity all assist in classifying a person as having a specialist interest. The specialisation concept is intertwined with the career concept, and both offer a way to assess and think about tourist involvement in activities and the growth of the involvement (Chipman & Helfrich, 1988; Kuentzel & McDonald, 1992; McFarlane, 1994).

When applied to tourist travel in general, the term 'career' has some further specific implications. It has been proposed that many people systematically move through a series of stages or have predictable travel motivational patterns. One pattern proposed is that over time some people may be seen as moving towards more self-esteem and self-actualisation

relation to
travel motivat ?

needs, while others may stay at a relationships or stimulation level, depending on contingency or limiting factors such as health and financial considerations. Broadly, the TCL theory proposed that, as people accumulate travel experiences, they progress upward through the levels of motivation.

Some empirical studies demonstrated that this research model was an acceptable initial tool in understanding travel motivation (Kim, 1997; Lee, 1998; Loker-Murphy, 1995; Mills, 1985). As Ryan (2002b: 50) reports, the evidence was not always clear cut but 'at a descriptive level it has an obvious appeal'. Furthermore, it has been proposed that the travel career ladder can be utilised as a blueprint for the design of motivational studies for special markets such as for ecotourists and for theme park patrons (Blayney, 1998; Pearce & Rutledge, 1994).

Although there is some promise with this travel motivation theory and its emerging applications, issues for further development have been identified. Ryan (1998, 2002b), for example, questioned the empirical validity of the approach. In particular he considered the number of items used to assess the ladder levels to be inadequate. Further appraisals suggested there was a lack of predictive certainty in the approach and there were inconsistencies in the formulation of the model (Ryan, 1998: 953). Such an appraisal, however, along with other comments concerning the methodological reactivity of measuring motivation, can take researchers towards the view that tourist behaviour is irrational, unmeasurable and unknowable (cf. Ryan, 2002b: 57). The author rejects this view while recognising the need to appreciate the socially embedded complexity of how people respond and the need to assess a diversity of response options.

At times, commentary of the Travel Career Ladder theory has focused on the explicit use of the term *ladder* in the formulation (Kim *et al.*, 1996; Ryan, 1998). The power of an effective theory lies partly in its ability to be clearly understood by its target audiences (cf. Pearce, 1993b). In this context, the term ladder has perhaps drawn too much attention to an analogy with a physical ladder with a concentration on ascending the steps and being on one step at a time. The present approach will therefore de-emphasise the hierarchical elements in the travel career ladder theory and propose a travel career *pattern* approach. In this reformulation the dynamic multi-level motivational structure, which is seen as critical in understanding travel motivation, can be seen as forming patterns that reflect and link to travel careers. The concept of a travel career remains important even though the ladder concept is no longer employed. The view persists that travellers will exhibit changing motivational patterns over their life-stages and/or with travel experience. Table 3.2 provides some conceptual definitions regarding key terms pertinent to this discussion.

Some of the challenges in developing travel motivation theory are met through these conceptual adjustments. It is also helpful to use empirical

Table 3.2 Key terms involving travel career pattern

Key terms	*Conceptual definitions*
Travel needs/motives	The forces that drive travel behaviour. These forces are both biological and socio-cultural.
Self/others-oriented motives	Travel motives can be internally oriented or externally influenced.
Motivation pattern	Travel motivation occurs in a pattern of multiple motives rather than in single dominant force .
Travel career	A dynamic concept arguing that tourists have identifiable stages in their holiday taking. The state of one's travel career, like a career at work, is influenced by previous travel experiences and life-stage or contingency factors. A pattern of travel motives should be linked to or characterise the state of one's travel career. (Empirical studies are useful to explore these links.) Travel careers can be operationalised by a conjoint consideration of travel experience, age and life cycle.
Travel career ladder (TCL)	An older theoretical model describing travel motivation through five hierarchical levels of needs/motives in relation to travel career levels.
Travel career pattern (TCP)	Conceptually modified TCL with more emphasis on the change of motivation patterns reflecting career levels than on the hierarchical levels.

analyses of traveller motivation to support and help refine the conceptual arguments. The purpose of the first study reported here was to provide comprehensive research-based information regarding travel motivation patterns and their development. While a detailed exposition of this work is provided in this chapter further details are also available in Pearce and Lee (2005).

The research approached travel motivation through a two-phased process – exploratory interviews and a major survey study. The interview phase of the study is reported in detail in Lee and Pearce (2002). Intensive interviews with a small number of travellers chosen because of their markedly different travel experience and life-cycle phases were conducted. The small sample consisted of Australian-based residents.

The concept of 'theoretical saturation' in the focus and small-group literature was used to guide the study (Krueger, 1994; Strauss & Corbin, 1990). Following grounded theory, theoretical saturation was defined as a situation obtaining when further sampling elicited no new or further information. In the interviews, the 12 diverse interviewees were asked about their motivation for previous and future international holiday travel. Following the interview, each participant completed a two-paged structured questionnaire containing a preliminary network of travel motive items. The coding of the full interviews was extensive and thorough, and was checked and verified with other researchers (Lee & Pearce, 2002). The results from these preliminary investigations indicated some dominant motives for international holidays. They included a search for novelty and self-development as well as cultural experiences, relationships and escape. Apart from these clear categories, other travel motives were difficult to identify because of the subjects' uncertainty about their travel needs. Nevertheless, the dominant types of motivations obtained had also been identified from the early key travel motivation literature that has shaped contemporary travel motivation research (Crompton, 1979; Dann, 1977, 1981; Iso-Ahola, 1982; Mill & Morrison, 1985; Pearce, 1988, 1991b, 1993b; Uysal & Jurowski, 1994).

It can be noted that when the respondents were asked to describe the reasons for travelling to a particular country, they sometimes simply provided their image of the destination from memory rather than employing motivational statements (cf. Uysal & Jurowski, 1994). This finding raises awareness that respondents are engaged in a social process of maintaining a successful interaction with an interviewer, and the way they respond reflects circumstances, moods and capacity. A very similar point about satisfaction responses in tourism studies will be made in Chapter 7. This issue of commenting on travel motives has been noted by previous researchers. For example, Dann (1981) classified the people's lack of awareness of their travel motives under four headings:

- tourists may not wish to reflect on real travel motives;
- they may be unable to reflect on real travel motives;
- they may not wish to express real travel motives;
- they may not be able to express real travel motives.

These issues focus attention once more on the purpose and style of motivational research and conceptualisation being developed in this chapter. The core goal of the present approach is to inform large-scale survey work conducted about travellers' motives and reasons for travel. In this kind of work, which is largely atheoretical at the moment, there is a need for a structured rationale for including travel motivation items and for describing and just possibly anticipating emerging motivation patterns.

Surveying Travel Motivation

In order to set these preliminary motive categories into a larger frame of reference, a major survey phase of research followed the exploratory interview phase. Throughout this study, travel motivation was viewed as a multi-dimensional construct comprising numerous motives. A pool of 143 initial motive items was therefore obtained from the existing tourism and leisure literature (Beard & Ragheb, 1983; Crandall, 1980; Crompton, 1979; Dann, 1981; Driver & Manfredo, 1996; Fisher & Price, 1991; Gitelson & Kerstetter, 1990; Hollender, 1977; Iso-Ahola, 1982; Iso-Ahola & Allen, 1982; Krippendorf, 1987; Lee & Crompton, 1992; Loker & Perdue, 1992; McIntosh & Goeldner, 1986; Manfredo *et al.*, 1983; Pearce, 1988, 1991b; Shoemaker, 1989; Tinsley & Kass, 1978, 1979). These efforts were directed at overcoming Ryan's (2002b) criticism that previous work did not offer a definitive listing of items for measuring a motivational development process. The diversity and comprehensiveness of motivational items assembled from all the previous studies was considerable. A focus group panel then reviewed the initial motive items for content validity and overlap. The list was thus reduced to 74 items, each detailing a subtly distinct motivation for travel. These items were then utilised in the questionnaire for quantitative data collection. A four-page self-administered questionnaire was used to gather information on subjects' general motivations for travel. In the questionnaire, subjects were asked to to indicate the importance of each of the travel motivational statements on a 9-point Likert-type scale (from 'not important at all' to 'very important'). Australian and international tourists were sampled in Northern Australia at major shopping centres, express coach terminals, and the boarding gate areas of domestic and international airports.

Sample profiles

The sample consisted of 1012 respondents of whom just over half (57%) were Australian, 22% were from United Kingdom and the rest (21%) were from other Western countries. The percentage of male (47%) and female (53%) respondents was quite closely balanced. Slightly more than half (53%) were relatively younger respondents under 36 years of age. Nearly one quarter (23%) of the sample held professional or technical positions and more than half (56%) had completed their tertiary education. For the respondents' travel experience, nearly half (47%) were quite experienced in their domestic travel, indicating at least 26 separate travel events each while more than 53% had travelled overseas five times or more.

Principal component analysis (PCA) was employed to identify the underlying motive dimensions. K-means cluster analysis was used to classify the respondents according to their travel experience levels. A number of checks on the importance of the items contributing to the travel experience levels were also conducted (Lee & Pearce, 2002). The factor scores from the PCA analysis results were computed and independent *t*-tests were

utilised to examine differences in the motivation factors between the identified travel experience level groups. The results are presented here to:

(1) gain an overview of travel motivation;
(2) describe the analysis of travel experience in this preliminary study;
(3) relate the travel motivation and the travel experience measures.

Travel motivation analysis

The underlying dimensions of the 74 selected motive items were
assessed using principal component analysis (PCA). A varimax rotation
was followed (West, 1991). Principal component analysis is a standard
statistical procedure that identifies a hidden structure in a set of variables. It
is appropriate for large numbers of items and large sample (Bernstein *et al.*,
1988; Smith, 1995). A check on the adequacy of the sample size was made
using the Keiser-Meyer-Olkin (KMO) measurement of sampling adequacy.
This measure is expressed in a value ranging fom 0 to 1, and the higher
value represents a good basis on which to proceed. In this study the value
was 0.96, indicating a very satisfactory sample size. When eigen values
greater than 1 were considered, the procedure produced 14 factors. Eigen
values are a measure of the coherence of the factor and depend on the
number of items loading or defining the underlying dimension of interest.
Usually when eigen values are 1 or more, the underlying dimension in the
data is considered to represent a strand of meaning worthy of further
consideration. Only items where the factor loadings were above 0.40 were
used to explain the factor (Child, 1972). The percentage of variance
explained by this solution was 67.9%. Cronbach's coefficient alpha (α) was
used to measure the internal consistency among the items. Baloglu and
McCleary (1999) report that this is the most generally used reliability
measure to estimate the degree to which the items on a measure are representative of the domain of the construct being measured. The criteria of 0.70
for the coefficient alpha is usually considered reliable (Ryan, 1995a). Apart
from the novelty factor (0.70), all factors resulted in a Cronbach's coefficient
alpha score above 0.80, which indicates strong consistency among the items
in each factor. The results are shown in Table 3.3.

The 14 resulting motivation factors, in the order of importance, were
labelled as (1) novelty, (2) escape/relax, (3) relationship (strengthen), (4)
autonomy, (5) nature, (6) self-development (host–site involvement), (7)
stimulation, (8) self-development (personal development), (9) relationship
(security), (10) self-actualisation, (11) isolation, (12) nostalgia, (13) romance
and (14) recognition. The results indicated that *novelty, escape/relax*, and *relationship* motivations are the most important factors in forming travel motivation. The least important factors were recognition, romance and nostalgia.

The four common and main travel motivations (escape/relax, novelty/

Table 3.3 Travel motivation factors ranked by factor mean scores and indicating item importance of mean scores and loadings

Factors	Motive items	Importance mean	Factor loadings
Novelty (7.62)[a] (1.7%)[b] (α = 0.70)[c]	having fun	8.23	0.48
	experiencing something different	7.61	0.53
	feeling the special atmosphere of the vacation destination	7.45	0.52
	visiting places related to my personal interests	7.2	0.45
Escape/relax (6.92) (5.8) (α = 0.82)	resting and relaxing	7.34	0.43
	getting away from everyday psychological stress/pressure	7.33	0.8
	being away from daily routine	7.3	0.66
	getting away from the usual demands of life	7.23	0.8
	giving my mind a rest	6.57	0.65
	not worrying about time	6.44	0.52
	getting away from everyday physical stress/pressure	6.24	0.68
Relationship (strengthen) (6.69) (2.20%) (α = 0.83)	doing things with my companion(s)	7.00	0.70
	doing something with my family/friend(s)	6.83	0.83
	being with others who enjoy the same things as I do	6.83	0.43
	strengthening relationships with my companion(s)	6.58	0.60
	strengthening relationships with my family/friend(s)	6.54	0.82
	contacting with family/friend(s) who live elsewhere	6.34	0.54
Autonomy (6.57) (1.80%) (α = 0.85)	being independent	6.92	0.78
	being obligated to no one	6.42	0.85
	doing things my own way	6.38	0.77
Nature (6.44) (2.40%) (α = 0.92)	viewing the scenery	7.11	0.65
	being close to nature	6.42	0.84
	getting a better appreciation of nature	6.29	0.84
	being harmonious with nature	5.94	0.8
Self-development (host–site involvement) (6.2) (2.9%) (α = 0.84)	learning new things	7.24	0.43
	experiencing different cultures	6.82	0.65
	meeting new and varied people	6.53	0.56
	developing my knowledge of the area	6.48	0.72
	meeting the locals	6.29	0.73
	observing other people in the area	5.61	0.77
	following current events	4.42	0.4

Table 3.3 *continued*

Factors	Motive items	Impor-tance mean	Factor load-ings
Stimulation (6.19) (28.80%) (α = 0.89)	exploring the unknown	7.05	0.53
	feeling excitement	6.59	0.74
	having unpredictable experiences	6.46	0.69
	being spontaneous	6.38	0.50
	having daring/adventuresome experience	5.92	0.86
	experiencing thrills	5.78	0.85
	experiencing the risk involved	5.15	0.79
Self-development (personal development) (6.16) (7.00%) (α = 0.92)	develop my personal interests	6.43	0.74
	knowing what I am capable of	6.2	0.68
	gaining a sense of accomplishment	6.19	0.64
	gaining a sense of self-confidence	6.11	0.69
	developing my skills and abilities	6.09	0.77
	using my skills and talents	5.93	0.69
Relationship (security) (5.86) (4.10%) (α = 0.87)	feeling personally safe and secure	6.36	0.53
	being with respectful people	6.23	0.73
	meeting people with similar values/interests	5.99	0.69
	being near considerate people	5.95	0.73
	being with others if I need them	5.45	0.47
	feeling that I belong	5.16	0.58
Self-actualise (5.78) (2.10%) (α = 0.89)	gaining a new perspective on life	6.52	0.5
	feeling inner harmony/peace	6.15	0.58
	understanding more about myself	5.53	0.68
	being creative	5.39	0.55
	working on my personal/spiritual values	5.32	0.76
Isolation (5.72) (1.90%) (α = 0.81)	experiencing the peace and calm	6.71	0.52
	avoiding interpersonal stress and pressure	5.84	0.52
	experiencing the open space	5.79	0.55
	being away from the crowds of people	5.15	0.73
	enjoying isolation	5.1	0.79
Nostalgia (5.43)(1.5%) (α = 0.92)	thinking about good times I've had in the past	5.51	0.79
	reflecting on past memories	5.35	0.81

Table 3.3 *continued*

Factors	Motive items	Impor-tance mean	Factor load-ings
Romance (5.10)(1.5%) (α = 0.78)	having romantic relationships	5.32	0.71
	being with people of the opposite sex	4.87	0.68
Recognition (4.27) (4.40%) (α = 0.87)	sharing skill and knowledge with others	4.9	0.63
	showing others I can do it	4.23	0.74
	being recognised by other people	4.14	0.72
	leading others	4.07	0.7
	having others know that I have been there	4	0.72

67.9% of variance explained; motive items with factor loading <0.40 is discarded
a = mean score of the factor, *b* = variance explained
c = Cronbach's alpha reliability coefficient
Source: Pearce and Lee, 2005

stimulation, relationship and self-development) revealed in the previous interview-based phase of the study could then be further divided into two types. In the PCA results escape/relax was further classified into escape/relax and isolation, novelty/stimulation into novelty and stimulation, relationship into relationship (strengthen) and relationship (security), and self-development into personal development and host–site involvement.

One way to think about the factors obtained from the principal component analysis which are independent is to interpret them as defining a multi-dimensional space. For further analyses and in order to locate individuals within the 14-dimensional space, factor scores were calculated. First, the loading of each variable on a factor was multiplied by the individual's original value for that variable. In the next step of the procedure, the same calculation was repeated for all variables in the factor for that individual. These scores were then summed. The process was repeated for all factors for that same individual and then repeated for all other individuals. Finally, all scores were standardised to a mean of 0 with a standard deviation of 1. These procedures facilitate further statistical treatment of the motivational patterns and other variables of interest such as travel experience.

Travel experience levels analysis

The first study reported in this chapter made a modest attempt to consider life-cycle issues and travel experience variables. Since this effort illustrates and represents the developmental nature of conducting research it is included here for its demonstration value rather than as a definitive incorporation of life-cycle factors into travel motivation study. The second

Table 3.4 Cross-tabulation-profiles of travel experience level group

Profiles	Categories	Travel experience levels			
		High	(%)[a]	Low	(%)[a]
Gender*	Male	243	(50.7)	196	(43)
	Female	235	(49.1)	260	(57)
Educational level**	High school	120	(25.2)	204	(44.7)
	Technical/trade qualification	111	(23.3)	73)	(16)
	University degree	122	(25.6)	116	(25.4)
	Postgraduate degree	76	(16)	31	(6.8)
	Others	47	(9.9)	32	(7)
Occupational category**	Home maker	27	(5.6)	36	(7.9)
	Professional/technical	142	(29.6)	79	(17.4)
	Executive administrator	17	(3.5)	8	(1.8)
	Labourer	3	(0.6)	20	(4.4)
	Middle management	43	(9)	11	(2.4)
	Tradesman/machine operator	18	(3.8)	21	(4.6)
	Retired	33	(6.9)	9	(2)
	Sales/marketing	31	(6.5)	29	(6.4)
	Self-employed/business owner	56	(11.7)	33	(7.3)
	Student	26	(5.4)	85	(18.7)
	Clerical or service	33	(6.9)	45	(9.9)
	Others	50	(10.4)	78	(17.1)
International travel experience**	Inexperienced (0)	18	(3.8)	184	(40.4)
	Somewhat experienced (1–4)	66	(13.8)	173	(37.9)
	Experienced (5–10)	118	(24.6)	69	(15.1)
	Very experienced (>10)	277	(57.8)	30	(6.6)
Domestic travel experience**	Inexperienced (0–9)	14	(2.9)	194	(42.5)
	Somewhat experienced (10–25)	111	(23.2)	180	(39.5)
	Experienced (26–50)	141	(29.4)	58	(12.7)
	Very experienced (>50)	213	(44.5)	24	(5.3)
Age *	<26	28	(5.8)	188	(41.2)
	26–35	128	(26.7)	162	(35.5)
	36–45	118	(24.6)	71	(15.6)
	>45	205	(42.8)	35	(7.7)

Table 3.4 *continued*

Profiles	Categories	Travel experience levels			
		High	(%)[a]	Low	(%)[a]
Nationality **	Australian	190	(39.7)	324	(73.1
	United Kingdom	167	(34.9)	41	(9.3)
	Other Western countries	122	(25.5)	78	(17.6)

Note: *a* = % within travel experience level group
chi: *= $p<0.05$ ** = $p<0.001$
Source: Pearce and Lee, 2005

study explored the travel experience variable in more detail with a wider range of variables but the presentation of this first phase might help assist readers in understanding the genesis of the ideas about travel experience.

Three basic variables – domestic travel experience, international travel experience and age – were taken into account in an initial attempt to characterise travel experience levels and to consider dimension of life-cycle and experience. A set of cluster analyses established that two distinct groups, an experienced and an inexperienced traveller group, were present in the sample. These groups also differed on a range of other demographic variables. These differences are reported in Table 3.4.

Travel motivation and travel experience level

The links between the motivation factors and different levels of travel experience were explored with independent *t*-tests. The travel experience level was used as the independent variable, and motivation factors as the dependent variables (Table 3.5).

The following motivation factors resulted in significant differences for the two levels of travel experience: nature, self-development (host–site involvement), stimulation, self-development (personal development), relationship (security), self-actualise, nostalgia, romance and recognition motivation factors resulted in significant differences. Several other motivation factors including novelty, escape/relax, relationship (strengthen), autonomy and isolation were not significantly different. The nature and host–site involvement motivation factors were generally more important to people with greater travel experience levels (0.09, 0.24) than those with lesser travel experience levels (-0.11, -0.22). By way of contrast, the stimulation factor was not as important to the respondents with greater travel experiences (-0.09) compared to those with lower levels (0.13).

The findings identified some new patterns in the motivational landscape. Personal development and self-actualisation, which comprised the upper levels of the previous TCL theory, were emphasised more by people

Table 3.5 Independent *t*-test, motivation factors by travel experience level groups

Motivation	High travel experience level		Low travel experience level		t-score	Sig.
	Factor score	Mean	Factor score	Mean		
Novelty	0.01		0.01		-0.11	0.91
Escape/relax	0.04	6.92	-0.03	6.96	1.11	
Relationship (strengthen)	-0.05	6.49	0.04	6.87	-2.58	0.23
Autonomy	-0.07	6.37	0.05	6.78	-1.75	0.08
Nature**	0.09	6.59	-0.11	6.32	3.01	0
Self-development (host–site involvement)**	0.24	6.42	-0.22	6.03	-6.96	0
Stimulation**	-0.09	6.05	0.13	6.39	-3.16	0
Self-development (personal development)**	-0.1	5.9	0.1	6.49	-2.88	0
Relationship (security)*	-0.08	5.63	0.09	6.11	-2.58	0.01
Self-actualise*	-0.09	5.57	0.1	6.05	-2.81	0.01
Isolation	-0.01	5.69	0.01	5.81	-0.34	0.74
Nostalgia*	-0.08	5.07	0.07	5.81	-2.15	0.03
Romance**	-0.14	4.55	0.13	5.64	-4.13	0
Recognition**	-0.13	3.86	0.11	4.66	-3.49	0

**= $p < 0.05$ ** = $p < 0.001$
Source: Pearce and Lee, 2005

with less travel experience stage (0.1, 0.1). The relationship (security) factor was also emphasised more by those with less travel experience (0.09) compared with more experienced travellers (-0.08). The least important motivations, romance and recognition, were also more important factors for the group with lower levels of travel experience. Importantly, the three most important motivation factors, novelty, escape/relax, and relationship (strengthen), were not statistically different in their significance as motivation factors for the two levels of travel experience. These patterns will be discussed in more detail later, but a preliminary observation is that they imply that the three dimensions of motivation function as the core factors in all travel motivation patterns regardless of travel experience levels. In other words, it could be suggested that, though people travel for various reasons, these three factors could nevertheless be the common backbone for all kinds of travel.

Developing a Travel Career Pattern Framework

In the two phases of the study travel motivation seems to have been identified as patterns and combinations of multiple motives. Certainly these motives are influenced by previous travel experience and age. Earlier, Pearce and Caltabiano (1983) and Woodside and Jacobs (1985) argued that previous travel experience would provide insights when studying travel motivation. In this first set of results linking travel motivation and travel experience level, _escape/relax, novelty, relationship_ and _self-development_ were the most important overall, and were core to all travellers. People with high travel experience levels gave more emphasis to motivations regarding self-development through host–site involvement and nature seeking. People with less travel experience stressed other factors such as stimulation, personal development, self-actualisation, security, nostalgia, romance and recognition. These findings show a marked similarity to the work of Shoe-maker (1989) derived from the senior travel market. Shoemaker's study did not directly measure previous travel experience, but the majority of the respondents (62%) indicated that they travelled more than twice a year. For the experienced seniors market visiting new places and experiencing new things, escaping and relaxing, spending time with family and visiting museums and historical sites were considered to be more important as travel reasons. By way of contrast, being with the opposite sex, engaging in physical activities, seeking spiritual enrichment and telling friends about the trip was less important for these travellers. The findings of Shoemaker's study, as noted in the next section, form just one set of previous motivational results in close accord with the present findings.

For both phases of the present study, the outcomes point to several common and notable findings. Firstly, the results from both phases of this first study indicated that the motivational dimensions of escape/relax, novelty, relationship, and self-development within the new travel career pattern approach are the most important travel motivation factors. A number of studies have endorsed and reinforced these kind of results. For example, the novelty-seeking motive has received considerable attention in tourism research since it was introduced into the tourism literature by Cohen (1972). It is one of the main forces behind all travel behaviour and has been explored in a number of empirical studies (Bello & Etzel, 1985; Cohen, 1972; Crompton, 1979; Dann, 1977, 1981). While novelty-seeking is a need to pursue stimulation, escape-seeking has been understood as a need to get away from over-stimulation (Iso-Ahola, 1982). Mannell and Iso-Ahola (1987) theorised that escape from routine responsibilities and stress is a major motivation for recreational travel. This perspective has been confirmed by several researchers (Crompton, 1979; Hollender, 1977; Lounsbury & Hoopes, 1985; Woodside & Jacobs, 1985). Additionally the self-development motive too, has been understood and defined as seeking personal growth and/or a desire to learn and interact with host cultures and communities (Calantone & Johar, 1984; Crompton, 1979; Dann, 1981; Etzel & Woodside, 1982; Goodrich, 1977; Woodside & Jacobs, 1985). This view of self-development is consistent with some of the subtleties in Marlow's revised writing on the social nature of human fulfilment and competence (Rowan, 1998). The relationship-seeking motive has been viewed as the desire to affiliate or socially interact through vacation travel (Tinsley & Kass, 1978, 1979). Research here too has been considerable, noting the need to establish permanent or temporary relationships as well as enhancing kinship relations (Crompton, 1979; Lounsbury & Hoopes, 1985; Woodside & Jacobs, 1985).

In this first study, travel motives reflecting self-development through host–site involvement (such as 'experiencing different cultures' and 'meeting the locals') were considered more important at the higher levels of travel experience than at lesser levels. As reported in the interview phase of this study, some respondents tended to start their initial travel experiences from Western-culture-based countries such as Europe and then travel to Asia or so-called 'exotic' destinations as they gained travel experiences. Again the direction of the findings is consistent with previous work. Robie *et al.* (1993) report that the desire to seek a more meaningful existence and to feel as if one belongs to a community or group was central to their motivational work and consistent with that of Figler *et al.* (1992).

Important contradictions to the original TCL theory were also obtained. It was found the travel experience group with less experience rated the self-*actualisation* and *self-development* motives as more important. Indeed that group tended to rate most travel motivational factors as more important. Seven out of the nine motivational factors, which were identified to be significantly different in importance, were emphasised more by the people with less travel experience. This finding was consistent with the qualitative results.

The three most important motivational factors identified in the quantitative results were *novelty*, *escape/relax*, and *relationship*. These factors showed no significant difference in their importance between the two levels of travel experience. Similarly, the interview results also suggested that these three factors, along with *self-development*, are the main psychological forces driving travel. A preliminary statement on the structure of travel motivation is possible here. There is a strong likelihood that people may have certain dominant and constant travel motivations that act as a common backbone to travel regardless of their travel experience level. In particular, the outcomes from these studies suggest that travel motivation patterns can be described as having *novelty, escape/relax, relationship,* and *self-development* related motives as a foundation regardless of one's travel experience. Therefore, these four central motivation factors can be understood as the 'skeleton' in travel motivation and for travel career patterns. *Self-development* motives however can be classified into two categories of personal development and host–site involvement. Personal development motives are emphasised more by people with less travel experience, whereas host–site involvement motives become more evident as their travel experience develops. Such a perspective may explain why the subjects in the interview study were not sure about their travel motivation apart from the core motivation factors. It also appears that these core motivations may not change to any great degree. It can be argued, however, that a change in or alteration of other less-dominant motives do transform the overall travel motivation patterns. Similar to a human body undergoing maturation, the physical appearance may change but the skeleton does not.

From this first study several achievements can be noted. An extensive list of travel motivation items, which provided a broad coverage of possible motives of travel, was employed. Motivation factors were effectively and clearly identified. Many of the motives were shown to be influenced by the levels of travel experience. Furthermore, the identification of four important motivation factors that persisted through two contrasting levels of experience led to the theoretical possibility that there is a 'mainframe' or 'backbone' in the travel career patterns.

Travel Career Patterns: Further Analysis

The next phase of the motivational research was designed to further confirm and expand the theoretical concepts of the travel career patterns approach. In particular, this study was designed to investigate the cross-cultural applicability of the theory by using a Korean sample. While the previous studies and outcomes represented travel motivation within Western culture, this second study investigated the travel motivation and travel career patterns of one Asian culture, that of Korea. In this context, it is notable that much work on travel motivation has been with US-based samples. It is important, given the global nature of tourism to test ideas, concepts and theories developed in Western countries with other emerging traveller nationalities.

The focus of this second study was guided by three general aims.

(1)   to empirically confirm and further develop the conceptual ideas of the travel career pattern approach;
(2)   to further explicate the travel career concept and to establish methods for its measurement;

(3)   to investigate the relationship between Koreans' motivation patterns and their travel career development and examine the cross-cultural applicability of the travel career pattern approach.

To achieve the above aims, a six-page self-completion questionnaire was constructed. The purpose of this study required the questionnaire to address the areas of travel motivation, previous travel history and experience, and demographic details. From the first study, 74 travel motivation items were again employed to investigate travel motivation patterns. A 9-point Likert-type scale (from 'not important at all' to 'very important') was provided to indicate the importance of each of the 74 general travel motivational statements. The questionnaire was first constructed in English and then translated into Korean. Then, in order to improve the reliability of the translation and to recover any subtle expressions lost in the translation process, the translation was verified by retranslating the entire content back into English. Therefore, in this process, any unclear or inappropriate vocabulary or terminology in the translated Korean questionnaire that might confuse or cause respondents to respond in an inappropriate way were corrected.

Distribution of the questionnaire was predominantly achieved through a snowball sampling method of university and professional networks in Daegu, Daejon, and Seoul in Korea in 2001. During this period, a total of 1176 questionnaires were collected, of which 824 were validated as useful responses.

In order to investigate the motivation patterns in relation to travel career levels, it was necessary to measure the travel career levels. This was done by identifying different levels of travel experience, life-stage and age. Therefore, the entire analysis procedure performed in this study could be classified into three major sections. In the first section of the analysis, principal component analysis (PCA) was again employed to identify the underlying motivation dimensions of the Korean respondents. The second section involved a sequence of analyses to classify the respondents according to their levels of travel experience. Kruskal-Wallis analysis was first employed to screen out the variables that are irrelevant in differentiating respondents' travel experience levels. K-means cluster analysis was next utilised to classify the samples according to their travel experience levels. Then discriminant analysis was performed in order to assess the clarity of the classification and identify the travel experience parameters that best discriminate the identified travel experience groups. On this occasion respondents were asked to record their perceived travel experience as a further variable to check the demographic and descriptive indices being collected. Finally, a multiple regression was used to help determine the ranking and ordering of the experience groups. The final section of the analysis involved choosing different travel career levels and relating the levels to the identified travel motivation factors. Using the classified groups of different travel experience level, life-stage and age, the travel career levels were identified using k-means cluster analysis. In this process, high and low travel career levels were highlighted. Two travel career level groups were then related to the travel motivation factors and the overall travel career patterns of Korean respondents were examined.

Within the sample of 824 useable responses, male (49%) and female (51%) respondents were closely matched. The majority (67%) were relatively younger respondents who were under 32 years of age. There were numerous occupational groupings but students were the highest single group (38%). In terms of achieved education level, 41% of the respondents had completed their high school education. Nearly one-third (31%) indicated that, including themselves, there were 4 persons in their household, and 52% lived with their mother and 35% with their father.

Travel Motivation Patterns Analysis

The 74 travel motivations were subjected to PCA in order to identify the underlying factors defining travel motivations. Prior to this procedure, adequacy of sample size was verified using the Keiser-Meyer-Olkin (KMO) measurement of sampling adequacy. Expressed in a value ranging from 0 to 1, with scores closer to 1 representing better sampling adequacy, the measurement resulted in a score of 0.95 indicating a satisfactory sample size. Following this, through verification of the statistical validity from the produced results, varimax rotation was followed which resulted in orthogonal factors. Considering eigen-value scores greater than 1, the procedure resulted in 14 factors with all factor loadings above 0.40, which indicated that the items contributed adequately in explaining that factor. The results are shown in Table 3.6. The 14 motivation factors, in the order of mean scores on each factor, were labelled as: (1) novelty, (2) escape/relax, (3) self-actualisation, (4) nature, (5) kinship, (6) self-enhancement (7) romance, (8) kinship (belonging), (9) autonomy, (10) self-development (host–site involvement), (11) nostalgia, (12) stimulation, (13) isolation, and (14) recognition. All factors and the motive items identifying the factors were very similar to the results of previous study. These findings provide strong empirical support for the cross-cultural similarity of the structure of the motivation patterns.

The percentage of variance explained by this solution was 67.9%. Internal consistencies among the items in the factors were again measured using Cronbach's coefficient alpha. In this study, all alpha (α) scores were between 0.78 and 0.99, which indicated strong internal consistency among the items in each factor (Baloglu & McLeary, 1999). Factor scores were then computed for each case. The factor scores, representing the values of the identified factors, were used in subsequent analysis as the basis for comparing the travel motivation patterns according to the groups with different levels of travel career.

Table 3.6 The Korean sample: 14 factors and their importance as travel motives

Factors	Items	Importance mean	Factor loading
Novelty (7.18)[a] (3.26)[b] (α = 0.80)[c]	Having fun	7.29	0.73
	Feeling the special atmosphere of the vacation destination	7.29	0.55
	Experiencing something different	7.22	0.65
Escape/relax (7.07) (5.89) (α = 0.85)	Being away from daily routine	7.33	0.76
	Giving my mind a rest	7.31	0.65
	Getting away from everyday psychological stress/pressure	7.25	0.75
	Resting and relaxing	7.05	0.61
	Getting away from the usual demands of life	7.02	0.78
	Getting away from everyday physical stress/pressure	6.82	0.66
	Not worrying about time	6.72	0.48
Self-actualisation (6.91) (5.7) (α = 0.87)	Gaining a new perspective on life	7.14	0.72
	Experiencing things I have always wanted to do	7.07	0.64
	Working on my personal/spiritual values	7.03	0.68
	Feeling inner harmony/peace	6.87	0.54
	Understanding more about myself	6.81	0.68
	Being creative	6.51	0.48
Nature (6.82) (4.74) (α = 0.86)	Viewing the scenery	7.07	0.65
	Being close to nature	7.03	0.77
	Being harmonious with nature	6.62	0.8
	Getting a better appreciation of nature	6.57	0.8
Kinship (6.61) (4.59) (α=0.84)	Strengthening relationships with my family/friend(s)	6.85	0.69
	Doing something with my family/friend(s)	6.84	0.74
	Being with others who enjoy the same things as I do	6.56	0.62
	Being with others if I need them	6.40	0.44
	Doing things with my companion(s)	6.38	0.73

Table 3.6 *continued*

Factors	Items	Impor-tance mean	Factor load-ing
Self-enhancement (6.39) (9.55) (α = 0.93)	Gaining a sense of self-confidence	7.03	0.66
	Learning new things	6.83	0.43
	Knowing what I am capable of	6.81	0.61
	Gaining a sense of accomplishment	6.68	0.72
	Develop my personal interests	6.48	0.7
	Developing my skills and abilities	6.27	0.71
	Being recognised by other people	6.12	0.72
	Showing others I can do it	6.11	0.69
	Using my skills and talents	6.02	0.74
	Sharing skill and knowledge with others	6.02	0.64
	Leading others	5.94	0.56
Romance (6.37)(3.01) (α = 0.99)	Having romantic relationships	6.77	0.90
	Being with people of the opposite sex	5.97	0.90
Kinship-belonging (6.35) (4.83) (α = 0.86)	Being near considerate people	6.58	0.73
	Being with respectful people	6.49	0.71
	Meeting people with similar values/interests	6.49	0.64
	Strengthening relationships with my companion(s)	6.49	0.46
	Contacting with family/friend(s) who live elsewhere	6.32	0.58
	Feeling that I belong	5.72	0.6
Autonomy (6.07) (2.78) (α = 0.78)	Being independent	6.50	0.52
	Being obligated to no one	6.02	0.75
	Doing things my own way	5.99	0.71
Self-development (host–site involvement) (6.07) (4.64) (α = 0.85)	Experiencing different cultures	6.73	0.46
	Meeting new and varied people	6.53	0.52
	Following current events	5.94	0.68
	Developing my knowledge of the area	5.89	0.65
	Observing other people in the area	5.74	0.71
	Meeting the locals	5.61	0.73
Nostalgia (6.04)(2.51) (α=0.91)	Thinking about good times I've had in the past	6.09	0.77
	Reflecting on past memories	5.98	0.79

Table 3.6 *continued*

Factors	Items	Impor-tance mean	Factor load-ing
Stimulation (5.89) (6.48) (α = 0.91)	Exploring the unknown	6.47	0.73
	Having daring/adventuresome experience	6.17	0.79
	Having unpredictable experiences	6.16	0.78
	Experiencing thrills	5.85	0.76
	Feeling excitement	5.57	0.71
	Experiencing the risk involved	5.12	0.73
Isolation (5.9) (4.89) (α = 0.81)	Experiencing the peace and calm	6.56	0.53
	Avoiding interpersonal stress and pressure	6.37	0.67
	Feeling personally safe and secure	6.08	0.48
	Being away from the crowds of people	6.04	0.73
	Getting away from my family	5.1	0.62
	Enjoying isolation	4.84	0.64
Social status (5.73) (3.85) (α = 0.84)	Having others know that I have been there	5.79	0.63
	Experiencing fashionable/trendy places	5.78	0.76
	Experiencing luxury	5.63	0.69

Kaiser-Meyer-Olkin measure of sampling adequacy: 0.95
Bartlett's test of sphericity: approx. chi-square = 40695.73/df = 2701/sig. = 0.00
67.9% of variance explained; motive items with factor loading <0.40 is discarded
a = Mean score of the factor, b = Variance explained,
c = Cronbach's alpha reliability coefficient

Travel Experience Levels Analysis

Re-scaling the variables

In analysing travel experience levels, 8 travel experience variables were used in this second study: international trips level, domestic trips level, total international travel time, number of usual travel companion(s), proportion of international pleasure travel, proportion of domestic pleasure travel, level of organised/package travel experience, and self perceived level of travel experience. Before employing cluster analysis to identify different travel experience level groups, the variables were standardised; variables subject to cluster analysis must be measured on equal scales as variables with large values contribute more to the calculations of distance measures than those with small values (SPSS Inc., 1999). One way to avoid this problem is to re-express the variables on the same scale, such as a ratio scale ranging from 0 to 1 (Coakes & Steed, 1999; SPSS Inc., 1999).

Screening the variables

Prior to cluster analysis, these re-scaled travel experience variables were initially evaluated to determine which ones were relevant in differentiating travel experience levels. Using 'self-perception of travel experience level' as the independent variable, the other 7 travel experience variables were subject to Kruskal-Wallis analysis. This procedure attempted to establish a face validity for using the specified variables to describe travel experience by relating them to the respondents' own perception of their travel experience. Kruskal-Wallis analysis, which is the non-parametric equivalent of one-way ANOVA, tests whether several independent samples are from the same population (SPSS Inc., 1999). This test was selected as the correct procedure since heavily skewed data were involved and the Kruskal-Wallis is suitable for this situation (Diekhoff, 1992). The results are presented in Table 3.7.

As the results indicate, except for 'number of usual travel companions', all variables describing previous travel experience showed significant differences between the levels of self-perceived travel experience. There are some subtleties in the data that indicate that the perception of oneself as an

Table 3.7 Travel experience variables by self-perceived level of travel experience

Travel experience variable	Self-perception of travel experience level			Chi-square	df	Proba-bility
	Low	Mod-erate	High			
International trips level	308.92	380.26	438.25	36.78	2	0
Domestic trips level	284.99	396.36	484.95	79.08	2	0
Proportion of international pleasure travel	196.29	244.87	247.43	13.04	2	0
Proportion of domestic pleasure travel	284.17	360.55	356.83	22.97	2	0
Level of organised/package travel experience	348.39	412.73	343.5	17.29	2	0
Number of people I usually travel with	372.39	375.9	367.22	0.15	2	0.93
Total amount of international travel time	313.29	383.95	445.67	38.64	2	0

experienced traveller initially rises with an increase in some variables, and then remains steady or falls. For example, the proportion of domestic pleasure travel as well as the level of organised/package tour experiences initially enhance respondents' self-perception of travel experience but this relationship is diminished for the highest self-perceived travel experience group. The important implication of the results of Table 3.7 is that, except for the 'number of people I usually travel with', it was worthwhile including all of these travel experience variables in subsequent analysis. It appears that all six play a role in helping to understand different clusters of experienced travellers.

Identifying the travel experience levels

Cluster analysis was then employed on the six travel experience variables to classify the sample into identifiable travel experience groups. Cluster analysis is a class of techniques used to classify objects or cases into relatively homogeneous groups called clusters. Within the range of different clustering methods, and following the procedure in the previous study, k-means cluster analysis was employed as it is useful in analysing samples exceeding 200 cases and has the advantage of being more reliable than hierarchical clustering (SPSS Inc., 1999). The procedure indicated that the most easily interpretable solution involved three clusters and the distances among the clusters were measured using analysis of variance (Table 3.8). The first cluster consisted of 231 respondents (28.9%) while

Table 3.8 Cluster analysis: Travel experience levels

Travel experience variables	Cluster 1	Cluster 2	Cluster 3	ANOVA Significance level
	Experienced travellers	Inexperienced travellers	Experienced domestic travellers	
International trips level	0.72	0.23	0.33	0
Domestic trips level	0.70	0.4	0.69	0
Proportion of international pleasure travel	0.59	0.20	0.87	0
Proportion of domestic pleasure travel	0.67	0.53	0.74	0
Level of organised/package travel experience	0.44	0.43	0.50	0.01
Total amount of international travel time	0.90	0.22	0.34	0
Cases (%)	231 (28.9)	332 (41.6)	236 (29.5)	

there were 332 respondents (41.6%) in the second cluster, and 236 respondents (29.5%) in the third cluster. As shown in the table, the clusters were labelled as *experienced travellers, inexperienced travellers,* and *experienced domestic travellers,* respectively. As might be anticipated, experienced traveller groups had high levels of travel experience both internationally and domestically with extensive time spent in international travel. The inexperienced traveller group generally showed low levels of travel experience for all travel experience variables. The experienced domestic traveller group was low on international travel experience level but high on domestic travel and most of their previous international and domestic trips were for pleasure.

Relating Travel Motivation Patterns to Travel Career Levels

Operationalising travel career levels

In this research the concept of a travel career is viewed as the combined level and stage of travel experience, life-stage, and age (see Table 3.2). K-means cluster analysis was used to identify the different travel career levels. Travel experience level, life-stage and age variables were included in the analysis. As age was measured in an open format in the questionnaire, the responses were classified into five groups with each group containing similar number of respondents. The five age groups were: under 26, 26–30, 31–40, 41–50, and over 50.

The life-stage variable, an important integrating element in the total research plan, was determined by the domestic living arrangements of the respondents. A younger at-home group, an independent living group, a mid-life family group and a senior without-family group were used as core dimensions. Then, the groups of travel experience level, life-stage, and age were recoded into new variables with values ranging according to the number of the groups. Following this, owing to the requirements for the cluster analysis, the three variables were standardised into ratio scales, ranging from 0 to 1 and were subject to the analysis. The procedures resulted in the five clusters shown in Table 3.9: low travel career, mid-life and moderately experienced, mid-life and experienced, high travel career, and younger and experienced. As the major focus of this study is to establish a general understanding of the travel career and travel motivation patterns, two clusters were selected from the resultant five clusters for further analysis:

- Cluster 1: low travel career (a younger group in lower life-stage with less travel experience);
- Cluster 4: high travel career (an older group in higher life-stage with more travel experience).

Table 3.9 Cluster analysis: Travel career groups

Variables	Cluster 1	Cluster 2	Cluster 3	Cluster 4	Cluster 5	Sig.
	Low travel career	*Mid-life & moderately experienced*	*Mid-life & experienced*	*High travel career*	*Younger & experienced*	
Age	0.25	0.59	0.52	0.76	0.22	0
Life-stage level	0.3	0.76	0.35	0.86	0.3	0
Travel experience level	0.33	0.52	0.98	0.96	0.77	0
Cases (%)	238 (30.9)	172 (22.3)	70 (9.09)	121 (15.7)	169 (22.0)	-

It would, of course, be possible to conduct further and more comprehensive comparative analyses on all of the travel career levels. However, it was decided that, at this developmental stage of the theory, a clear explication of the career-motivation pattern links would be best served by contrasting the high-level and low-level samples.

Relating travel motivation patterns and travel career levels

Using one-way ANOVA, the travel motivations were compared according to the two travel career groups. Tukey *post hoc* comparison tests were conducted to determine which motivations were significantly different. The results for the travel motivations and travel career levels are shown in Table 3.10.

Examining the factor scores, between the two travel career level groups, the nature ($t = -4.73$; $p = 0.00$), self-enhancement ($t = 5.05$; $p = 0.00$), romance ($t = 4.82$; $p=0.00$), kinship (belonging) ($t = 2.47$; $p = 0.01$), autonomy ($t = 3.71$; $p = 0.00$), and self-development (host–site involvement) ($t = -2.29$; $p = 0.02$) motivation factors were significantly different. On the other hand, other motivation factors including, novelty ($t = 1.06$; $p = 0.29$) escape/relax ($t = -0.97$; $p = 0.33$), self-actualisation ($t = 1.33$; $p = 0.18$), kinship (bonding) ($t = -1.07$; $p = 0.29$), nostalgia ($t = 0.06$; $p = 0.95$), stimulation ($t = 1.72$; $p = 0.09$), isolation ($t = -0.18$; $p = 0.86$), and social status ($t = 0.79$; $p = 0.43$) resulted in non-significant differences.

From Table 3.10, it can be understood that emphasis on nature and self-development (host–site involvement) increases as the individual's travel career stage changes while the other 6 travel motivations decrease. The factor scores of the 7 other travel motivation factors (stimulation, escape/relax, self-actualisation, isolation, kinship, social status, novelty, and nostalgia) for the two travel career groups resulted in a concentration near zero, indicating less difference between the groups. This suggests that these motivations are common to both travel career levels. In particular, the fact

Table 3.10 Independent *t*-test: Travel motivation by high/low travel career levels

Motivations	Low travel career		High travel career		t	Sig.
	Factor score	Mean	Factor score	Mean		
Novelty	0.10	7.43	-0.02	7.23	1.06	0.29
Escape/relax	-0.03	7.15	0.08	7.08	-0.97	0.33
Self-actualisation	0.09	7.16	-0.06	6.61	1.33	0.18
Nature**	-0.11	6.74	0.40	7.21	-4.73	0
Kinship	-0.06	6.66	0.07	6.44	-1.07	0.29
Self-enhancement**	0.14	6.70	-0.46	5.71	5.05	0
Romance**	0.21	6.91	-0.34	5.29	4.82	0
Kinship-belonging*	0.13	6.62	-0.14	5.71	2.47	0.01
Autonomy**	0.16	6.61	-0.27	5.56	3.71	0
Self-development (host-site involvement)*	-0.12	6.06	0.13	6.07	-2.29	0.02
Nostalgia	0	6.35	-0.01	5.61	0.06	0.95
Stimulation	0.02	6.04	-0.18	5.48	1.72	0.09
Isolation	-0.01	5.9	0.01	5.71	-0.18	0.86
Social status	0.06	6.00	-0.03	5.28	0.79	0.43

Note: ** = $p<0.01$ * = $p<0.05$

that four of them (novelty, escape/relax, self-actualisation, and kinship) are among the five most important motivations suggests they are the core motivations in Korean travellers' travel motivation patterns. These multiple empirical findings provide rich consistencies across the two studies in this chapter and facilitate some promising conceptual developments in travel motivation theory.

Confirming the Travel Career Pattern Approach

This study was conducted to meet three aims: to empirically assess and further develop the conceptual ideas of the travel career pattern approach, to further explicate the concept of travel career and establish methods for its measurement and finally, to investigate the cross-cultural applicability of a travel career pattern conceptual scheme through the use of a Korean sample.

Overall, the results of the second study were very supportive and parallel to those in the first study. It was demonstrated that travel motivation can be identified as patterns linked to different levels of a travel career, which in turn can be assessed by previous travel experience, life-stage, and age. While the first study investigated travel career using only international and domestic travel experience and age, the second study involved a more diverse range of variables relating to travel experience. The expanded range of variables was seen to help provide a better view of travel career.

In understanding the relationship between travel motivation and travel career level, escape/relax, novelty, kinship and self-actualisation were the most important and common motives for all travellers. Within the identified 14 travel motivational factors, respondents with the higher travel career levels gave greater emphasis to externally-oriented motivations such as self-development through host–site involvement and seeking nature. On the other hand, respondents with lower travel career levels placed more stress on internally-oriented motivation factors such as self-enhancement, romance, kinship (belonging), and autonomy. Other motivations such as nostalgia, stimulation, isolation, and social status were less important to both high and low levels of travel career.

The similarity between these outcomes and those from the first study, which was conducted in a Western cultural context, suggests a potential cross-cultural applicability of TCP theory. The common and notable findings of both studies are that the identified 14 motivation factors were very similar in terms of number of factors, appropriate labels, and the associated items in each factor. Furthermore, for both high and low travel career levels, novelty, escape/relax, and kinship were the most important travel motivations, while social status and isolation were the least important ones.

There is a close congruence between the findings of both studies and the work of numerous previous authors writing about travel motivation. Travel motivations such as seeking novelty, escape or relaxation, and kinship or affection have received considerable attention in tourism research as the main forces behind all travel behaviour (e.g. Crompton, 1979; Cha *et al.*, 1995; Dann, 1977; Mannell & Iso-Ahola, 1987; Woodside & Jacobs, 1985). In terms of the cross-cultural universality of these motivations, similar findings to the study of Yuan and McDonald (1990) are noted. When they compared tourists from four countries – the United Kingdom, Japan, France and Germany – Yuan and McDonald found that, while the rankings between the motivation factors were similar, the level of importance attached to the factors differed from country to country. More importantly, novelty and escape were ranked 1 and 2 for all four countries, which indicates that these two motivations were cross-culturally important and fundamental. Again there is a close alignment between this previous research and the present findings.

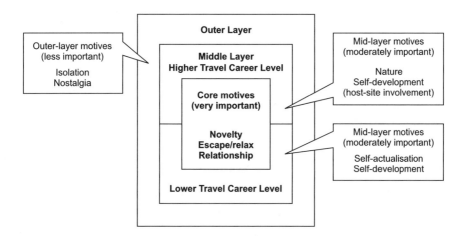

Figure 3.1 Travel career patterns (TCP) concept

Importantly, the findings from both the first and second study imply that the travel career patterns approach can be conceptually illustrated as three layers of travel motivation, where each layer consists of different travel motives (Figure 3.1).

The core in the centre shows the most important common motives (e.g. novelty, escape/relax, enhancing relationships). The next layer, surrounding the core, includes the moderately-important travel motives that change from inner-directed travel motives (e.g. self-actualisation) to externally-oriented motives (e.g. nature and host–site involvement) as one's travel career develops. The outer layer again consists of common and relatively stable travel motives, but these are less-important ones (e.g. nostalgia, isolation, social status). In terms of cross-cultural differences in the motivation patterns, while the emphasis on individual motivation factors may vary between cultures, the overall patterns of travel motivation and its change according to developing travel career structure are suggested to be similar.

As far as pleasure travel is concerned, all travellers, regardless of their travel career levels, are influenced by the most important and central travel motives (such as novelty, escape/relax, and relationship) as well as by less important motives (such as isolation, nostalgia, and social status). As their travel career level develops, in other words, as they grow older, pass through stages in their life-cycle and gain more travel experience, their moderately important travel motives will shift from internally-oriented needs (such as self-development) to externally-oriented needs (such as experiencing nature and host–site involvement).

Overall, the development of the travel career patterns (TCP) approach has resulted in de-emphasising the original ladder metaphor. The research discussed in this chapter does not negate the value of other motivational theories or approaches to tourism study. It does suggest, however, that a revised model of the travel career ladder approach holds promise for cross-national research in this field. Further studies to explore the levels of the travel career approach, rather than simply identifying low-scoring and high-scoring respondents, could add to the understanding, particularly if linked to more cross-cultural work.

Extending the Analysis: The Northern Australian Study

The detailed work on travel motivation that has been reported so far in this chapter only partly utilises the full power of the life-cycle or life-stages concept. The concept of different segments for age and domestic arrangements segments was incorporated in the second study, but is better illustrated in an applied example of tourist behaviour research rather than an analysis of general motivational patterns. The specific example is drawn from the work of Moscardo and Pearce (2004) and describes the intersection of motivation and life-cycle and experience factors as it relates to self-drive holidays in Northern Australia.

Life-cycle is an integrative term that combines the person's age, family status, income, health and well being (Jafari, 2000). It is used frequently to suggest categories of activity preferences (Mill & Morrison, 1995). Life-cycle factors and other psychographic approaches can be seen as forces that intersect with and are expressed in the motivation of travellers. While motivation remains the basic and initial driving force for tourist behaviour, the actual motives that individuals express are strongly shaped by life-cycle forces. It is argued here that life-cycle stages (e.g. young pre-marriage adults, mid-life adults with families, older travellers without children) are loose descriptions, and motivation provides a more exacting account of activity preferences and choices than do broad demographic factors (Moscardo, Morrison *et al.*, 1996).

The links between traveller motivation, life-cycle, the role of transport and the experiences from these links are presented in Figure 3.2.

Case study: The travellers' experience and automobile tourism

The case study described here was not constructed around the full set of motives reviewed and empirically explored earlier in this chapter. Nevertheless it does offer some analogies and links to the work already presented and suggests that the multi-motive patterns described do have life-cycle links particularly as they are expressed in preferences for activities in the particular setting.

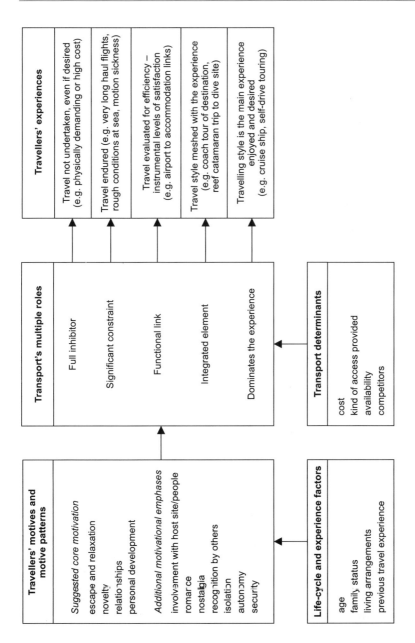

Figure 3.2 A conceptual map of the links between motivation, life-cycle, transport roles and the travellers' experience

Source: Pearce and Moscardo, 2004

The data for the present case study are drawn from a specific survey of 1513 visitors conducted in 1999. The surveys were distributed throughout the North Queensland region and included surveys in the main city of Cairns as well as amongst visitors in a number of smaller towns in the region.

The greater Cairns region has a population of approximately 150,000 residents and a total tourist visitor profile estimated at over 1 million domestic and international tourists annually (Queensland Government, 2001). Two World Heritage Areas (the Great Barrier Reef and the Wet Tropics) are key regional attractions. Analyses of the visitor market segments to this region have been conducted in a number of previous studies (Morrison *et al.*, 1995). Broadly, these analyses reveal that there is a substantial number of domestic visitors varying in age and also a sizeable international visitor market who tend to be either in the 18–35 age group or else in a later life-cycle phase (Pearce *et al.*, 1996). The sample is thus well suited to exploring life-stage and motivational differences. The international visitors are predominantly from UK/Europe, New Zealand, North America and Japan, with rising numbers from other Asian countries.

Three groups of visitors are of particular interest.

International self-drive market

The information pertaining to this group is drawn from 292 respondents, predominantly from the United Kingdom/Ireland (35%) and Europe (33%). The group consists of a large number of couples (66%), the balance families and friends. The group is not exactly typical of all international visitors to the region since the two largest age groups are 21–30 (45%) and 31–60 (40%). The older age group of senior travellers, which is apparent in the broader demographics of the region's visitors (Tourism Queensland, 2002) is under-represented in this self-drive market. The most common amount of time spent in the region is two weeks. The mean satisfaction for this group is 7.89 on a 0–10 scale. The locational information indicates that 11 sites are visited by at least 25% of these visitors – a statistic that indicates a modest reach in their travel behaviour compared to the other self-drive subgroups.

Domestic self-drive market, without children

The information pertaining to this group is drawn from 388 respondents, predominantly from the Eastern states of Australia. This group is also characterised by people travelling with their partners (65%), but other family and friends are also common companions. The group is most likely to be over 51 years of age, with 52% in their 50s and 60s. Many of these visitors (unlike the international visitors) are on a second or third visit to the region. They tend to spend a little less time in the region than the international visitors (just less than two weeks) and are highly likely to stay in a caravan (54%) or a motel/hotel (20%). The locational information indicates that 22 sites are visited by at least 25% of these visitors and while this indicates a considerable effort and achievement, it may be confounded by previous visit recollections. The mean satisfaction for this group is 8.32 on a 0–10 scale, a figure that is statistically significant in terms of being the highest satisfaction score recorded for the subgroups.

Domestic self-drive, with children

The information pertaining to this group is drawn from 71 respondents, predominantly from the state of Queensland itself (49%) as well as the Eastern states of Australia. The adults are most often accompanied by either one or two children (32%). Like the other domestic visitors, they have visited the region on multiple previous occasions but their length of stay is typically 7 days rather than the 14 or more days or more of the other groups. Like the other domestic travellers, staying in a caravan (46%) or hotel/ motel (20%) are important accommodation options for this group, and there is also some accommodation with friends and relatives. The locational information indicates a visit to 17 locations by at least 25% of the sample. A distinctive feature of this group is the amount of planning for the holiday, with 69% of these travellers having planned five months in advance of their travel. The corresponding figure for the other two self-drive segments are 50% for the international travellers and 57% for the domestic self-drive without children group. The mean satisfaction for this group lies between the scores of the other two segments – on this occasion the mean satisfaction with their visit to the North Queensland region was 8. 01 on the 0–10 satisfaction scale.

This broad demographic, trip planning, localised and satisfaction information on these three self-drive market subgroups helps interpret the motivational profile responses for the three groups. This material is presented in Table 3.11.

The material presented in Table 3.11 reinforces the view that the motivation and destination attribute features can be seen as a pattern of responses. The percentage data displayed represent the percentage of people who consider this attribute to be very important, so that even a low percentage still indicates that some people think it is very important and further, it is highly likely that a large number of people think it is somewhat important. This finding and presentation of the data corresponds to one of the attributes of a good approach to motivational studies noted in the introductory sections of this chapter. Specifically, the presentation of findings on motivation should reflect a multi-motive view of human behaviour. Further, this notion was effectively incorporated in the conceptual map of Figure 3.1, where a range of core motives common and important to many tourist situations was outlined but was supplemented by a further set of motives likely to be highly important in some situations.

Table 3.11 Motivational responses coded according to travel career pattern motives for self drive markets

Motivation factor	Examples from the case study	Inter-national	Domestic no children	Domestic with children
Novelty	Interesting small towns/villages	13.6	23.8*	21.4*
	Chances to see wildlife not normally seen	42.3*	31.8	28.6
Escape/relax	Chance to escape a busy life	36.1	41.6	43.5
	Warm sunny weather	49.5*	49.9*	31.4
	Beaches for sunbathing/swimming	29.5	23	27.5
Relationship (strengthen)	Activities for the whole family	10.9	14.5	42.9*
Autonomy	-			
Nature	Opportunities to visit rainforest	51.2	48.9	44.3
	Chance to visit the Great Barrier Reef	61.5*	34.1	36.3
	Outstanding scenery	49.1*	50.4*	34.3
	Access to wilderness/undisturbed nature	38.7	38.6	30
Self-development (host–site involvement)	Experience indigenous culture	15.5*	4.5	7.1
Stimulation	Wide variety of things to do	33.7	36.2	31.4
	Outdoor adventure activities	36.4*	24.7	29
Self-development (personal development)	Opportunities to increase knowledge	22.6	19.8	15.7
Relationship (security)	Friendly local people	29.6*	28.6*	11.4
Self actualise	-			
Isolation	-			
Nostalgia	Pleasant rural scenery	32	34.5	22.9
	A familiar well-known place	7.5	12.7*	17.1*
Romance recognition	A place I can talk of when I get home	26.2	29.4	30
	A fashionable place to go	2.5	3.5	2.9

* repeats significant group differences.

Figures are percentages rating the motive 'very important' on a 5-point scale

An inspection of the numerical information in Table 3.11 confirms sets of patterned responses where motives fluctuate in importance. In this specific context the transport dominates the tourist experience and the motivations portrayed reflect this setting and the local destination attributes. For example, the domestic self-drive group with children considers a number of motives/features to be very important. But the group is distinctive in clearly identifying activities for the whole family, interesting small towns and villages and a familiar well-known place as relatively more important items than do the other groups. The effect of life-cycle factors (in this case the presence of usually one or two children as a part of the travel party), expresses itself in the greater importance given to these motivational statements. Similarly these same domestic travellers with children place relatively less importance (although these features are not unimportant) on opportunities to visit family and friends, view outstanding scenery, interact with friendly local people and experience indigenous culture.

A consideration of the traveller motivation, life-cycle and demographic links manifested in the self-drive transport choices can be developed in a similar way for the 'domestic, no children' travellers. This group places a relatively greater importance on outstanding scenery and warm sunny weather, interesting small towns and villages, opportunities to visit family/friends and friendly local people. These results are consistent with the core-motives emphasis of the travel career pattern approach but in this context the motives find expression in activities.

The international travellers are distinctive in relation to the other two self-drive groups, with defining and contrasting items being the importance of having the chance to visit the Great Barrier Reef, outstanding scenery, warm sunny weather, outdoor adventure activities and chances to see wildlife not normally seen. Friendly local people and the chance to experience indigenous culture are also relatively more important for the international self-drive group. These findings for the most experienced travellers in the group are entirely consistent with the travel career pattern reported in the two major empirical studies reported earlier in the chapter.

Motivation is a complex topic in tourist behaviour, and its study requires a mix of conceptual skills, awareness of the history of the concept and a view of its role as both an instrumental and interpretive tool in studying people who travel. The exposition here of just one developing approach to tourist motivation has been directed at initiating further work on the levels of tourists' travel careers. It is hoped that researchers and analysts might now have another promising system to explore the transitions experienced by travellers as well as understanding large-scale patterns of visitor needs. In particular, case studies that directly use the motive items discussed in this chapter might be able to confirm or qualify the present work.

Chapter 4

Perceiving and Choosing the Destination

Introduction

The study of destination characteristics, destination images and the destination choice process are all central to this volume. Indeed, in many appraisals of tourist and consumer behaviour, the choice of a product (or destination) is viewed as the central topic in the whole area of study (Bagozzi *et al.*, 2002). Additionally it can be noted that destination-related topics are of major interest to regional tourism marketers. In choosing a destination, tourists are making multiple financial and expenditure commitments, which are of key interest to the businesses providing these services. Academic and scholarly studies that can better understand and even help to influence the product choice process are therefore likely to be seen as amongst the most relevant tourist behaviour research for practitioners. The substantial emphasis on these issues in tourism research may be linked directly to the orientation of researchers who believe that facilitating business success is the dominant goal of their work (cf. Gunn, 1994b).

It would be premature to claim that tourism scholars understand all the elements of this destination imaging and selection process. This chapter will review critically the core themes in the existing literature and will offer some novel organising frameworks and directions for further analysis.

Characterising Tourist Destinations

Tourist destinations, even more than basic consumer products such as food or household items, are viewed and presented in selective and diverse ways. Tourist places are not just 'used' or 'promoted' by the tourism industry, but are frequently shaped by marketing efforts. In this sense tourism forms and reforms its own product. At the same time, other community and economic forces also shape the destination. As Hughes suggests:

> There is nothing 'natural' about the various landscapes (and places) valued by tourists since they are the result of the history of human intervention which has manipulated nature in ways conducive to economic growth. (Hughes, 1995: 53)

Table 4.1 Six systems for characterising tourist destinations

Label	*Emphasis*	*Characteristics and examples of the system*
Activities	physical	Listings, profiles, GIS approach
Settings	physical	Public management agencies use of zones using a biophysical basis
Facilities	physical	Micro-environments and servicescapes: the immediate physical features of the tourist space
Service	social	Personnel: the characteristics of personnel in the service quality framework
Hosts	social	Community responses and reception; Social representations of tourism and differences in community views
Management	social	Marketing labels and management actions and branding using existing and new tourism infrastructure and themes

Similarly Jakobs writing about Canada's Eastern Arctic argues:

There is little hope and less purpose in freezing the north within a framework of traditions that no longer exist. (Jakobs, 1996: 72)

Destination marketing efforts in tourism do attract frequent criticism of this type because of suggested distortions in the way communities and settings are presented; the argument being that there is a tendency to emphasise the clichéd past rather than the evolving complexities of the present (Moscardo & Pearce, 2003; Saarinen, 1998). In order to understand the basis of this distortion argument, it is useful to review the multiple ways in which destinations can be characterised.

Six systems or approaches to viewing tourist destinations can be identified, three of which emphasise physical dimensions while a further three have a more human and social face. The six systems are presented in Table 4.1.

Activities

The first of the organising systems can be labelled an activities approach. In response to the question 'What is this destination like?', listings of available activities in an area are frequently drawn up, thus defining both the commercial and the public opportunities available to visitors to the region. At times the overall listing is supplemented by profiles of activities for a particular market. For example, adventure-oriented tourists may be targeted in publications that list companies offering adrenalin-rush opportunities.

The listing and profiling approach to characterising destinations has also been developed in a more complex way. Gunn (1988, 1994a) amongst others has employed a geographic information systems framework not only to list activities but also to layer them in mapping summaries so that clusters of activities can be identified. This work, carried out initially in Texas, is akin to constructing nodes or clusters of compatible activities built around physical resources such as forests, water and road routes. Clusters of resources and activities formed in this way are likely to appeal to such groups as long distance touring visitors or day trip visitors. Contemporary work on the application of geographic information systems (GIS) continues this tradition of layering resources and activities for tourism planning.

Settings

A different tradition of describing tourist destinations is found in the natural environment management literature. More recently it has also crept into regional tourism appraisals (Font & Tribe, 2000). The term 'setting' is frequently used in this approach and a popular distinction is to define different parts of the space as 'zones'. This approach is intimately linked to the biophysical aspects of the setting such as when national parks, world heritage or wilderness areas are being described. Typically the plans of the public management agencies specify a number of zones for different kinds of tourist use. These zones are built on and linked to the vegetation, soils, fauna and geology of the sites (cf. Page & Dowling, 2002). In this approach Zone 1 might be a high-use area, often effectively confirming existing use patterns, where there are picnic facilities as well as existing roads and tracks in a well-signed and richly interpreted open space. Zone 2 might be a moderate-use area where there is a paved track to a specific feature but here there are, for example, few toilets, no drinking water and only occasional safety measures such as hand rails. The biophysical basis of this zone might be more fragile vegetation, softer soils, and less common fauna. Zone 3 might be a very rough, difficult walking track that follows a river system with steep gradients and strong restrictions on user behaviour to protect river edges and riparian vegetation. It is unlikely to be accessible to many visitors. Zone 4 might be a scientific conservation zone with little expectation that the public will use the setting but permits may be available for conservation study and scientific research.

Facilities

A related but more fine-grained approach to describing destinations combines the notion of the facilities in a setting and the immediate micro-environment of the visitor. This work, described in the studies of Bitner (1990, 1992) and Yang and Brown (1992), is sometimes referred to as servicescapes. It pays particular attention to the physical comfort of the visitor and presses the case for landscape architecture to be considered in tourist destination design. As such there is an emphasis on surfaces, vegetation, colour, sound, airflow and the physical comfort of tourists in the destination. It is a somewhat specialist approach to characterising destinations, but has an influence in the specifics of place design and can be utilised in conjunction with zoning approaches and activity appraisals. The facilities and servicescape tradition can be seen as the focused but applied heir to the older tradition of characterising tourist destinations by climate, specifically thermal comfort and seasonality fluctuations (Baum & Lundtorp, 2001; Boniface & Cooper, 1987).

Services

The tourism management literature has developed a number of specific appraisal schemes for describing the 'friendliness' of the service encounter situations (Noe, 1999). In one of these schemes, referred to as the RATER approach, five dimensions of friendliness or, more specifically, service quality are detailed: reliability, assurance, tangibles, empathy and responsiveness. What are these attributes? *Reliability* is that things will happen as expected: the guide will take the visitor on a full-day tour, the travel agency will be open as expected and the hotel will deliver on the promised no-smoking room. *Assurance* refers to the service person's competency. It is not the same as friendliness or attractiveness and the distinction is emphasised when a very engaging waiter, both personable and witty, totally confuses the order. Assurance and competence are partly to do with the training of a destination's service personnel. *Tangibles* in turn can be defined as the appearance of settings and the personnel who work in them. The Welsh coal miner turned bed-and-breakfast operator who still has the legacy of his working life in terms of a hacking cough and stained hands does not convey a desirable set of 'tangibles' to customers at the breakfast table.

Empathy and *responsiveness* are intertwined components of service quality. They are defined by service providers expressing appropriate concern about the tourists' views and concerns, and then attempting to act on the problem in a timely manner.

The adequacy of these five dimensions and of systems like them remains an active part of service quality debates (Kandampully *et al.*, 2001). Further aspects of this dimension of tourist research will also be explored in Chapter 5, where the concern is with tourists' relationships. In the present context of Chapter 4, the quality of the service personnel in the region is one of the important social descriptions of destinations.

Hosts

A further social and cultural appraisal of destinations obtains from the larger population of the destination, not just those who work in tourism businesses. The ways in which host communities view tourism, how much they welcome tourists, and what perceptions they hold of tourists and tourism impacts constitute a substantial literature in tourism study (Singh *et al.*, 2003). As Pearce, Moscardo and Ross (1996) report, there is no one simple way to characterise destinations and local communities, but there is a range of organising everyday theories or social representations about how tourism works, what it is doing to the local destination and how much it is desired. Any attempt to characterise a tourism destination by the attitudes of its community needs to consider the multiple voices and representations of segments of the community, and these voices are the complex dynamic outcomes of power, contested identities and economic struggle (Burr, 1991). Viewed in this light the cliché of uniformly 'friendly locals' represents a particularly glib marketing generalisation.

Management

A recurring theme of this section on characterising destinations has been an emphasis on the ways in which selective accounts of the attributes of destinations are emphasised in each system. The final system to be reviewed is that of the marketing and management of the destination. This theme does not simply repeat the previous assertions that marketing appraisals may exaggerate elements of promoted places, but reaches further into the issue of how tourism influences the management of destinations. The twin forces of civic pride and potential economic profit often combine for the managers of destinations to reconstruct the destination they oversee for future tourism. Sometimes these very ideas, like the Mainstreet USA programmes, actually come from tourism settings such as Disney's theme parks (Ashworth, 2003). In this example streetscapes created for tourism in controlled settings become a desirable past for communities. They are then constructed for residents with the side benefit of potentially attracting tourists. These kinds of circular, inverted and dynamic changes in destinations reveal that an attempt to understand how to view destinations should not overlook the managerial, economic and political forces that are constantly modifying them for and because of tourism. It was this phenomenon of destination marketers reconstructing areas and staging spaces that was originally noted by MacCannell (1976) when he stressed tourists seeking authenticity.

In all of these views of destinations, there is one missing component: how tourists image the places they might and will visit. The ways of characterising destinations reviewed in the present section represent inputs and considerations deriving from the destination itself and its management. These forces in turn shape a central concern of this book – how tourists view potential destinations. Destination information collides with the experience and psychological profile of the customer to produce the images that are the ultimate precursors to destination choice.

Communicating the Destination Characteristics

It is now quite well documented that there are multiple information pathways that help shape the would-be travellers' destination image. Building on the characterisation of destinations already presented it is possible to define the way in which this information is picked up by the consumer. Gartner (1993), developing the categories initially labelled by Gunn (1972), reports eight image formation agents.

(1) The first agent (or set of forms) is labelled *Overt Induced I* and consists of traditional forms of advertising through television, radio and brochures.

(2) *Overt Induced II*, a second category of destination information transfer, applies to material received through travel agents, tour operators and wholesalers.

(3) When destinations are supported or recommended by well known celebrities and their spontaneous behaviour the source of information is referred to by Gartner as *Covert Induced I*.

(4) Impartial sources such as unsponsored travel writing are termed *Covert Induced II*.

(5) *Autonomous image formation* agents consist of movies, news articles and documentaries (Riley *et al.*, 1998). The effect of autonomous image formation agents is often very immediate and powerful, particularly when dramatic large-scale news events are involved (Gartner & Shen, 1992). Not surprisingly, major images of world events such as the Tiananmen Square conflict are profound in their impact on international destination images.

(6) Unsolicited organic image formation agents refer to information received from individuals who have previously visited a destination or who claim to be knowledgeable about the destination. Such information is not requested, but is offered in everyday conversation

(7) The category *solicited organic image formation*, is a relabel for the well-known word-of-mouth advertising, an important information source since the early days of tourism. It is suggested that solicited organic image material is sought from friends and relatives. The distinction Gartner makes between solicited and unsolicited organic image formation is subtle and many other commentators would see both the unsolicited and the requested information as word-of-mouth advertising.

(8) Gartner's eighth and final category is termed *organic* and refers to the experience of having personally visited the site

Destination Image

In an earlier account of the term 'image', the author offered the following observations on the concept:

> For many social scientists 'image' is one of those terms which will not go away. A term with vague and shifting meanings, it has been variously linked to advertising and consumerism, attitudes, memories, cognitive maps and expectations. (Pearce, 1988: 162)

Additionally, in responding to the literature of that time, an emphasis on the visual or sensory components of the term image was stressed as researchers had neglected this element of the concept. The destination image of Hong Kong, for example, is more than a set of ratings along

Table 4.2 Tourism research and destination image definitions; from the historic to the contemporary

Researcher	*Definition*
Hunt (1975)	Perceptions held by potential visitors about an area
Lawson and Baud-Bovy (1977)	An expression of knowledge, impressions, prejudice, imaginations and emotional thoughts an individual has of a specific object or place
Crompton (1979)	Sum of beliefs, ideas and impressions that a person has of a destination
Stringer (1984)	A reflection or representation of sensory or conceptual information
Dichter (1985)	Overall impression with some emotional content
Phelps (1986)	Perceptions or impressions of a place
Frigden (1987)	A mental representation of an object, person, place or event which is not physically before the observer
Ahmed (1991)	What tourists as buyers 'see' and 'feel' when the destination or its attractions come to mind as a place suited for the pursuit of leisure
Gartner (1993)	A complex combination of various products and associated attributes
Kotler (1994)	Net result of a person's belief, ideas, feelings, expectations and impressions about a place or an object
Baloglo and McLeary (1999)	An attitudinal construct consisting of an individual's mental representations of knowledge, feelings and global impression about an object or destination
Tapachai and Waryszak (2000)	A mental prototype

semantic differential scales; it must also be able to embrace respondents' mental pictures of dramatic urban high rise, crowded harbour traffic, steep mountains, the throng of people, and subtropical humidity. Table 4.2 provides a contemporary account of how researchers have and are defining the term destination image. The material in Table 4.2 will be used as a resource to provide a new definitional statement of destination image and its components that is at once holistic and encompassing but amenable to assessment.

The notion that the destination image concept contains a multisensory component has gained currency across time in the definitions reviewed. Further, there is mounting agreement that the destination image represents a totality of beliefs, feelings and expectations and that it is an accessible mental schema or information store. In formulating a useable definition of destination image for tourism research, attention needs to be paid to incorporating all of these elements, but in a way that assists researchers to collect data. Both a statement and a diagram provide the joint tools to realise these requirements. It is proposed that destination image be viewed as a complex schema including an attitude towards a location complete with cognitive, affective and implicit behavioural components interfaced with a multisensory dimension. Further, destination image is best viewed in full with a cognitive map or orientation component organising the available information spatially. Figure 4.1 illustrates this statement and indicates the kinds of research directions deriving from the components.

Several necessary observations arise from the presentation of destination image featured in Figure 4.1. The discussion of these issues occupies the remainder of this section. All parts of the figure will be discussed, including the methodologies suited to appraising destination images.

Attitude

From the perspective of the would-be tourist, the three-part classification presented may seem unusual, as the individual's conception of his/her image is likely to be an integrated and holistic one. For the purposes of analysis however it is often useful, comprehensive and more precise to go beyond everyday conceptions of psychological processing and mental products. As Baloglu and Brinberg (1997) suggest, components may not be separated in people's minds unless they are questioned in a certain way, but from a theoretical and ultimately applied point of view an approach that provides a better representation of image and the structure of behaviours is to be preferred.

Secondly, since the formulation provided in Figure 4.1 is innovative there are unlikely to be clear research examples where all the components have been assessed. In a different tradition of research, that of landscape architecture, some of the early work conducted by Kevin Lynch on city

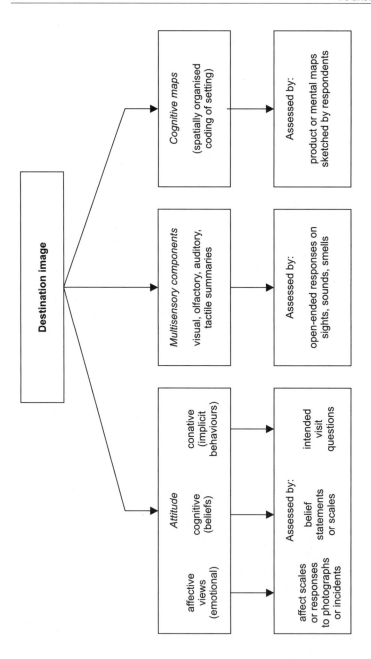

Figure 4.1 Components of destination image and sample research procedures

images represents a study where most of the components identified in Figure 4.1 were assessed (Lynch, 1960; Pearce & Fagence, 1996). In this early approach, which focused on residents' images, researchers not only conducted interviews on the respondents' attitudes but they also considered the sensory qualities of city districts and elicited citizens' sketch maps of their homes. In the same tradition, some early researchers appraised the sensory qualities of urban environments and routes and produced auditory and olfactory maps of places (Sommer, 1978; Southworth, 1969).

A hidden element in Figure 4.1 is that of the conative or behavioural intention component of attitude. Attitudes are typically seen in the social psychological literature as having the components of affect and cognition, but they also include a component of conative or behavioural intention. Curiously this is rarely discussed in the work on destination image, but may be assumed to be covered by tourism researchers when destination choice models are built. The present analysis suggests instead that, even at the destination image level of analysis, there is a clear if muted behavioural intention. For example, destination images of some of the world's most troubled or challenging destinations (such as Zimbabwe or Antarctica) arguably include more than just a set of beliefs and emotional reactions to the country or continent. In addition they include a restrained behavioural response that embraces such behaviours as envisioning oneself participating in activities, not wanting to seek further information or possibly simply not being interested in any travel to that location. The view that destination images contain their own initial behavioural inclinations could prove to be important in thinking about marketing and destination selection processes. It may be more important than tourism researchers have realised to measure the kinds of implied behaviours that are integral to destination images so that these potential actions can become the focus of communication efforts. It is worth labouring this point because it is ultimately visitor behaviour that interests business personnel even more than the nature of people's beliefs and affective appraisals. Further, it is very likely that the same affective and cognitive views may lead to different behavioural components for people with different values and skills, such as those who are motivated to travel to Antarctica by challenge and an enthusiasm for remote environments compared with those who seek comfortable and safe travel. The affective responses and cognitive beliefs may in this example be very similar but the implicit behaviours markedly different.

The sequencing and ordering of the component parts of attitude has received considerable attention in psychological research (Bagozzi *et al.*, 2002). Under some circumstances it appears that strong affective responses precede cognitive elements, while on other occasions emotional reactions may become associated with or tied to certain beliefs. There is a detailed literature but as yet no definitive answer to the question of precedence in these component parts of attitude. One suggestion is that, when respondents are more involved in a topic, cognitive appraisals take precedence while for low-involvement situations affective responses are powerful and primary (Miniard *et al.*, 1990).

The complexity of these debates and research efforts in attitude theory as well as in emotion and attitude models will be explored further in Chapter 7 on the outcomes of tourist behaviour; specifically the post-experience attitude of satisfaction. There is a developing awareness amongst those who write about attitudes and applied topics that some modifications to general attitude theory may be necessary in specific domains of human action. For example, some researchers downplay the behavioural element of the three-part classification of attitudes. Others have suggested that, where attitudes relating to difficult-to-perform behaviours are concerned (e.g. giving up addictive substances) then new components of attitude theory such as attitudes towards success and failure are needed (Bagozzi & Warshaw, 1992). From the point of view of tourist behaviour research, this kind of researcher realisation implies that models that use attitudinal constructs to characterise destination image and tourist satisfaction may also have their own distinctive, topic-dependent additions and extensions. This view is consistent with a theme in this volume that tourist behaviour requires an elaboration and application of ideas and concepts in other fields of inquiry.

Cognitive maps

Two core and somewhat familiar traditions of research are included in the model: the affective, cognitive components of attitudes and the mental maps of places. For example, the prevailing traditions of tourist destination image research often focus on the cognitive (belief statements) component of attitudes, with some recognition of affective elements (Baloglu & Brinberg, 1997; Dann, 1996b; Echtner & Ritchie, 1991). An existing but parallel tradition uses the cognitive mapping methodology (Oliver, 2001; Pearce, 1977, 1981b; Walmsley & Jenkins, 1991, 1992; Young 1999). Much of the latter work focuses on how the experience of visiting places is encoded in respondents' memories for places and spaces. Few attempts have been made to use the cognitive mapping approach with potential visitors who have no actual experience of visiting a destination, although this can be seen as a possibility when there is substantial public material on the destination (Downs & Stea, 1977). Certainly, cognitive maps (or, more accurately, the product maps that are sketched to represent the mentally stored information), show substantial sensitivity to experience of the destination, and can properly be thought of as helping to summarise the state of the individual's destination image.

Multisensory components

A final feature of Figure 4.1 is the connections between the multisensory components of destination image and the other two core facets. In the early work on cognitive mapping Downs and Stea (1977) and Pocock and Hudson (1978) demonstrated the importance of tactile, auditory and olfactory cues in shaping images of places. More recently Dann and Jacobsen (2002) emphasised the importance of olfactory cues in tourists' experience thus building on a line of clinical and physiological work that has linked the sense of smell to mood, memory and meaning (Classen *et al.*, 1987). It is not surprising therefore that Figure 4.1 connects the multisensory component to the attitudinal elements particularly as mood and emotion have strong sensory underpinnings. A link can be drawn here to some of the research discussed in Chapter 2, where Selanniemi (2003) emphasised the sensory stimulation and affective appeal of Mediterranean destinations for Northern Europeans. As an illustration of this affective-sensuality link de Botton (2002) notes that a number of European literary figures, including Beaudelaire and Byron, considered the Mediterranean countries with their sensory qualities to be totally synonymous with happiness.

Methodology

The methodological layer presented in Figure 4.1 also deserves attention. More than a decade ago, Echtner and Ritchie (1991) lamented the rather one-dimensional approach to assessing destination images. The work they reviewed at that time demonstrated a dominance of text-based scales where respondents typically rated dimensions that described the location. One illustration of destination image conducted in this way in the Asia-Pacific region is found in the work of Yau and Chan (1990). Their study considered the image of seven major Asian cities assessed along a number of dimensions such as price, nightlife, beaches, entertainment and attractions, shopping and the presence of friends and relatives. The spatial depiction of the results as reported in Figure 4.2 is typical of this kind of work and provides a quick, user-friendly appraisal of the perceived similarities in the study. The sample consisted of over 700 visitors to Hong Kong mainly from the USA, Australia and Europe. In a powerful sense, Figure 4.2 is a Westerners' view of Asian cities amongst those favourably disposed to visiting Hong Kong.

In the terminology employed in this chapter the destination images realised in Yau and Chan's (1990) study are heavily dependent on the cognitive and implicit behavioural component of attitudes. There are clearly many ready extensions to this kind of work – other samples of travellers from different source markets such as mainland China, Japan or Singapore could be studied. Additionally the effects of a specific marketing campaign, a

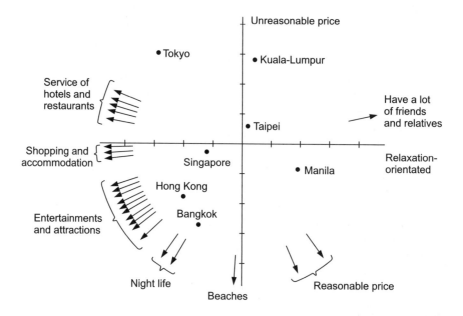

Figure 4.2 Joint space of vacation destinations and attributes

feature film or a turbulent event could be monitored if benchmark information existed. That is, studies of this sort can explore how destination images
change with time.

It is necessary to turn to other methodological styles to assess the affective, multisensory and locational–spatial components of destination image.
Several authors have drawn upon historical accounts including literature,
photographic and film archives to trace the origins of destination images.
This tradition, which relies more on traditional scholarship and historical
methods rather on than empirical appraisals, is illustrated by the work of
Butler (1998) in assessing Scotland's image. Butler reports that the current
tourist image of Scotland has been reinforced for over two centuries and is
tied to primary features such as mountains, tartan, bagpipes, castles and
kilts and secondary features such as highland dancing, whisky, haggis,
heather, golf, Balmoral and lochs/lakes. The persistent and complex historical construction of this image is seen as under-emphasising Scotland's
modernity, but it is a highly recognisable image and a basis for marketing
modernisation.

While Butler points out that the derivation of Scotland's image relies on
largely literary texts and political history, Douglas (1997), examining South
Pacific tourist destination images, reveals that the use of documentary

films and photographs were dominant in formulating an understanding of Melanesian locations and cultures. The early films partly appealed because they provided titillation to a socially conservative viewing audience in Australia and Europe. Importantly, Douglas observes:

> The early images of Melanesia and Melanesians convey the paradoxes which are perpetuated in the tourism marketing images for the region in the 1990s. The pictures of Melanesians in customary clothing (or little clothing) are juxtaposed with those of smiling waiters in Western clothing; tribal rituals are performed in hotel lobbies ... they are perceptions of the suave and the regulated, the exotic and the safe. (Douglas, 1997: 59)

Crawshaw and Urry (1997) discuss research illustrating how these provided destination images are integrated into or with the visitor's own experience and expectations of destinations. They report work from the Lake District of England where the Cumbria Tourist Board asked 350 people to view 120 colour photographs that represented a variety of subjects in the region. Participants were then asked to select typical images. Four photographs dominated the selection and 80% of responses were restricted to just 10 photographs. There are clearly stereotypical views of destinations, and the English study revealed a strong identification with scenes that depicted ordinary visitors gazing at and over scenes they would like to experience or which they felt reflected their experiences. Crawshaw and Urry argue that visual consumption of places is a dominant tourist mode and their work illustrates the consensus that can occur in the visual component of images.

As depicted in Figure 4.1, the visual and other sensory components of destination image are interwoven with the affective responses to places and destinations. One line of work that has explored the emotional images of places is that of Ward and Russell (1981) and subsequent developments of that work (Russell *et al.*, 1989).

Son (2004) using the kinds of semantic differential scales to measure affective responses developed by Russell and colleagues, assessed over 100 international students' images of two Australian cities, Melbourne and Sydney. Importantly, Son's study also assessed cognitive and spatial dimensions of the students' images, thus permitting some links to be made among dimensions set out in Figure 4.1. For the affective responses, Son found that both cities were perceived as pleasant and favourable, but Sydney was significantly more likely to be perceived as exciting – 70% of respondents in Sydney compared with 40% in Melbourne thought of their city as exciting. The other affective scales such as relaxing, pleasant, arousing did not differentiate between the cities.

In comparing the sketch maps of the two cities drawn by the international student sample, Son and Pearce (2003) noted a number of differences.

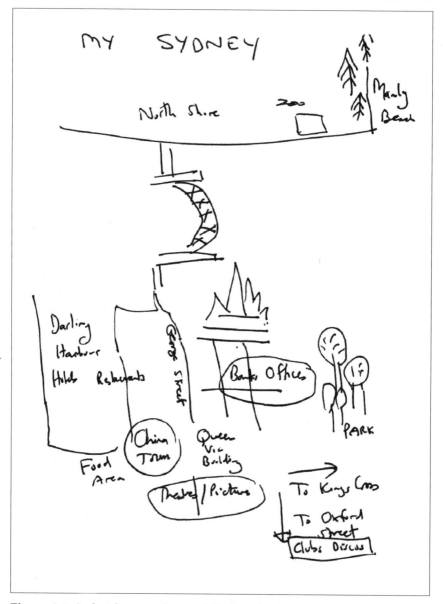

Figure 4.3 A sketch map of central Sydney by 21 year old Polish female

Landmarks take on a greater importance in the sketch maps of Sydney than is the case in Melbourne where the students' sketch maps have more paths or routes. Districts or areas too are more commonly reported in the Sydney sketch maps. The kinds of sketch maps produced by the students are illus-

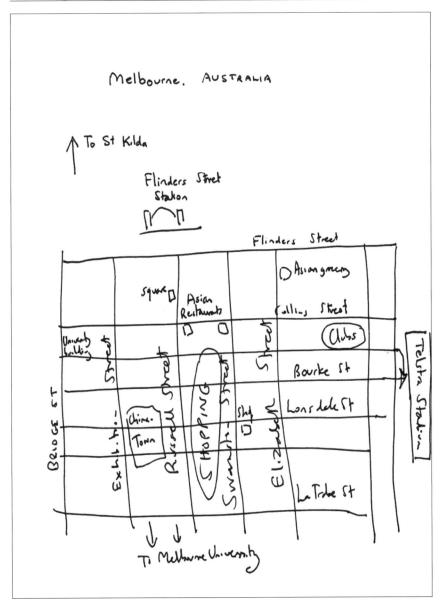

Figure 4.4 A sketch map of central Melbourne by 23 year old Japanese female

trated in Figures 4.3 and 4.4 and summaries of the overall map images constructed by profiling the most common elements are provided in Figure 4.5 and Figure 4.6.

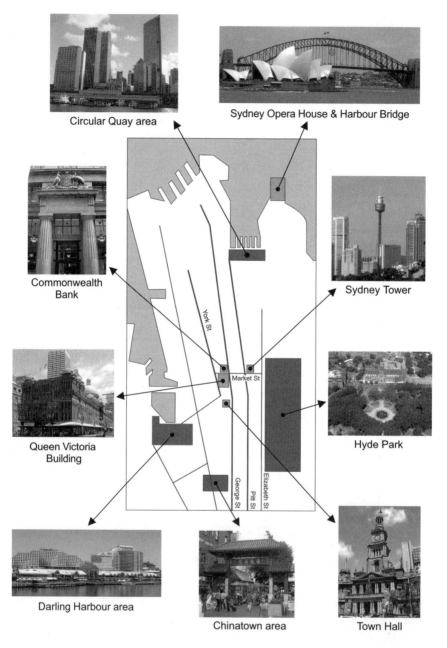

Figure 4.5 The public image of the downtown area in Sydney based on the top 15 image factors

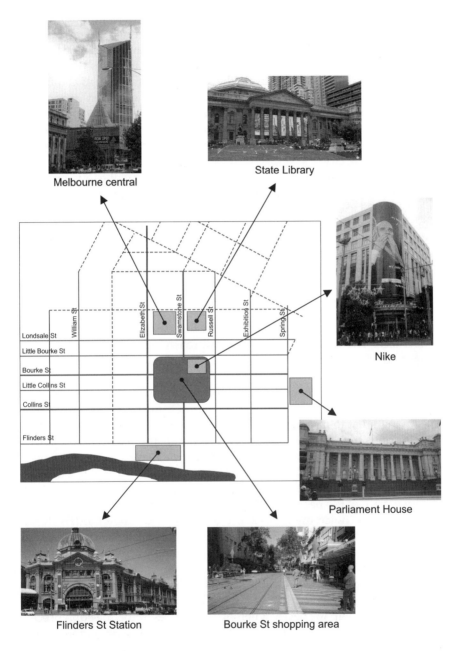

Melbourne central

State Library

Nike

Parliament House

Flinders St Station

Bourke St shopping area

Figure 4.6 The public image of the downtown area in Melbourne based on the top 15 image factors

Unlike the previous studies, the multiple assessment techniques used in this Australian work promise to provide a well-integrated picture of destination image. In addition to the material already reviewed Son (2004) asked each of the two city samples to nominate the top attributes or cognitive dimensions of their city – effectively the leading beliefs they had about their city. For Sydney, the top five statements were the tourist attractions, beaches, multicultural society, friendly people and the variety of food. For Melbourne the images were beautiful gardens, numerous restaurants and cafes, good nightlife, cold and unpredictable weather and the trams that run through the city.

In summary, destination image studies are evolving in the tourism literature. Armed with more comprehensive and holistic definitions, the work has begun not just to consider basic ratings of destination attributes but to facilitate a wider coverage of the term with affective and orientation components built on the sensory and particularly visual qualities of places. This development in tourist behaviour research represents a useful precursor to the applied topic of how people choose their travel destinations.

Destination Choice

Two kinds of models dominate tourist behaviour research on destination choice. The structured economic approach emphasises the idea that tourists' decisions depend on pricing issues and economic exchange rates, and there is indeed some evidence that flows between tourism-generating and tourism-receiving countries are influenced by exchange rates and price variables (Crouch, 1993; Morley, 1994). Despite substantial problems with specifying what to measure and include in exchange rate studies, a broad conclusion is that a 1% decrease in exchange rate (i.e. a shift favourable to the travellers' home country) produces a mean increase in travel demand of 0.8%. The effects noted by Crouch and others appear to be greatest in countries where there is substantial packaging and control by travel agents on the total price of the package. A highly rational and quantitative approach to destination choice underlies these economic exchange models. It has been appreciated for some time that such highly structured approaches have to confront a particular challenge – when does price enter the decision-making process for the consumer.

The greatest emphasis in the tourist behaviour literature has been directed towards a second group of models, broadly referred to as *choice set* models. These help to specify when price operates in the selection process and also help to articulate the interplay between destination image, psychological profiles of the visitor and destination selection.

The model of Um and Crompton (1990) will be taken as a leading exemplar of this choice set approach, and Figure 4.7 is built on this work with

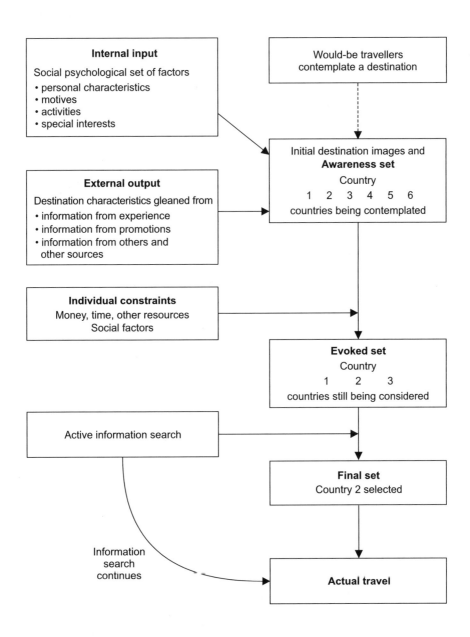

Figure 4.7 A model of the destination choice process

After Morrison and Rutledge, 1998; Moscardo *et al.*, 1996; Um and Crompton, 1990

some attention to the extensions offered by Crompton and Ankomah (1993) and Moscardo, Morrison *et al.* (1996). The model is very similar in spirit but differs marginally in labelling from the model presented by Woodside and Lysonski (1989).

Many of the concepts already discussed in this volume re-appear in Figure 4.7 as contributors to the destination choice process. In particular, the destination images are seen as the result of the destination characteristics, how they are presented and how they are integrated with the social psychological factors such as motives and interests.

Several other features of this choice set approach are noteworthy. Figure 4.7 illustrates the approach using just three layers of choice sets. Other more comprehensive views of the choice set approach include five or more layers of set selection, with the number of candidates for final travel slowly being reduced at each stage (Crompton & Ankomah, 1993).

It is consistent with the aim of this volume to report on innovation and to present some challenges to the existing conceptual schemes employed to understand themes in tourist behaviour. The challenges to the choice set models for destination selection come from three sources. First, much pleasure travel features not just one destination but several interwoven locations. The problem is described by Stewart and Vogt:

> It is time to revisit destination choice research ... multi-destination trips represent the choice of a cluster of destinations. On what basis does the traveller compose that cluster? Are transportation and access the only considerations or are travellers mentally grouping destinations based on some perceived similarity (all historic sites) or difference (seeking variety) in destination image. (Stewart & Vogt, 1997: 459)

A potential answer to Stewart and Vogt's questions will be presented, but two other challenges are noteworthy. A second issue is that the choice models typically represent an individual's choice process. Arguably the role of other people is implicated in the individual constraints section, but the notion of shared, joint or social decision making is not fully developed in the existing literature. Nevertheless there is research suggesting that, at least in Western countries, the family vacation decision is most often the result of a joint decision-making process (Fodness, 1992) or at least one with multiple family influences (Lee & Beatty, 2002; Zalatan, 1998).

A third issue relates to the kind of decision making. The destination choice models are typically designed for countries or whole regions. A valid question is, do the destination choice models describing a sequence of choice sets apply to decisions within an area (such as choosing an attraction) or do different models apply? Similarly, are the decisions made for day trips or short-break holidays made in the same way as for longer vacations or do heuristics and short-cuts apply as has been suggested by Murphy

(1997) in describing the budget youth travel market? Further, several researchers have argued that the decision making for travel is a set of processes, not just one decision and that family members or groups play different roles at different stages of the process (Shoham & Dalakas, 2003; Turley, 2001).

An activity-mediated choice model

It may be that a combination of these challenges to the omnipotence of a choice set approach to tourist destination choice can be met with some elaborations and modification. First, a potential answer to Stewart and Vogt's concern to identify a basis for travellers comparing multi-destination clusters lies in the use of activities as a mediating mechanism. There is a substantial basis in the tourism literature for choosing activities as a linking mechanism between destinations and the motives of tourists (Gitelson & Kerstetter, 1990; Gunn, 1988; Hsieh *et al.*, 1992; Pyo *et al.*, 1989). As Moscardo *et al.* (1996) suggest:

> Motives can be seen as providing travellers with expectations for activities and destinations seen as offering activities ... Existing destination choice models can be both more destination-specific and bring travel motives more clearly into the choice process by including activities as attributes of destinations. (Moscardo *et al.*, 1996: 112)

Importantly an activities elaboration of destination choice models also helps to address the two other concerns noted about existing models. A social decision process involving family members, partners or groups deciding on where to travel can be seen as a problem-solving task of selecting the suite of activities to best accommodate all group members. This view is built on the important premise that people travel to see attractions and participate in activities there rather than to stay in types of accommodation or benefit from support services (cf. Gunn, 1988; 1994a). The power of different members of the group may be unequal but a social approach to destination choice can be handled with an activities elaboration of the basic approach (Meikle, 2003).

The issue of the generality or universality of choice set approaches has also been raised. It can be suggested that the choice set approach will apply in circumstances where the tourist decision involves selecting from regions or tourism products involving several sets of activities. By way of contrast, when travellers are choosing one or two activities it may be that the choice set approach is replaced by one-dimensional heuristics such as convenience, proximity or price. In this way an activities focus alerts researchers to the range of convenience or scope of the choice set models and suggests that such models can co-exist with other approaches to tourist choice behaviour for more limited product ranges.

The activities emphasis also achieves two other conceptual links that help to integrate the study of tourist behaviour. The emphasis reinforces the view, expressed previously in this chapter, that destination image appraisals should not ignore the conative or behavioural dimension of attitude as a part of the destination image schema. The issue of what people can do in a destination or more subtly how they image themselves and their potential behaviours in a location is a part of destination image. It is difficult to imagine a visitor thinking of Las Vegas, for example, without involving a behavioural component that embraces activities such as gambling, shopping and seeing the sights.

A second important conceptual link achieved by an activities emphasis is to develop the value of the motivational research on tourist behaviour. Krippendorf (1987) amongst others has argued that many of the motives quoted by researchers are inherently vague, effectively empty containers which individuals will fill with quite different contents. In this criticism the motive of escape will, for some, result in a desire to be in a quiet natural setting while for others escape may be realised through continuous partying and nightlife. The criticism that motives are empty concepts is perhaps a little unfair, since there is a basic issue of at what level of detail researchers are working. General motivation theories (such as presented in Chapter 3) represent a broad blueprint or framework for understanding motives in any context. There is also a level of analysis for specific market segments and here there is a need to fill the empty containers that Kripendorff observes. Such specificity is assisted by noting that an activities emphasis is one way to define more closely for a particular group what escape, self-fulfilment and status amount to in relevant holiday settings.

It might be objected here that certain experiential states, rather than activities per se, are the desired goals of visiting a destination. The view being expressed in the activities emphasis does not disagree with this perspective, but asserts that it is not possible for travellers to effectively choose or plan for a memorable experience, and that such outcomes are a by-product or epiphenomenon of a suite of activities. In this view activity preferences are a result of motives and the participation in activities is the way to realise desired experiences. It is worth noting that activities as being used here can be quite passive contemplative behavioural sequences rather than always physically demanding pursuits.

This activity emphasis results in a redrafting of Figure 4.7 as Figure 4.8.

Studies by Moscardo, Morrison *et al.* (1996) and Meikle (2003) provide some initial evidence consistent with the model outlined in Figure 4.8. Using archival data based on the Pleasure Travel Markets Survey, Moscardo and colleagues analysed the responses of 1503 outbound Australian travellers to a detailed interview on international travel behaviour. Three groups of travellers who emphasised different sets of travel motives

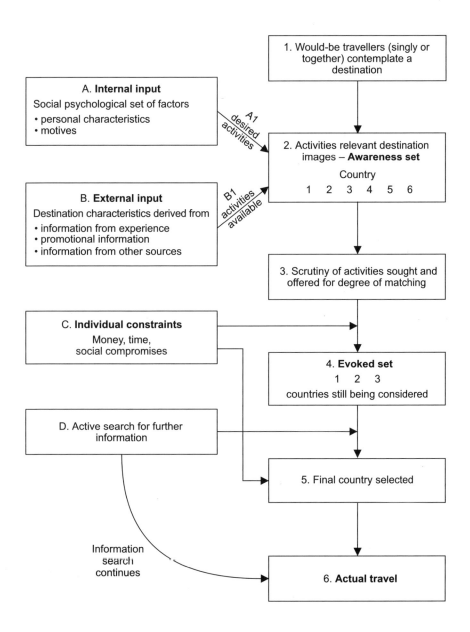

Figure 4.8 An activities-mediated destination choice model

were identified: one group characterised by a greater emphasis on escape, one by an emphasis on self-development and a third by higher responses to items defining social status concerns. For the purposes of Figure 4.8, these groups, together with their distinctive demographic profile represent Box A, the Internal Input component of the figure. Importantly, the researchers established that the motive clusters showed different frequencies of participation in a range of activities. Members of the self-development group, for example, were significantly more likely to emphasise getting to know local inhabitants, visiting galleries and museums, seeing historic and archaeological sites and sight-seeing in cities. This kind of finding, which also applied to the other motive groups links Box A to Box A1 – the motives–desired activities link. The Pleasure Travel Markets Survey format also presents destinations as consisting of activities, facilities and other features. It further asks respondents to rate the importance of these attributes in their vacation decisions. Effectively in specifying activities as a part of the destination profile, the survey delivers a view of destinations consistent with the B to B1 framework in Figure 4.8. The critical empirical question that is needed to support the importance of the activities-mediated destination model is, will there be a link between the destination characteristics and the three travel motive clusters? It has already been established that A and A1 are connected, but are A (and A1) connected to B1? It does not necessarily follow that destination activities will be consistently related to the motives. It can be noted that the profile of destinations provided in the survey also describes service facilities, hygiene, climate features and price related accommodation categories. If the activities-mediated destination choice model is to receive empirical support, then the motives–destination activities must be strong and must not be swamped by these other destination features. The evidence was somewhat surprising. The data reported by the researchers did show distinct links between the motive groups and activities available in the destination. Additionally, however, there were also clear and distinct links between the motive groups and the facilities to support those activities, including the climate and contextual factors providing the means to enjoy the activities. In this account, activities matter and while they are not all that matters they provide a useful organiser to link destination characteristics. This pivotal empirical study goes someway towards justifying Figure 4.8 but provides an implicit caution that activities need to be widely interpreted and understood as available and embedded destination characteristics. Figure 4.8 can be seen as justified in its emphasis on an 'activities offered and desired' approach. It further asserts the continued scrutiny and checking of this relationship as the destination choice process develops.

Another source of evidence supporting Figure 4.8 comes from an explicit study of the perceived roles of adults and children in making destination-

Table 4.3 Major decision makers for different types of vacation decisions

	Initial suggestion	*Finding the information*	*What to do*	*Spending amount*	*Final decision*
Australian day trips	male & female	female	children	female	male & female
Australian holidays	female	female	female	female	male & female
Singaporean day trips	male, female & children	male & female	male, female & children	male	male & female
Singaporean holidays	male & female	male & female	male & female	male	male & female

relevant travel decisions (Meikle, 2003). On this occasion, unlike many
other studies it was not just one 'decision' that was the focus of attention but
five components of destination decision making – making the initial
suggestion, finding out about the destination, what to do at the destination,
how much to spend and making the final decision. The study was
conducted in both Singapore and Australia, with 200 adults being interviewed in each setting. For both day trips and longer holiday travel, the
respondents were asked to assess the importance of the role of both the
adults and the children in the travel party. Statistical treatment of the data
revealed a pattern of findings identifying the key participants in the decision areas. Table 4.3 summarises this pattern.

The findings in Table 4.3 suggest a rich and complex interplay of family
decision-making influences with each decision type being governed by
different actors. From the perspective of Figure 4.8 this analysis of the social
forces at work in vacation decision making sees the potential for an interaction amongst partners and group members in constructing the final decision.
It represents a much more fluid and dynamic view of vacation decision
making than the formal choice set models. It raises the possibility that
survey work on destination choice that concentrates only on the final decision may be ignoring the input of activity preferences of group members.
These preferences may feature in the final decision, but not actually belong
to or be a part of the profile of the individuals making that decision.

Several conclusions can be drawn from this close examination of tourists
perceiving and choosing their destination. It was suggested in the
introductory section of this chapter that not all of the elements of destination imaging and selection have been satisfactorily resolved in tourist
behaviour research. There are, however, some strong indicators of what is

important and what needs to be considered both academically and in tourism industry practice in this area. First, a rich view of destination image is required. Depending on the academic or the applied interests, select facets of this total image may be a basis for further attention. Second, understanding motives and the visitors' preference for activities represents a promising direction in linking visitors' needs and the attributes of destinations. This does not imply that activities are all that matter to the tourist, but it does suggest a convenient route for understanding destination choice. Third, destination decisions have several components and where groups of travellers are involved several different sub-decisions may contribute to the final outcome. Much of the work on destination decisions has been carried out with large-scale survey methodologies. It can be suggested that a range of studies using more qualitative and reflective accounts of ongoing and past decisions by individual and group travellers might augment and test the conceptual scheme of the activities-mediated destination choice scheme developed in this chapter.

Chapter 5
Social Contact for the Tourist

This chapter provides a comprehensive view of the social contacts and relationships that tourists may experience. These social interactions are a consequence of the active role of the tourist as an outsider, as a stranger, and as an observer of life. The tourists' social relationships are also a product of the organisation of much contemporary travel as well as the attitudes and perspectives of other travellers and the community members that tourists meet.

It can be stressed here that the view of a tourist adopted in this chapter and more generally in this volume is in accord with the view of, amongst others Gergen (1997), Crang (1997) and Moore (2002). These commentators explicitly posit the view that a full understanding of behaviour (and tourist behaviour) requires the interacting parties to be viewed as actively constructing their experience and their relationships. Tourists, like other social actors, are not passive bodies pushed from place to place and from group to group by mechanistic internal forces and external factors. Rather, they are best viewed as organisers of their social world and experiences, acting out roles, communicating their identities and purposefully structuring their time. Once stated, the perspective may seem obvious but it is not always manifested in psychology research on tourists when experience and action are described in multivariate statistical terms with well-defined independent and dependent variables.

Moore (2002) in particular has argued that it is necessary for researchers who study tourist behaviour to support and adopt this social constructionist view in order to meld together the sociological work about tourists, with its concern for the question of what being a tourist means for contemporary society (cf. Dann, 2002), and the more individual psychology tradition which focuses on the experience of the individual and often analyses this in a very positivistic framework (cf. Pizam & Mansfield, 2000).

As with other chapters in this volume the material presented considers some of the dominant themes and issues in tourist behaviour in this sphere and then explores the value of key conceptual frameworks which can illuminate these topics. Three content themes will be developed in this chapter:

- how tourists interact with and see other tourists;
- how tourists interact with service personnel;
- how local communities treat and are treated by their visitors.

Chapter 2 introduced the social role of the tourist in general, and noted that many tourist behaviours can be understood by utilising concepts such as role distance, and altercasting. Further, the outsider role noted in the early writing of Simmel was identified as insightful in exploring the intimacy and spontaneity of tourists' social relationships. In the present chapter the distinctive individual role of the tourist as flaneur, the casual observer of the passing crowd, will be added to the analysis (Benjamin, 1973; Jokinen & Veijola, 1997).

This chapter will also develop and extend the analysis of tourists' behaviours within the dynamics of social situations. The influence of cultural factors that shape social responses will also be considered.

Tourists and Other Tourists

With some exceptions (such as theme parks and festivals), the images of tourism destinations rarely portray a world full of other travellers. In particular, there are few promotional images of the waiting lines at passport control, of the delays in accessing historical monuments or more simply the press of other people who also require food, drinks and toilets.

Tourists, it can be argued, can have multiple perspectives on other tourists. Table 5.1 presents an array of possible tourist views of other tourists.

It can be suggested initially and following the work of Glasson *et al.* (1995), that the kind of tourist response to other tourists will depend on both the setting and the number of other visitors present. Glasson *et al.* propose a series of non-linear relationships describing tourist satisfaction with use levels in four types of settings. In the first of these settings, wilderness and natural environments, they argue for a reverse J curve, where high satisfaction is associated with low numbers and low satisfaction with high numbers. The proposed relationship is depicted in Figure 5.1.

This is an important figure for tourist–tourist contact in the tourist behaviour literature. The wilderness and natural environment context has been the dominant arena for the work of recreation user–user interaction (Graefe & Vaske, 1987; Mannell & Kleiber, 1997; Rathmun, 1995; Ruddell & Gramman, 1994; Schneider & Hammit, 1995; Vaske *et al.*, 1995). At the broadest descriptive level, there is support for the shape of Figure 5.1 from the North American recreation studies. It should be noted that the term 'satisfaction' here is being used jointly to represent satisfaction with the presence of other users and also satisfaction with the total experience. Three lines of work support Figure 5.1 in its general form.

A foundation piece of work in this area is that of Jacob and Shreyer (1980), who outlined 10 hypotheses that they thought defined user–user conflict. The key proposition in their work is that goal interference attributed to other people's behaviour is the driving force shaping conflict. Many

Table 5.1 The multiple perspectives tourists may have of other tourists

	Other tourist seen as	*Behaviours*
Positive views	Potential close friend	• friendly contact – intimacy • learn about and from them • learn about other culture
	Travel companion	• partner for activities • socialise, someone to be with
	Helper	• source of information • share costs • lend a hand
	Security guard	• look after possessions • prevent unwanted contacts
	Stimulation	• improve atmosphere of destination • excitement • 'marker' of good times
Neutral perspective	Background scenery	• just there • no impact
Negative views	Stranger	• minor discomfort • something unfamiliar
	Disturber	• noise source • adds to crowd • invades privacy • causes conflict, contributes to culture shock
	Competitor	• competitor for accommodation, tickets, space, access to people and setting

Adapted from Pearce, 2005

factors contribute to goal interference, and the key factors, themes and specific propositions for this approach are outlined in Table 5.2.

The research effort in the recreation and park management literature has been strongly influenced by the factors identified by Jacob and Shreyer. Watson *et al.* (1994) reported that the factor of intensity, that is the focus on the task, may be associated with hostility to interfering parties. Occasionally, however, the focus may be so intense that other people are simply not noticed. The relationships are often unbalanced or asymmetrical in these encounter situations. Participants in quiet and traditional activities

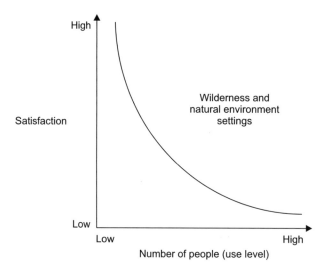

Figure 5.1 User satisfaction and use levels for a natural environment context

After Glasson *et al.*, 1995

may be more concerned with noisy newcomers than vice versa (Jackson & Wong, 1982; Ruddell & Gramman, 1994; Shelby, 1981). More specifically, a set of contrasting user groups can be depicted with the non-mechanised and passive-appreciation users experiencing greater goal interference than their mechanised or adrenalin-oriented counterparts. The first-mentioned group in the following pairings is likely to be the most troubled by other users: canoeists and motor boat users, swimmers and jet-ski users, walkers and horse-riders, cross-country skiers and snowmobilers, hikers and trail bikers (cf. Gibbons & Ruddell, 1995; Shelby, 1981). These kinds of findings reinforce the interacting forces of intensity, lifestyle tolerance and the respect for place dimensions of Jacob and Shreyer's propositions.

Rathmun (1995) noted some difficulties in working with Jacob and Shreyer's categories. In particular he observed that they tended to overlap and he proposed instead a more fundamental underlying psychological process shaping tourist–tourist conflict. Rathmun stressed the in-group out-group dimension in interpersonal relationships. His approach is in accord with fundamental social psychological research on group identity such as found in the work of Tajfel (1981). Further discussion of the adequacy of this dimension in tourist–tourist contact will be considered later in this chapter.

Table 5.2 Propositions potentially explaining user-user conflict in recreation settings

Factor	Specific theme	Proposition
Activity style	Intensity	1 The more intense the activity style, the greater the likelihood that social interaction with less intense participants will result in conflict
	Status disregard	2 Conflict results when one party ignores the status makers and attributes of a status conscious group
	Status snobbery	3 Status based intra-activity conflict occurs when a participant deserving high status must interact with others viewed as lower status
	Status disagreement	4 Conflict occurs between participants who do not share the same status hierarchies
	Quality judgement	5 The more specific the expectations of what constitute a quality experience, the greater the potential for conflict
Resource specificity	Respect for place	6 Evaluations of resource quality: when a person who views the place's qualities as unequalled confronts behaviours indicating a lower evaluation, conflict results
	'Ownership'	7 Sense of possession: conflict results when users with a possessive attitude towards the resource confront users perceived as disrupting traditional uses and behavioural norms
	Privacy of place	8 Status: conflict occurs for high status users forced to interact with low status users who symbolise devaluing the exclusive intimate relationship with place
Mode of experience	Focus	9 When a person in the focused mode interacts with one who is not, conflict results
Tolerance for lifestyle diversity	Lifestyle tolerance	10 If group differences are evaluated as undesirable or a potential threat to recreation goals conflict results when group members contract one another.

After Jacob and Shreyer, 1980

A process-based approach to user conflict was identified by Schneider and Hammitt (1995). The core of this argument is that conflict is an ongoing problem characterised by small incidents of annoyance that have a cumulative effect. The stress on the most annoyed group builds up over time. It is insightful to explore the phenomenon in a time frame by noting the accretion of small critical incidents rather than focusing on the final trigger for action and dissatisfaction. Vaske *et al.* (1995) provide the additional perspective that the triggers or defining points of annoyance may be indirect, such as reading a newspaper report or noting a new policy or park rule, rather than actual direct behavioural disputes. This approach is consistent with the view expressed at the beginning of this chapter that insights into tourist behaviour can be generated by plotting how actors see themselves and construct their social relationships over time. There is a strong suggestion here that more historical and longitudinal studies and accounts would benefit this research area rather than cross-sectional and unitary snapshots of attitudes.

There are several important comments to be made on this North American recreation-based work. At the broadest level wilderness settings and natural environments are just one kind of tourist–tourist context and even within such an 'environment' categorisation there are many variations. Recreational conflict appears to be particularly noticeable when the specific focused purposes of one group are frustrated by the cumulative actions of another. By way of contrast, in many tourist situations there are shared goals. The visitors in the setting have come to see, experience and enjoy the same features and activities. In this kind of scenario the tolerance for fellow visitors may be quite high.

Urry (1990) has developed this kind of argument in some detail. The term 'the tourist gaze' has been used by Urry to provide an integrative view of how tourists approach social and environmental encounters. In particular Urry distinguished those whose goals are largely to appreciate settings alone or with a very small number of like-minded companions from those who seek social experiences. The romantic gaze is the term given to this small group or individual appreciation style. This theme is rich in historical Western precedent as a way of approaching environmental sites. The collective gaze is the term reserved for those seeking socially rich recreational experiences. The collective gaze defines the presence of others as a positive rather than a negative experience.

Urry's perspective, now widely cited in the tourism literature, can be linked to three other tourism settings identified by Glasson *et al.* (1995). There is also a mounting argument from cross-cultural studies of tourist–tourist contact that other groups such as the Chinese, Japanese and Koreans prefer, or at least tolerate group-based and high-density natural settings (Kim, 1997; Ward *et al.*, 2001).

Figure 5.2 adopts and develops Glasson *et al.*'s depiction of other kinds of tourism settings where this interaction among visitors may function differently than in wilderness settings.

At a quick glance, the curves portrayed in Figure 5.2 are appealing as a convenient distinction among tourist settings. A more exacting analysis,

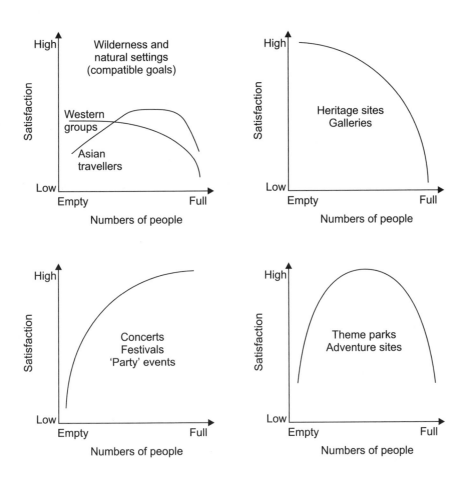

Figure 5.2 Tourist–tourist encounter reactions in diverse tourism contexts

however, raises critical questions about the number of people required to specify the high and low ends of the x-axis and the amount of difference in satisfaction which should be portrayed on the y-axis.

One of the additional issues that arises in considering these curves and relationships is that attention has been largely devoted in the research literature to the negative dimensions of tourist–tourist contact, or in terms of Figure 5.2 the lower values on the y-axes. The more positive and even the neutral outcomes reported, for example, in Table 5.1 have received less scrutiny.

A method for developing a greater understanding of tourist–tourist contact is to extend and explore the value of existing conceptual schemes and approaches. Two such concepts, the in-group out-group distinction and the concept of the familiar stranger will now be highlighted.

In-groups and out-groups

Rathmun (1995) cited the potential of the in-group and out-group categorisation system to inform the recreation conflict literature. In the tourism context there are some ambiguities in distinguishing among multiple in-groups and out-groups. For example, consider one subgroup of Western tourists, say from the United States and on a package tour, who are travelling throughout China. They might visit the Bund, home to Shanghai's famous heritage buildings and core to the city's commercial history; they might walk along the Great Wall of China or inspect the Terracotta Warriors site in Xi'an. There are several in-groups in these settings, varying in closeness and connection to the travelling party. First there are members of the same tour group, there are other Americans, and then other English-speaking Westerners. Yet again there are Asian tourists, domestic Chinese tourists and then local citizens. The existing in-group out-group appraisal does not specify how to treat these multiple groups. There may be some kind of algebra of affinity and consequences for the tolerance of other tourists but propositions in this area have yet to be developed. Further, the in-group out-group relationships may work differently in restaurants than at attractions or in accommodation establishments and on transport systems. In brief, advancing the understanding of tourist–tourist contact using the in-group/out-group distinction represents a significant measurement and definitional challenge for researchers.

Familiar strangers

A potentially more fruitful conceptual approach rests with the adoption of the familiar stranger notion originally described by Simmel (1950). A neglected dimension in many accounts of travel experience is the incipient relationships built with other travellers. For example, consider an international flight from Seoul to Sydney. While waiting in line, other travellers are noticed. It may be an unusual clothing style, a loud voice or simple physical proximity but a select number of fellow passengers are mentally recorded. On entering the aircraft and taking up one's seat further individuals are noticed, particularly those close to one's own position and those who are louder, more conspicuous or distinctive in their appearance. On embarking after the shared tedium and physical challenge of such overnight flights, the dishevelled passengers accumulate in tired lines for passport control and then baggage collection. There is a tacit community of fellow sufferers-adventurers. There are benefits and advantages in being attentive to these fellow travellers. Their behaviour can provide guidance, they may be able to help pass the time in conversation and they may even be sources of help in times of stress.

In Simmel's (1950) account of familiar strangers he noted their omni-presence in such contexts as urban commuting, in retail settings and in one's neighbourhood. In a quasi-experiment field study of Greyhound bus travellers in the United States, Pearce (1980) reported that these familiar strangers were consistently more helpful to fellow travellers on a range of small tasks than were total strangers. The familiar stranger is a potentially powerful concept for tourist analysis. As individuals sharing a common experience they are distinguished from the passing crowds. The flaneur, the social observer in the crowd, is not truly alone – there are indeed others walking the same path and it is to these others that fellow travellers may turn for confirmation of instrumental and possibly even expressive aspects of their experience.

Some further insights into the role of familiar strangers have been offered by Yagi (2003), who paid attention to the physical characteristics of other travellers. Visible characteristics of other people such as their race, gender, age and dress style are readily observable by all travellers, and of course by tourist service personnel. In popular tourism settings where there are numerous visitors of varied nationalities, it is likely that travellers of the same age, appearance and nationality constitute a special kind of familiar stranger. Even to the tourists who cast themselves as flaneurs (the quiet observers in the crowd), certain other strangers will stand out, visible points of reference in the throng of the passing mass.

In an extended programme of research addressing tourist–tourist rela-tionships Yagi (2003) asked whether or not tourists prefer to mix with familiar strangers of their own nationality. A variety of methods were used in this work. Internet diaries were accessed to review travellers' own accounts of their experiences with other travellers. Additionally electroni-cally-altered photographs of visitors varying in their appearance and placed in different environmental settings were used as a basis for assessing visitor responses in a survey format. Focus groups were also used to explore travellers' explanations of their preferences. The preferences of Japanese and Western (largely Australian and US) travellers towards mixing with Caucasian versus Asian visitors in natural environment settings were closely studied using the multiple methods.

It was concluded, using a sample of both Japanese and North American Internet stories, that the Japanese showed consistently greater awareness of the presence of other Japanese. The attitudes towards other Japanese travellers was not always positive because at times a desire to escape the confines of their own compatriots' expectations emerged (Yagi, 2001). In the electronically-altered photographic images, different mixes of tourist appearance and density were portrayed. It was found that, while the Western tourists examining the photographs preferred smaller numbers of people in natural environment settings, such as the rainforest, the Japanese travellers preferred moderate to larger numbers (Yagi & Pearce, 2002). Perhaps surprisingly, Japanese travellers expressed a preference for photographs with more Caucasian faces as opposed to those depicting more Asian faces. This is a somewhat surprising finding since it contains an apparent contradiction with the preferences for familiar strangers. The Western travellers revealed no marked preferences for Caucasian or Asian faces in the photographs.

Possible explanations for these results were revealed in the focus-group interviews. Japanese travellers have *'akogare'* (respect, enthusiasm and admiration) for the Western world, particularly in arenas where fashion and taste are implicated. More Western faces, in the Japanese view, enhance the international atmosphere of the site. This finding is congruent with Urry's analysis of the collective gaze. Importantly it extends Urry's perspective by incorporating a cross-national addition where the symbolic value of the personnel making up the crowd is important. Additionally, the in-group/out-group distinction is seen as a misleading conceptualisation for these findings. The familiar stranger approach was also unable to explain the results, but there is a strong possibility that it may be appropriate when actual behaviours are assessed and interaction is studied. The findings in Yagi's work relate to preferences for mixing, not fordirect interaction.

An additional emotional state and sequence of behaviours can be identified from the spectrum of tourist–tourist behaviours in Table 5.1. Armstrong (2003) identified the concept of 'katabasis', which is an appreciation of small and helpful acts in times of emotional stress. It is a heightened appreciation for other people that stems from their kindness and tenderness. Armstrong emphasises that it represents a vulnerability where people are confronted with loneliness and disappointment, and thus welcome stranger assistance. The focus of much attention in travellers' experience is the extraordinary, the life-enhancing episodes and significant encounters with others. Armstrong's insight suggests that the genesis of companionship and even key elements of tourists' social relationships in general may stem from quite simple acts of altruism (Herold *et al.*, 2001).

It is possible to use the familiar stranger dimension to integrate and synthesise the work done in the recreation settings and more recent cross-national studies. Travellers from Western countries construct their view of others in natural settings according to long-standing cultural traditions of the values of being in special environments. The traditions derive both from Christian views of the value of wilderness and the popularisation of nature in the literature of the 19th century. In this kind of environmental setting, relationships with other travellers are not desired. Other travellers are viewed as unwelcome intrusions since fellow users restrict the attainment of the travellers' goals. In more purpose-built tourist attraction settings, there are suggestions that familiar strangers may be tolerated and be useful companions. Indeed, as Urry has argued, the atmosphere generated by large crowd numbers is integral to the visitor experience. For travellers from more group-oriented or collectivist cultures, being with other travellers is marginally preferred even in natural environment settings as they are seen to enhance the appeal of the location because of the symbolic value of connoting a noteworthy site. For Japanese travellers especially, Western travellers at sites may provide a strong symbolic message that the attraction is worthy of time and attention (cf. Kagitcibasi & Berry, 1989; Triandis et al., 1998; Ward et al., 2001).

The use of the concept of the familiar stranger is of further value in interpreting the social interaction of tourists. Fellow travellers may fulfil roles such as providing friendship, offering assistance and aiding traveller safety and security. These positive roles may be seen as a consequence or as a part of a sequence of identifying people with whom one has only peripheral initial contact but who are seen as suitable people to approach to ease the tourist's journey. These relationships may be developed in good times or they may arise in times of minor stress where katabasis may play a role. Less positively, tourist–tourist relationships may also degenerate into hostile encounters. It has been established in the recreation literature that, when there is conflict over achieving goals or competition for limited resources such as tickets and space then a process of conflict commences. A further consideration of these poles of positive and negative roles for fellow travellers will be reiterated later in the chapter in considering the interactions of travellers with members of the local community.

Social situation analysis

Another conceptual scheme that can inform studies of tourist–tourist relationships is referred to as *social situation analysis* (Argyle et al., 1981). In the original publication, the researchers note that a 'situation could be described as the sum of the features of a social occasion that impinges on an individual person' (Argyle et al., 1981: 7). The approach is intentionally comprehensive and inclusive. In the kinds of situations already reviewed many features have been identified as impinging on tourist behaviour. Some of the features discussed include the traveller's social role, the environmental setting and the compatibility of the participants' behaviour. The social situations review conducted by Argyle et al., identifies eight organised topics, of which the factors already considered form a part. The core topics are presented in Table 5.3.

The social situations approach can be employed as a comprehensive organising framework for descriptive and interpretive accounts of tourist–

Table 5.3 Definitions for the eight features of social situations

Feature	Brief definition
Goals	Goals may be seen as the purposes or ends which direct social behaviour
Environmental setting	Environmental setting consists of the props, spaces, barriers, modifiers (the physical units and their arrangement) which influence the situation
Rules	Rules are the shared beliefs that regulate behaviour. The existence of many unstated rules is most clearly shown in the opprobrium attached to rule-breaking behaviours
Roles	Roles are the duties or obligations which attend the social positions people occupy
Repertoire of elements (behaviours)	The sum of behaviours which are appropriate to that situation
Language and speech	The interest in language and speech in this context focuses on how things are said, the code of speech, vocabulary, and social variation inherent in language
Sequences	The ordering of the repertoire of behaviours. Sequences may be very fixed or very fluid

tourist or tourist–host contact. It can also be used as a guide directing attention to what kinds of empirical information can be collected in survey or visitor evaluation data. It has been used in a number of tourist studies including analyses of farm tourism, critical encounters in marine tourism, analyses of bed-and-breakfast operations and to portray the character of backpacking or budget youth tourism (Murphy, 2001; Pearce, 1990a; Scarinci, 1997). The present interest in tourist–tourist contact is best illustrated by Murphy's portrayal of the social situations encountered by backpackers in their hostels.

Murphy (2001) highlighted the very social goals of backpackers, especially the desire to meet other travellers, to mix with them and to use them for information and companionship. Interestingly her work also contained observations that some backpackers tired of altercasting (playing out the social role into which they felt cast) – a role where being friendly and constantly telling one's abbreviated life story is a necessary pre-requisite to short-term relationships. The sociological traditions emphasising how tourists construct and re-invent themselves is particularly appropriate here (cf. Gergen, 1997). Murphy noted that some backpackers assumed other identities, they made themselves more interesting with a different life story in order to avoid the tedium of repeated renditions of their journey.

Other elements of the social situations framework were also described by Murphy as affecting the way tourist–tourist relationships developed. She noted the importance of the environmental setting and the facilities in the accommodation lodges and how this either enhanced or inhibited group conversation and mixing. Additionally, some backpacker lodges provided group activities to facilitate the atmosphere of the establishments and participation in these activities (such as beach games or free meals) was central to the kinds of positive relationships developed by individuals.

It is apparent from this brief example of the application of social situation analysis that comprehensive accounts of tourist–tourist encounters can be built from these core elements. The value of the social situation analysis lies not so much in its explanatory power – at core it is a descriptive summary scheme – but in the recognition that diverse components of the external context and participants' psychological functioning work together to structure tourist–tourist outcomes. It is entirely consistent with social situations analysis and contemporary motivational thinking that tourists construct their words in a teleological sense. They are thinking about where they want to go literally and metaphorically and, while it would be overstating the case to say that this applies consistently to all younger budget travellers, there is a clear sense in which many backpacker tourists are writing their own roles and playing out the encounters to deeply personal agendas.

Travellers' Relationships with Hosts

The presentation of information in this section uses the term 'hosts' as a convenient integrating expression for two groups of locals with whom visitors come in contact: service personnel and local citizens. Aramberri (2001) has suggested that the continued use of the term hosts in tourism is misleading. He argues that it continues an anthropological tradition that describes contact with distinctive traditional communities. Aramberri observes:

> The host–guest paradigm cannot be used to account for most types of what is called tourist behaviour. (Aramberri, 2001: 745)

The particular objection to the use of the term host resides in the connotation that there is a family-like and personal contract binding the host and guest. Further there is some future reciprocity anticipated by the host for the behaviour of caretaking the guest. Contemporary travellers and their service providers, it can reasonably be argued, do not fit this mould. There is an agreement here with the argument that it is not appropriate to embrace the more anthropological implication of the term, but instead it can be used as a simple integrative label referring to both service providers and other community members.

Much attention has been directed towards understanding the characteristics and performance of tourist service personnel. The relationships and social contact that the tourist has with the service personnel are rarely examined. As Noe (1999) reports, key dimensions used to assess service quality include the employees' reliability, the assurance they provide, the tangible aspects of their performance, and their empathy and responsiveness to client needs. These kinds of service provision evaluations have been developed by researchers such as Parasuraman *et al.* (1994a).

It is likely that tourists recall these multiple brief and routine encounters in a generalised or aggregated way, such as forming an overall impression of friendliness and service quality (Kandampully *et al.*, 2001). It is only when critical incidents (such as stressful or very rewarding brief encounters) take place that powerful memories are created and the service encounters become a noteworthy part of the tourists' recall (Lee-Ross, 2001).

It is worth noting that the present interest in tourist behaviour rather than in the behaviour of service personnel can be developed in several ways. Chapter 6 will consider tourist satisfaction and will highlight the contribution of service personnel to this satisfaction. Additionally, there is an opportunity to view the tourist–service encounter as a chance to better understand how tourists behave. This interest may be in the realm of how requests are phrased, the time and attention given to interaction with providers and the empathy (or lack of it) for the role of the guide, courier, waiter or attendant.

There is a view that tourists can be disturbingly rude towards the people looking after them. It seems worthwhile to explore under what circumstances, how frequently and by whom, these negative tourist behaviours are generated. Cataloguing and interpreting when and how tourists behave in ways perceived to be offensive and problematic to service personnel might illuminate the entire service process and interaction sequences.

Sexually-oriented encounters

A marked exception to the lack of research on two-way contact in tourist–local encounters involves sexual relationships. This is a complex topic incorporating many kinds of encounters, some of which are readily labelled, while others defy easy description. Traveller motivation is complex, local participation is complex and the broader effect on the host society is often both damaging and complex (Craik, 1997). Herold *et al.* (2001) use the term 'companionship tourism' to synthesise the multiple relationship possibilities inherent in the work of other researchers.

McKercher and Bauer (2003) highlight the relatively obvious point that tourism and travel can create new opportunities for sexual relationships. Factors such as anonymity, sensory stimulation, time, levels of affluence, and reduced social control all act to foster the possibility of new same-sex and opposite-sex partners (Selanniemi, 2003). One end of this multifaceted array of relationships is consensual adult sex involving males purchasing women's services. All the complex issues of power, exploitation and strategies for exploitation by and of both sets of participants serve to characterise these encounters (de Albuquerque, 1998; McCormick, 1994; Ryan, 1999; Truong, 1990).

Researchers exploring how female tourists develop relationships with local males are less inclined to characterise it as prostitution. Pruitt and La Font (1995) studying the links formed between European and North American women and young Jamaican males suggest that there are elements of courtship, emotional involvement and sometimes sexual intimacy. The ways in which the predominantly white affluent women pay for or reward male participation appears to be more indirect than direct. Purchases of meals, drinks, clothes and souvenirs are common. De Albuquerque (1998) has suggested that this is still prostitution rather than romance tourism. Herold *et al.* (2001) disagree, arguing that consensual romantic relationship is a more apt description and that the sexual component is not a predominant motivator.

The management of these relationships is carefully handled by the young males. The patterns appear to be widespread, and researchers note similar strategies and forms of intimacy in the Caribbean, Thailand (Cohen, 1982), Greece (Zinovieff, 1991), Crete (Du Cros & Du Cros, 2003) and Indonesia (Dahles & Bras, 1999). The working of the tourists is reported by Herold *et al.*:

> They use different strategies to indicate their lack of money to pay for drinks, admission to discos or taxi transportation ...
> (They) look sad and do not talk. This throws the woman off guard ... something is very wrong as he 'reluctantly admits to having money problem. (Herold *et al.*, 2001: 991)

Some of these relationships clearly provide temporary satisfaction and rewards to one or both parties. Lee (2002) studying Taiwanese male travellers reports that activities deriving from the sexual liberation of other parts of Asia are sought out and are synonymous with access to a better freer lifestyle. Additionally, as Cohen (2003) has documented, the sexually-oriented tourism relationships may not always be short-lived. Cohen analysed cross-national marital relationships, some of which commenced in tourism contexts and observed the persistent and expanding financial demands by the women on behalf of themselves and their family. The problems appeared to be the greatest when the foreigner stayed in Thailand. Although an initially difficult period was often encountered, a number of the relationships persisted, held together by children, common property and growing mutual understanding.

Such successful, albeit infrequent, marriages between tourists and local partners represent a positive pinnacle of tourist–local encounters. But there are also harmful and widely condemned consequences of such relationships. The interest here is on the impacts and consequences for the tourists although, of course, the hosts too are often seriously harried and harmed.

Negative encounters

Tourists themselves can be the victims of organised criminal stings and assault as well as being subject to disease and financial exploitation as reported earlier (Chesney-Lind & Lind, 1986; Craik, 1997; Hall, 1994; Harper, 2000). These negative encounters can vary from small opportunistic attacks (such as stealing, snatching handbags and wallets) to blackmail and assault. Some of the most vulnerable groups include those participating in compromising activities (Want, 2002). There are further forms of negativity. At times products purchased are exchanged for inferior substitutes and overcharging is a strategy to which many tourists are exposed (de Albuquerque & McElroy, 2001). For Westerners in Indonesia, casual street vendors touch, push and shove for attention causing distress to visitors (Pearce *et al.*, 1998). At a more extreme and global scale there is organised terrorism against identifiable national groups such as in Bali in October 2002.

As suggested earlier, it is likely that tourists recall the negative episodes even more than the positive ones as well-defined memorable encounters. Tales about the intrusive vendors, the overcharging taxi drivers and the sexually predatory street people are likely to be retold to others and define the nadir of tourists' social experiences (cf. Pearce, 1991a).

Travelling with family and friends

The foundation work on tourist behaviour has usually adopted a very individualistic orientation. Such a direction is partly linked to the dominance of questionnaire-based methodologies for exploring visitor behaviour, since surveys are typically filled in by individuals and the processing of the data aggregates individual responses. Many travel parties are however composed not of individuals but of couples, friends and assorted family groupings. There are multiple examples of these social dimensions of tourism. Senior couples dominate long-distance car touring in Australia (Pearce, 1999b), small shifting friendship groups characterise backpacker travel (Buchanan & Rossetto, 1997), family groups are common in zoos and attractions (Turley, 2001) and gay male couples are over-represented in many Mediterranean resorts (Clift *et al.*, 2002).

Three tourist behaviour topics can be identified from this social nature of travelling. There is the issue of who plays what roles in deciding where to travel (cf. Um & Crompton, 1990). At times some travellers visit places in which they apparently have only peripheral interest. For example, Moscardo and Pearce (1999) report that one cluster of visitors to a major Aboriginal cultural park in Northern Australia were merely motivated by 'accompanying others' and, perhaps not surprisingly, recorded the lowest satisfaction of all groups at the site. It can be suggested more generally that this kind of social motivation may account for some of the unflattering satisfaction scores obtained in select public tourist settings. For managers, those who are 'accompanying others' represent a challenge since, without attention, their disinterest may reduce the total party's satisfaction or even lead to destructive behaviours.

The particular role of fellow family members and friends in limiting the development of new tourist–tourist or tourist–host relationships is not well explored. There are anecdotal accounts that solo travellers have to be braver and more extroverted but the rich possibilities of exploring how existing relationships both inhibit and advance other social links await further attention.

Culture Contact and Culture Shock

One subdivision within the general theme of tourists' social contacts is that of contacts that involve contrasting cultures. Many of the general concerns and relationships already outlined in this chapter prevail in situations involving culture contact but there are some additional processes, outcomes and conceptual schemes for elucidating culture contact.

Cross-cultural contact is a part of many on-site tourist experiences. It usually occurs internationally but can develop in domestic tourism situations. 'Culture shock' is now a term in popular use that describes the difficulties of operating in a foreign culture. It derives from an applied article written by Oberg in 1960 in Practical Anthropology. Oberg, a missionary working in Africa, described some of the difficulties that Westerners, particularly North Americans, had in dealing with people in the African communities. The term was originally 'cultural shock' and was applied to nurses, doctors, missionaries, peace workers and volunteers abroad. Later it was used to portray the difficulties of international students studying abroad (Gullahorn & Gullahorn, 1963). In the 1970s it was expanded to include business people trying to deal with international trade, and in the 1980s it was applied to tourists (Furnham & Bochner, 1986). The original work by Oberg provided some practical advice that was mainly of a physical and health-related nature partly because, in tropical Africa, he was concerned with how people coped who had moved from a temperate environment to a tropical environment. He recommended behaviours such as

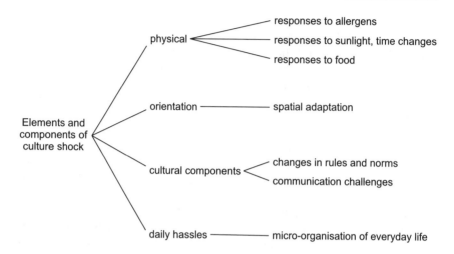

Figure 5.3 Expanded components of culture shock

being careful of the water, being careful of certain foods and watching out for sunstroke and mosquitoes. Oberg's original analysis has been expanded and the wider components of cultural shock are represented in Figure 5.3.

The diverse contributions to what is now simply referred to as 'culture shock' highlight the complexities of the concept. For the traveller, particularly the traveller moving across time zones into altered daylight and weather conditions, there are assaults on the body's immune system and functioning. A rich travel medicine literature has now developed and is replete with dramatic example of the difficulties faced by some tourists.

Orientation issues also affect tourists as well as other international travellers. In the grid-like street structures that prevail in modern Western cities, getting lost is rarely a problem. In Asian and Arab cities where there are circular and irregular patterns to street forms, substantial coping behaviours may be needed. Further, for many visitors there are complexities with subway and transport systems, and with road rules and driving practices. As Lynch (1960) reported, getting truly lost is a very alarming experience, particularly given the safety issues for tourists that prevail in a range of settings.

The difficulty in dealing with people whose value system and communication style may be markedly different is a major contributor to culture shock. The difficulties may arise in conceptions of honesty and bribery or, more simply, different meanings for friendship and social performance. This component of culture shock, the core of the phenomenon, will be discussed in more detail using two conceptual schemes.

It is valuable to complete the preliminary review of the elements of culture shock by reference to the term daily hassles. This component refers to the disruption of familiar behavioural routines caused simply by being somewhere else. It can include access to services, crossing the road under different traffic conditions, using different money and mispronouncing place names. All of these activities represent challenges to the tourist's effective performance in the novel setting. Together they can turn a normally competent individual into a dazed and inept performer.

Despite the contributions of daily hassles, orientation issues and physical challenges to the total culture shock phenomenon, the core of attention has been on the cultural values and communication component.

A rarely-used but comprehensive conceptual scheme to describe cultural contacts and exchange is the coordinated management of meaning (CMM) approach (Cronen & Shuter, 1983). CMM theory argues that for effective well-managed communication there are six elements to be considered; these are described and defined in Table 5.4.

Table 5.4 The core elements of the coordinated management of meaning approach to cross-cultural interaction

Element	Description
Verbal and non-verbal behaviour	The use of gestures, posture, eye contact and space combined with the vocabulary and actual words and labels for concepts may generate communication difficulty
Speech acts	The forms of address used including its formality and the respect shown to different interacting parties may be a source of difficulty
Episode	The sequences of behaviour that constitute meaningful units of everyday interaction may be organised differently (such as drinking rounds or farewell rituals) prompting social challenges
Relationships	The responsibilities and obligations that attend developing friendship and business relationships may vary prompting emotional reactions to behaviours not performed or over-elaborated.
Life scripting	The ways in which individuals view themselves in relation to others, their culture and their country can be different with problems arising in terms of decision making and respect for others and treatment of cultural institutions and leaders
Cultural patterns	The largest issues that inform a culture include the treatment of gender, honesty, guilt, freedoms of speech and spiritual values

It is noteworthy that the elements of CMM theory overlap with some of the social situation categories reported earlier in the chapter. In particular, there is a commonality in the area of rules and sequences of behaviour and a link between the cognitive structures or social knowledge and cultural patterns. The link should not be surprising, since the CMM elements are in effect a more focused treatment of social situations where it is already established that the goals of the participants are to interact successfully and the environmental setting component that appears in the social situations framework is not specifically considered.

Undoubtedly the greatest amount of conceptual attention in the cross-cultural and communication sphere has been devoted to the life-scripting and cultural patterns components described in Table 5.4. Much of the work has been pioneered by Hofstede (1980, 1997) but there are also significant contributions from Triandis (1972, 1990, 1994), Trompenaars and Hampden-Turner (1997), Gudykunst and Kim (1997), Gudykunst and Shapiro (1996), and E.T. Hall (1976, 2000). In reporting on this work for a tourism audience, Reisinger and Turner (2003) observe that some of the major dimensions used to characterise cultural differences include individualism–collectivism, high and low power distance, masculinity–femininity, weak or strong uncertainty avoidance and high and low context.

Not all of these dimensions are self-explanatory or independent. Collectivist cultures where saving face and harmony are highly valued tend to use a high-context communication style where the participants have to interpret meanings and nuances rather than receive blunt assertions and direct responses (Triandis, 1990).

There is a particular kind of difficulty for tourist behaviour researchers in using these dimensions that can be referred to as the 'levels of analysis' problem. While the dimensions employed can be seen to operate at a broad cultural (and sometimes national) level, it does take several dimensions to characterise the differences between two interacting parties. Further, some citizens (perhaps some of those predisposed to international travel), might be at the extreme ends of the distribution of that dimension in their own culture. Also many of the descriptions of tourist behaviour assume that the dimensions which were derived from considering certain kinds of situations are adequately refined to apply to tourist settings. There is a further complication residing in the view that cultures are changing rapidly on the dimensions described. It should be noted that some of these dimensions were first assessed almost two decades ago. These points do not amount to an argument that the assessment of cultural dimensions does not matter. Instead, the view is being expressed that the superficial characterisation of cultural contacts and distances by reference to global measures of cultural style is at best a first step in understanding the cognitive structures and meanings that participants employ in thinking about their encounters. In recent work Pearce and Moscardo (2004) have provided empirical evidence demonstrating that simple East–West distinctions in describing the social experiences of visitors to marine environments are weak, and there is substantial variation within the respondents from Western cultures and Eastern cultures.

The problems reported here are linked to the challenges noted by Moore (2002) at the outset of this chapter; the particular problem is one of how to connect the voice of empirical work, with its precise and measured statements, to the larger frameworks representing more theoretical social appraisals. Gergen (1997) has argued that the discourse of the individual in presenting him/herself and confronting the world is an important direction in theoretical social psychology. In this context the researcher armed with measured portrayals of how social interaction and culture shock works at the psychological level can be seen as a distinctive voice in the larger socio-cultural debates.

There is an important managerial dimension in stressing the value of the CMM approach to culture contact as compared with dimensions based on the work reported earlier of Hofstede, Triandis and Hall. The CMM approach, like its more generic counterpart social situations analysis, directs attention to levels of training and performance that can reduce culture shock. In particular, information-based approaches, where guidebooks and how-to manuals are deployed are useful starting points in understanding social episodes and language forms. In addition the analysis of episodes has led to culture assimilators, which are booklets where up to 40 troublesome cultural episodes are described and readers are required to choose the best of four or five explanations of the problem. Respondents learn by having to make a choice or commitment and if they are incorrect they receive immediate feedback when they read the correct explanation. There is mounting evidence that these culture assimilators are effective, albeit somewhat complicated to design and time-consuming to complete (Ward *et al.*, 2001). At a more detailed and demanding level of commitment, there is also social skills training and language learning as preparations for cultural immersion. For the purposes of this chapter, these kinds of active performance-based preparations for travel can be informed by the CMM approach (Pearce *et al.*, 1998). By way of contrast, the cultural dimensions account is a characterisation of the encounter rather than an impetus to training practices. Emerging possibilities for the culture assimilator training involve Internet sites with video feeds and replays for a fuller context and faster training of tourists.

The discussion and presentation of culture shock and the components that constitute its full complexity imply a ready acceptance of the term. Given that it was developed in the 1960s and was not specifically designed for the vagaries of contemporary travel, it is useful to clarify the continued appropriateness of this concept for studies of tourist behaviour. It can be suggested that the term culture shock is now a powerfully institutionalised label for the challenges and predicaments that most travellers face to varying degrees when moving across cultures. Hottola (2004) suggests a distinction between serious shock involving depression, failure, acute anxiety and insomnia versus the slighter problem of cultural confusion. In Hottola's view, *culture confusion* is a wider and more useful term that covers both the problematic part of the adaptation process and the simultaneous presence of enjoyment, success and learning. It is particularly clear from a number of tourism analyses that the models of the phases of culture shock (the earliest suggestions specified U-shaped curves describing stages of euphoria, disillusionment, hostility, adaptation and recovery) are unlikely to be widely or uniformly applicable to the diversity of tourist types and market segments already reviewed in this volume (Reisinger & Turner, 2003; Ward *et al.*, 2001). It is a significant challenge for future tourist behaviour studies, whether using the full term culture shock or its attenuated cousin culture confusion, to specify how select groups of travellers learn how to deal with and manage the challenges raised in cultural encounters. Based on a study of South Asian backpackers, Hottola (2004) proposes that some contemporary travellers may not experience confusion at all, others may be overwhelmed by the shock of seeing poverty and inequality, and others may be challenged by contact episodes that vary in success and pleasantness. Both to assist tourists and to understand tourism it appears that this area of tourist behaviour would profit from more detailed, grounded theory and evidence-based studies of adaptation, learning and personal control.

In summary, few would challenge the view that meeting new people and mixing with other tourists is a core part of the travel experience. Human beings are a notably social species with our sensory systems and psychological capacities directing much of our attention to other people, their behaviour and their likely responses to us. As the study of tourism develops as a social business it can be anticipated that the social dimension in studying tourist behaviour will become an even greater area of scholarly interest and a focus for potential management action.

Chapter 6

The Tourists' On-Site Experiences

Introduction

The focus of this chapter is tourists' on-site experiences with the sites and settings they visit. A major emphasis in this chapter lies in understanding and promoting sustainable tourist behaviours.

This account of tourists' on-site behaviour is organised by initially presenting a simple integrative model of place. This neat summative approach is then used to structure the discussion on experientially enhancing features of visited destinations. Attention is directed both to specific attractions and to the broader natural and social environment. Two special topics pertaining to the on-site visit experience will themselves be visited: *visitor skills* and *authenticity*. The importance of sustainable on-site behaviours is then identified, and a number of mechanisms to enhance sustainable tourist behaviours outlined. Interpretation, and the conceptual scheme of mindfulness to underpin the work on interpretation, are reviewed. Finally, tourist behaviour at a specific location, Australia's Kangaroo Island, is considered. The discussion of this site will cast it as a microcosm of Australian tourism and a globally useful exemplar of tourists' on-site experiences.

A Place Model for Tourist Sites

The earlier work of Canter (1977) and Lee (1976) helps collate a range of ideas about the sites and locations that tourists visit. Canter (1977) in particular has synthesised and reviewed major bodies of work in the literature on psychology, geography, planning and design. The work has resulted in a concise diagram summarising three interlocking components required for visitors or other users to gain a sense of place. Pearce, Morrison and Rutledge (1998) and Pearce (1991c) have specifically applied the tripartite system to tourist attractions and locations. Figure 6.1 shows the place model applied to tourist sites to assist in structuring the understanding of tourists' on-site experiences.

In Figure 6.1 the central portion of the diagram states the core premise of the approach. A good tourist site (one likely to promote positive on-site experiences), offers the public clear conceptions of what the place is about, the activities available are understood and accessible, and the physical elements that constitute the setting are distinctive and aesthetically

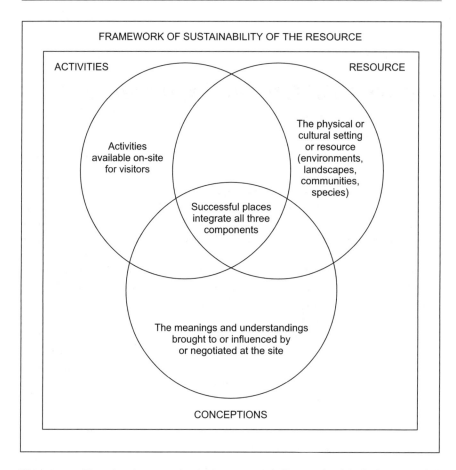

FRAMEWORK OF SUSTAINABILITY OF THE RESOURCE

ACTIVITIES

RESOURCE

Activities
available on-site
for visitors

The physical or
cultural setting
or resource
(environments,
landscapes,
communities,
species)

Successful places
integrate all three
components

The meanings and understandings
brought to or influenced by
or negotiated at the site

CONCEPTIONS

Figure 6.1 Tourist sites, a tripartite sustainability embedded place model

pleasing. The outline presented in Figure 6.1 is framed within a sustain-ability approach. This addition to Canter's original work represents an extension of the application of the ideas in earlier writing, but one that is consistent with contemporary emphases on managing tourism.

There is a growing and extensive archive of research on tourism's impacts that documents the specific negative effects of on-site tourist behaviour. Tourist activities have numerous consequences for biophysical environments and the species and human societies they support (Newsome *et al.*, 2002). As pointed out some time ago by Nicholson (1972), many people (including tourism advocates), fail to grasp the number of socio-cultural and ecological factors that are negatively affected by tourists (Ryan, 2003). The biophysical list includes impacts arising from water pollution, energy abuse, erosion, litter and fuel consumption (Liddle, 1997). There are also localised and often cumulative effects on habitats resulting in disturbance to the breeding patterns and reproductive efficiency of many native species (Hammitt & Cole, 1998; Shackley, 1996). The sociocultural list identifies insensitive and culturally-offensive behaviour, lifestyle changes and the transfer of disease (Pearce *et al.*, 1996). The developmental pressures of facility construction, the seasonality of tourism in some locations and the larger effects of the tourism industry are arguably indirect consequences of tourist behaviour. The negative accounts are sometimes juxtaposed with more positive appraisals including improvements in local leisure opportunities, enhanced economic wellbeing of residents and justification and support for conservation efforts (Newsome *et al.*, 2002).

In order to illustrate the sustainability enhanced place model for tourist sites, discussion of a specific example, that of Romeo and Juliet's balcony in the Italian city of Verona, is instructive. The physical resource consists of a second floor balcony jutting out from a two-metre square window. The balcony is in a quadrangle framed by low-rise Venetian-style residential apartments. Visitors bring a clear concept to this setting – it is the physical prototype and supposed inspiration for Shakespeare's use of the balcony scenes in Romeo and Juliet. The site, in the minds of many young travellers, is a shrine to passionate love, a romantic staging post in European travel. Its explicit tourist promotion as an embodiment of Italian courtship and passion undoubtedly informs many participants. The activities on-site include locating the balcony, an initial inspection of the small courtyard suggests several options, and then simply gazing at, photographing and contemplating the setting. A few tourists participate in elaborate displays of romantic affection and affectation. There is, however, another activity – the whole courtyard is 'decorated' and emblazoned with statements written in marking pen and proclaiming friendship and love relationships, often set in Valentine Day style hearts. The overwhelming impression is akin to a child's bedroom where all the walls have been used as a canvas. The damage to the walls, doors, window ledges and entrances to the apartments is considerable. The sustainability dimension surrounding the place model for tourist sites is most relevant since while the site activities, conceptions and resource are all powerfully enmeshed and communicated, the long-term sustainability and appeal of the location is severely threatened.

Attributes of Tourist Site Success

A parallel approach to understanding tourists' on-site experiences reviews the visitor-related attributes that are considered when tourist sites are awarded prizes and public honours. Such awards frequently highlight the physical beauty of the setting and the powerful display of cultural practices. This theme is congruent with the *resource* component of Figure 6.1. Environmental protection, profitable operation and environmental sympathy between the setting itself and associated tourist facilities are frequently considered and fit into the sustainability framework already discussed. The use of clear symbolism and public understanding of the attraction or site are two criteria that are also employed and match the *conceptualisation* segment of Figure 6.1. Activities, particularly if they are novel or distinctive, are a part of many successful award protocols (Pearce *et al.*, 1998). An additional emphasis raised by the archival material refers to the management styles and processes in operation which are likely to influence tourist behaviour. These management processes, such as legislation, permits, infrastructure controls and education/interpretation, form an important basis for further discussion in this chapter.

Skilled Tourist Behaviour

Two further distinctive frameworks shape tourists' on-site experiences. First, the level of skill required for the behaviour can be an important factor influencing tourist performance, satisfaction and learning. Skills may be thought of at the cognitive level such as knowing how to act or respond in cross-cultural situations (cf. Chapter 5). Additionally the skills required on-site might be a combination of knowledge and physical abilities. In the tourist behaviour literature there is rarely an explicit mention of skills as a key variable influencing behaviour. This lack of investigation and consideration can be contrasted with leisure research, where levels of challenge, skills and abilities are a part of the research commentary (Bammel & Bammel, 1992; Mannell & Kleiber, 1997).

There are, arguably, two reasons why skill-based assessments are hidden or ignored in tourist behaviour research. One view is that much tourist behaviour is gaze oriented, a simple observing of the visited scenes and communities and so participants are not differentiated by the concept of skill. Similarly Rojek and Urry (1997a) observe that sometimes tourists take photos simply because, confronted with remarkable vistas and sights, they simply do not know what else to do.

The issue of the level of skills can also be seen as partly embedded in a differently labelled tradition of research already reported in Chapter 2. Attention has been directed to the influence of specialisation or levels of previous experience in understanding tourist behaviour (Cole & Scott, 2000; McFarlane, 1994; Martin, 1997). It is certainly possible to see that more experienced travellers and those who specialise in activities are more likely to have a higher skill base.

The notion of skills is important to the on-site tourist experience in a number of ways. First, it helps to explain why there are sometimes low levels of participation in certain activities (such as swimming and snorkelling) by some Asian tourists in marine settings. If individuals feel inadequate and unprepared for the tourist activity, they will actively avoid it. Second, it helps explain why some damaging and destructive environmental behaviours occur. For example, residents of cold temperate environments with some previous outdoor camping experiences are much more likely to be economical in their use of firewood to keep warm than are those whose life experiences are entirely in tropical zones. Faced with the prospect of maintaining thermal comfort in a camping adventure, it is clear that the skilled travellers will use fewer resources more efficiently. Similarly skilled and competent snorkellers will be less likely to damage reef structures by inappropriately standing on coral when their face masks fill with water (Pearce & Greenwood, 1999). In an ethnic tourism context, Moscardo and Pearce (1999) identified an older group of travellers who felt self-conscious and underskilled in interacting with indigenous Australians in a cultural theme park. It is important that skills be considered as both physical abilities and social interaction abilities (Argyle *et al.*, 1981).

A skills analysis also provides insight into the issue of intentionality in tourist behaviour. Often social commentators write about fellow travellers as if the tourists were deliberately breaking rules, infringing on others' behaviour and acting in a destructive fashion (Horne, 1992). At times such a perspective is justified: if a person travels to Bangkok or Manila to buy drugs or engage in abusive sexual behaviour, and such activities are morally and legally indefensible in his/her own culture, then a clear intention is involved. Arguably, however, a good deal of unsustainable and less desirable tourist behaviour arises because tourists are underskilled, mentally and physically underprepared for the challenges to be met.

There is a prevailing view in travel medicine that physical preparation is required for the more arduous travel behaviours such as mountain climbing. Acclimatisation, adjustment to higher altitudes and reduced oxygen levels, as well as carefully-thought-out diets, represent a part of the well-prepared travellers' planning and skill development (Ashcroft, 2001). It is at least curious that the problematic traveller behaviour of interacting with contrasting cultures or visiting fragile settings is not met with parallel levels of preparation. This lack of individual responsibility and sometimes limited industry control towards travel behaviour means that several government-based mechanisms are required to moderate on-site impacts. In short the less-skilled traveller, as well as the traveller who intentionally breaks rules and laws, requires managerial guidance.

Authenticity and Tourist Behaviour

A major tradition in assessing and understanding tourists' on-site experiences has developed around the concept of authenticity. The concept has roots in philosophy, notably the work of Heidegger (1962) who emphasised the fusion of self and the external world – effectively the attainment of what he termed 'desain' or an awareness of all being. These metaphysical connotations were only partly pursued when MacCannell (1973, 1976) used the expression to characterise the purpose of tourist travel – to seek authenticity. MacCannell emphasised the quest for spontaneous, transparent, insightful views of places as a driver of all tourist behaviour. In an earlier account of this tradition, Pearce (1988) noted that authenticity has an openness, an unexpected gift-like quality. One particular direction in which MacCannell manoeuvred the authenticity concept was to link it to the Goffman-inspired terminology of front and back-stage environments. Goffman (1959), who in turn is associated with the dramaturgical view of social life where actors perform both publicly and privately, used the stage analogy as an extended characterisation of everyday interaction.

Initially it appeared that MacCannell had effectively operationalised authenticity as a measurable construct by applying Goffman's terminology. In brief, tourist spaces could be labelled as either gradations or exemplars of back stage and front stage settings. Cohen's (1979) elaboration of MacCannell's work also appeared to take this view as he developed a four-cell model of tourist situations (see Figure 6.2).

As researcher attention and commentary mounted on this topic, several elements of the earlier formulations were questioned. Did all tourists seek authenticity? Was it indeed the case that settings could be classified in an a priori or etic fashion by researchers? Did it in fact matter to visitor satisfaction and experience that tourists recognised that the space was contrived?

| | | Tourists' impressions of the scene ||
		Seen as real	Seen as staged
Nature of the scene	Real	Authentic and recognised as such	Suspicion of staging – authenticity questioned
	Staged	Failure to recognise contrived tourist space	Recognised contrived space

Figure 6.2 Cohen's four-cell model of tourist sites

Table 6.1 Dimensions of the authenticity debate

Topic	Key concern	Perspectives
1 Universal applicability	To what extent do all tourists seek authenticity?	Post modern analyses and empirical studies both view seeking authenticity as relevant to only some travellers some of the time (Moscardo & Pearce, 1999; Prentice *et al.*, 1998; Redfoot, 1984; Urry, 1990).
2 Criteria to determine authenticity	Can authenticity be determined by external assessment of staging or resource appraisal?	Legislation and regulation may specify hard architecture criteria for construction, and cultural commentators highlight historical versus contemporary ways of behaving, but the values of the assessor not the viewed scene determines authenticity (Cohen, 1988; Ehrentraut, 1993; Salamone, 1997).
3 Negotiated nature of authenticity	Who decides and determines authenticity and how is this achieved?	Performances and audiences form a network of collaboration judging the quality of the encounter (Daniel, 1996; Salamone, 1997; Taylor, 2001).
4 Fusion with other concepts	What are the links between authenticity, hyper-reality, self-actualisation, effort, sincerity, and related terms?	Authenticity is weakening as an academic concept with more specific terminology replacing its former function (Prentice *et al.*, 1998; Taylor, 2001).
5 Commercial persistence of authenticity	Why are promotional efforts richly imbued with promises of real, authentic experiences and opportunities?	Social differentiation and status markers for tourists and promoters maintain the commercial use of the term (Silver, 1993).

How could the effort put into constructing heritage sites, with all their striving for historical accuracy, be reconciled with the view that they were, inevitably, inauthentic because they were staged? Was it just the tourist space that was staged, or should this concept be extended to people and people's behaviour? How can an archetypal tourist attraction such as Disneyworld be inauthentic if in its totality it is not a copy of something else? Why are the terms 'authentic' and 'authenticity' widespread in promotional literature? These questions and allied concerns are summarised in Table 6.1.

Several perspectives that are noted in Table 6.1 warrant further attention and shape the continued use of the term *authenticity* in tourist behaviour research. It is suggested in the table that authenticity is weakening as an academic concept. This claim, which some may see as controversial given that there were more than 25 authenticity-related publications recorded in the Annals of Tourism Research alone in its 2002 index, is built around the view that the term, as MacCannell used it, has been carefully dissected and frequently appraised as inadequate. It appears not to apply to post-modern tourists so well as it did to travellers three decades ago, and it is not possible to classify settings on an a priori basis using the staging metaphor (Cohen, 1988; Ehrentraut, 1993; Moscardo & Pearce, 1986b). Nevertheless, in the redirections and reformulations of the concept some interesting perspectives for the on-site analysis of tourist behaviour can be highlighted. Sincerity, effort, involvement and the quality of the encounter become the new currency of on-site tourist appraisal and represent the key terms that are evolving from the authenticity traditions (cf. Daniel, 1996). Taylor suggests:

> By introducing the notion of sincerity, experiences in culture may be stripped of the temporal connotations implied by the concept of authenticity. Instead they become tied to selves in the present, both local and tourist. (Taylor, 2001)

Taylor's work and ideas were conceived in the context of studying tourism and Maori communities in New Zealand. Salamone (1997) working in the context of the San Angel Mexican restaurants in Disney-world and Mexico City reaches a very similar conclusion:

> The tourist and resident collaborate in forging identities, assembled from bits and pieces of real and imagined cultural heritages ... emphasis is on the creative and negotiated nature of culture as opposed to a given and static conception of it. (Salamone, 1997: 313)

These views are closely aligned to a perspective offered by Daniel (1996), who records that dance as a medium of cultural expression is creative and mutually involving. The physicality of dance for the performer, and the tendency for the audience to get involved in the rhythms and spectacle, results in a form of concerted communication across any staging and supposed authenticity barriers.

Following these perspectives, the evolution and dissolution of the authenticity concept has its successors in a dramaturgical conspiracy where performers, stages and audiences are locked in a concentrated communication to manage meaning, value and identity. There is something quite embarrassing about being in a tourist site that is poorly presented and inadequately serviced with all participants maintaining only a token effort at enacting their roles. The desire to leave is analogous to the feeling one gets when viewing a poor film (Bruner, 1994). In addition, the poor performance is not just a commentary on the participants but a reflection on one's own judgement, an indictment of one's poor decision making, and frustration with the lost opportunity of using tourist time well. In this view, it matters little whether or not the performance is staged in MacCannell's original sense of it being particularly 'put on for tourists'. Instead what matters is the effortful sincerity of the encounter, a sense of mutual immersion in making the experience the most it can be for all participants. This line of thinking even begins to recover some of the original thinking of Heidegger's (1962) desain – an awareness of all being and a fulfilment of being fully alive and mindful.

The discussion of authenticity has focused largely on cultural settings, but its applicability and its current reformulations also apply to environmental experiences and wildlife encounters. On these occasions the access and management practices in place become the co-conspirators in establishing the forum for meaning and value. Again, an earlier conception of authenticity that highlighted its gift-like quality re-emerges, particularly for wildlife viewing, which in many natural settings is at best unpredictable and at times magical. Some specific research applications of these reformulated views of authenticity will be briefly illustrated later in this chapter.

Sustainable On-site Tourist Behaviour

In Chapter 2, the work of Swarbrooke (1999a) was cited as defining the role responsibilities for sustainable tourist behaviour. It was noted that it was difficult to carry out some of these behaviours (such as boycotting exploitative businesses) owing to the complexities of appraising local practices and standards. More simply, ignorance of local customs and skill deficits, as discussed in this chapter, as well as intentionally selfish behaviours, may all be contributors to undesirable on-site actions.

Instead of simply prescribing generically-desirable ideal roles as Swarbrooke and others have done, one can adopt a more explicitly remedial and practical approach. Middleton (1998) has identified '10Rs' for environmental actions for the tourism industry as a whole. These suggestions may be re-applied to tourist behaviour itself and represent a comprehensive action-oriented approach to maintaining the sustainability framework of tourist settings. These actions are presented in Table 6.2.

Regrettably, a global consciousness and an awareness of sustainability issues are not reliably pursued by tourists in many contexts. As a consequence of the impacts of tourist behaviour briefly reviewed at the start of this chapter, governments and public management agencies have instituted a set of control and influence mechanisms to shape negative tourist behaviours that alter on-site experiences for all participants. Five such mechanisms can be identified.

Table 6.2 Tourist actions leading to sustainability

Actions	*Elaboration and example*
Recognise	Tourists need to recognise and identify that their behaviour creates a problem, e.g. nesting bird species such as albatross, if frightened from nesting sites, may not reproduce again for 2–3 years: a small action with substantial consequences but, unless the impact is recognised, the motivation to alter activities is low
Refuse	Faced with purchasing products from endangered animals or being offered illegal products, simple refusal is a sustainability enhancing action by reducing demand, e.g. blanket refusal to all vendors selling drugs
Reduce	Lowering consumption of local resources by reducing needless use of lights, power, water, e.g. turning off room air-conditioners, if possible, when leaving a hotel for the day
Replace	Finding substitute experiences with fewer or no impacts on environments and settings, e.g. using photography rather than extractive souveniring to record one's experience
Re-use	One-time use of products can be costly and environmentally unfriendly, e.g. re-using conference badges, towels, soap, bed linen and china cups rather than disposing of them and requiring a new round of products
Recycle	Either re-use for the same purpose or different purposes a line of products, e.g. recycle paper, cans, bottles and clothing
Re-engineer	Redesign or restructure behaviour through active personal intervention, e.g. specifying to guides that as a tourist you do not want to disturb wildlife but are happy to view from a distance
Retrain	Develop physical and personal skills to cope better in new situations, e.g. learning a few words of language to overcome basic difficulties, learning how to thank and appreciate the lives of those who are different
Reward	Take advantage of incentives or use one's personal resources as an enticement to promote sustainable activities, e.g. becoming a donor or sponsor of organisations to support communities or the environment, tipping sustainable host behaviours, commenting favourably on effective management practices
Re-educate	Long-term changes to personal behaviour resulting from tourist experiences may help the overall sustainability effort, e.g.when they get home, tourists may stop their long-term use of plastic recently experienced as a hazard to marine tourism

Mechanisms Shaping On-site Tourist Behaviour

Legal

One potentially powerful mechanism for shaping unacceptable tourist behaviours lies in the use of the legal framework to prosecute offending individuals. Additionally the organisations that facilitate the behaviours may also be prosecuted and penalties exacted. An illustration of the approach is provided by the legislative actions of some 20 countries that are trying to put an end to sex tourism with children. As McFeely (1996) observes, this kind of tourist behaviour is universally condemned, but very difficult to stop. The prosecution of citizens in their home countries for child-sex-related crimes in international settings has resulted in more than 100 investigations worldwide (Coday, 2000). This figure can be seen as disappointing, considering the resolution by 122 countries in a 1996 conference to attack the problem on sexual exploitation of children (Gampbell, 1999). As Bosong (2002) emphasises in writing about Cambodia, legal mechanisms are potentially effective but only if supported by an increase in police to monitor and mount the case for prosecution. The comment applies not just to child-sex tourism but to all legal efforts to pursue problematic tourist behaviour.

Legal mechanisms can be seen as offering a final point of action when other systems of control and management have not worked. The organisation ECPAT (End Child Prostitution, Child Pornography and Trafficking) has a multi-faceted approach to the problems of child-sex tourism, with an emphasis on training hotel staff to identify the people at risk, on rehabilitation programmes for the exploited and on anti-sex tourism promotional campaigns (Platt, 2002). An emphasis on restricting both international demand and the supply of children is thus seen as buttressing the largely symbolic legal deterrents that are hard to enforce.

Permits and passes

Another kind of regulatory framework lies in the use of prohibitions, permits and passes to structure behaviour in zones and designated areas. O'Meara (2003) reports that 660 establishments have been put off-limits to United States servicemen because of the alleged human trafficking and prostitution of Russian and Filipino women confirmed at these sites. Prohibition also operates in controlling tourist behaviour in sensitive cultural and environmental sites such as the inner sanctums of cathedrals and temples and the creation of no-entry zones for protecting animal breeding and habitat locations.

In areas where a well-defined and controlled space is involved, such as in national parks or in privately-owned tourist sites, visitors may be given permits to participate in supervised or restricted activities. Examples include permits to hike or heli-ski in wilderness areas, sanctioned collection of plants and animals and conditional access to indigenous community lands provided there is no photography and no alcohol used (Altman & Finlayson, 1993; Gale & Jacobs, 1987).

Passes too form a control mechanism in tourist behaviour, and typically alter the access conditions to crowded sites. For example, the Disney parks use a 'Fastpass' system whereby visitors can ensure that they join a themed ride with minimum waiting at a designated time in the day's outing. Fastpass systems at Disney control tourist behaviour powerfully by effectively providing an incentive to plan the day and avoid the waiting queues. Other forms of access control in attractions have an analogous function to fastpasses; these include quotas on the amount of time spent viewing a site and/or limits to the number of people viewing the setting at a time. Visitors to the Sistine Chapel in the Vatican to see Michelangelo's ceiling mural are admitted in small groups of 30–40 people and are given 10 minutes in the inner vault.

Fees

Passes and permits in particular are often considered within an economic regulatory framework as they can be a part of a 'user pays' system that further limits use. The public acceptability of fees and charges to access managed sites appears to vary from country to country and there are strong feelings about the issue. In Australia, for example, local tourists were much more prepared to accept fees for site access to world heritage areas and ski resorts than they were for beaches and urban parks (Lee & Pearce, 2002). The collection of park fees and the management of passes is itself an expensive activity requiring personnel to administer and monitor the system. Such costs can be justified when there are large numbers of people or when high charges are involved, but there is often a practical limitation to the use of personnel for such purposes in more remote, less crowded settings. In situations where much of the tourism is entirely based on groups or tour operators, the problems are eased because of the efficiency of collecting from a few specific industry personnel.

Social norms

Social norms, effectively the reaction of others to public behaviour, can also shape sustainable on-site behaviour. An example is smoking, an activity that can be a fire risk in many outdoor and natural environment settings. As one visitor proceeds to light up, a derogatory comment or a pointed stare can operate to control or stop the action. This 'para-police' role of other tourists may result in conflict, as in waiting lines, for example, where some people push in and ignore the protocol of joining the queue. Not surprisingly these kinds of inter-tourist prohibitions and restrictions, while effective, may not result in harmonious behaviours and may need to be managed by the authority figures if they are to continue to be influential.

Infrastructure design

A further mechanism shaping sustainable tourist behaviour is better infrastructure design. This function has been briefly noted in the 10Rs analysis, following Middleton's appraisal and was reported earlier in this chapter as 're-engineering'. Table 6.2 describes re-engineering as the tourist specifying to the guide or setting manager that certain experiences or types of access were not in fact required. The more environmentally deterministic approach to infrastructure design is to build and organise the setting so that negative tourist behaviours are difficult to perform. This may mean designing better zones or meeting places between groups of people or (more usually) the construction of barriers, railings, walkways and surveillance systems that inhibit undesirable behaviours. Improved infrastructure design can work well in areas where there is congestion and waiting in line is an inevitable consequence of large seasonal visitor concentrations. Attending to visitors' physical needs (such as queue width, resting points, water fountains and shade) may make the experience less negative. In addition, the visitors' psychological needs can be met by providing information about the forthcoming activity, by specifying the waiting time and by using the opportunity to inform visitors about other attractions or local features. A combination of these techniques, and in some settings the incorporation of the queue into the themed atmosphere of the main attraction, can jointly restructure the experience (Pearce, 1989). An array of safety and health-promoting infrastructure mechanisms is also vital to promote desirable tourist behaviour. Such efforts may include the use of non-slip surfaces, adequate lighting, controllable air-conditioning systems, the provision of facilities for the disabled, and a host of other pro-environment architectural and engineering applications.

One of the most widespread tourist behaviour shaping mechanisms is that of visitor education. While all of the preceding mechanisms are important, and some (such as infrastructure design), apply to both the tourism industry and the tourist, education and its corollary in the tourism context interpretation is a major dimension shaping tourist on-site behaviour

Interpretation and On-site Behaviour

Interpretation is defined in subtly different ways but at core it is the process of explaining to people the significance of the place or culture they are visiting, with the dual goals of promoting appreciation and assisting conservation (Knudson *et al.*, 1995). In the model of place analysis outlined at the start of this chapter, interpretation is a key process that influences the conceptions visitors hold and negotiate with others as they experience the site. Interpretation is also referred to as both public environmental education and visitor communication, and has an extensive literature involving the principles and pragmatics of good practice (Ham, 1992; Moscardo, 1999; Tilden, 1977). It can be argued that interpretation as a topic of academic inquiry in tourism studies is under-represented in the mainstream journals. This limited attention arises in part because interpretation has its own existing publication outlets and in part because it was first developed in settings such as museums, national parks and zoos where historically there was less emphasis on commercial tourism. The emphasis has now changed, and interpretation is a well-integrated management practice in both public and commercial settings and warrants detailed research attention in tourism.

A range of communication efforts constitutes interpretive activity: there are direct forms of communication such as guides and guided tours, there are visitor centres where the opportunity to communicate with advisory personnel is possible but not always central, and several forms of communication where no personnel are present. The challenge of communicating with visitors without direct contact is usually met by the use of signs, display panels, brochures, booklets, audio tapes, touch screens and guide books.

A discussion of some key issues in interpretation and how they influence on-site tourist behaviour needs to avoid treating interpretation as a set of products imposed on tourists with consistent effects. Throughout this volume tourists are viewed as active social agents who take charge of their experiences in a socially negotiated world. In accord with this view interpretation will be seen as perceived and valued differently by visitor subgroups (Ballantyne *et al.*, 1998; Klenosky *et al.*, 1998). Whether it is the information in a visitor centre, the text on a sign or the story being told by a guide, individual responses will vary and it is valuable to refer to communication theory and models of cognitive functioning to understand the impact of the interpretive activity.

Before reporting on conceptual schemes, three distinctive issues pertaining to interpretation need to be explored to understand this on-site influence on tourist behaviour; these are *intrinsic impact*, *information organisation*, and the *challenge of selectivity*.

Intrinsic impact

The intrinsic impact of places and settings refers to their unadorned power to capture visitor attention and evoke strong emotional responses. De Botton (2002) writing about reactions to dramatic landscapes unearths and re-uses the term 'a sense of the sublime' to indicate human responses towards precipices, vast deserts, grand mountains and ocean vistas. He argues that these unconnected landscapes can be categorised together:

> by virtue of their size, emptiness or danger ... such places provoke an identifiable feeling that (is) both pleasurable and morally good. (De Botton, 2002: 165)

The particularly distinctive human response to these grand landscapes and vistas lies not so much in their beauty and composition but in the recognition of power greater than that of humans. Such sublime settings are capable of placing personal achievement in a larger context and impress on the viewer his or her individual human frailty.

De Botton's argument about the raw power and intrinsic impact of grand landscapes can be transferred to some monumental human achievements – cathedrals, temples, ruined cities and other traces of vanished civilisations. An argument can also be made that certain encounters with large powerful animals can evoke this sense of human frailty induced by power, grace and the elegance of a charismatic species (Broad & Weiler, 1998; Kellert & Berry, 1980; Woods, 1998). There is, however, a problem with pursuing too enthusiastically the intrinsic ability of all sites, exhibits and cultural displays simply to impress tourists. In some settings the sublime and a sense of power may generate a powerful on-site experience, but at other times the features themselves are asked to do too much – to affect the viewer without explanation and without interpretation. For many tourist attractions, including those where interpretation evolved (such as museums, zoos and national parks), it is imperative that quality communication assists the engagement of the visitor, as only in a limited range of settings and exhibits does this eventuate through intrinsic impact.

Information organisation

The organisation of information is pivotal to effective interpretation. Rojek (1997), borrowing from contemporary computer terminology, uses the terms 'indexing' and 'dragging' to mirror the mechanisms that visitors use to assemble meanings for tourist sights. To extend the metaphor, the providers of site information in interpretive contexts can be viewed as sometimes displaying the wrong screen written in the wrong language. The challenge of organising appropriate visitor information and interpretive services is considerable.

Many tourist sites, particularly in urban environments, represent a historical layering of human effort; the settings or buildings to be viewed are the interwoven outcomes of power struggles, preservation efforts and cultural values. Tourist travel as a physical means of assessing sites contains its own inherent logic, which is at core geographical. Visitors are in a setting viewing wildlife or a landscape or a human cultural product that is contextualised by adjacent environments and products. For example, the great Sphinx, once magnificently isolated, now lies within suburban Cairo. Similarly, Indian tigers are habitually displayed next to African lions as if the species naturally co-existed. Museum displays frequently leap centuries and continents from room to room. Such juxtapositions make it difficult for visitors to focus and concentrate on the foreground. At times visitors need basic orientation information (material that connects to their on-site presence), in order to behave in appropriate ways and to make sense of their immediate view of the world.

A contrast can be made between the geographic logic of tourist travel (visiting exhibits and places according to their spatial propinquity) with the more usual form of information gathering, which is at core thematic. Reading about Niagara Falls, for example, usually includes a predictable account of geology, rainfall and water volume, as well as its discovery, its adventurers and its management. In visiting Niagara Falls the reader may be distracted by the journey, the nearby MacDonalds, the advertisements for the honeymoon motels and the manicured gardens. The problem for the on-site visitor who is distracted by the surroundings but seeks to understand the feature is compounded when the signs or guides provide highly specific scientific and one-dimensional facts. For the visitor, reading the information provided feels analogous to reading the wrong page in the wrong language (Woods *et al.*, 1998). Remedies to the problems of information organisation include theming, maximising personal relevance, encouraging participation and orienting visitors (Ham, 1992; Mack & Thompson, 1991; Miles *et al.*, 1982).

The challenge of selectivity

It will be apparent that one of the challenges of on-site interpretation is that of selecting what to interpret. This selectivity issue can be seen as having two dimensions.

The theme of power, or more specifically who interprets the setting in which way, is an enduring concern for cultural and environmental commentators (Prentice, 2003). At times there may be a loss of community support for the interpretive activity or facility if the muted voices of the local community or perceived disenfranchised groups are not represented. For example, in the Strahan Visitor Centre in the Australian state of Tasmania controversial themes and the very design of the centre were seen by several groups of citizens as presenting unacceptable views of local events and environments (Fallon & Kriwoken, 2003). More generally, and in line with assessments of the gendered and selective nature of existing tourism practices, there is a common view that the storytelling of traditional interpretation under-represents women, indigenous groups and the losers of military, cultural and environmental struggles (Horne, 1984; Hughes, 1987; Rojek & Urry, 1997a).

Selectivity can also be thought of as central to the influence of interpretation on the visitor. In an important sense interpretation (like other forms of art) can educate visitors in how to imaginatively construct and look at the world. This is more than just focusing on what to perceive and which stories are told, but embraces what might be termed training the mind or building the skill to see and experience more. For example, this essentially educational component of interpretation can be seen to build skills in looking at artworks when it directs readers to look for details of style and recurring symbolism that might otherwise go unnoticed. Similarly insightful interpretation concerning a wildlife species may alert the visitor to recurring behaviour patterns and the spatial organisation of animal groups. This kind of information is likely to remain with the observer as long-term learning, so that a subsequent sighting of the same or even a similar species might prompt the visitor to look more closely for the patterns and locations experienced on this occasion.

It is essential to the theme of this chapter that quality interpretation shapes visitors' on-site experiences and helps promote sustainable behaviour. There is only limited evidence for this claim, and more work needs to be carried out more creatively in this area. In a number of individual studies learning and educational efforts as well as enjoyment have been demonstrated as mutual outcomes of interpretive efforts (Moscardo, 1998). Additionally, interpretation can clearly structure a visitor's time at a site, both in the activity itself and in the ways in which the material digested shapes further on-site activity. It is less clear that tourist-related on-site interpretation fosters long-term behavioural changes that serve the overall conservation of the planet. Nevertheless for select groups predisposed to certain kinds of tourism, existing attitudes, appear to be consolidated (Lee, 2002).

Mindfulness/mindlessness

The subtitle of this volume stresses that the themes in tourist behaviour are to be understood by and linked to conceptual schemes. The topic of interpretation is well served by the conceptual scheme of mindfulness/ mindlessness (Langer, 1989). The *mindfulness* model of cognitive processing emphasises that mindfulness is a cognitive state where people are developing new routines, paying attention to the setting and its features and they are open to learning. *Mindlessness*, by way of contrast, is not a scenario where people are not thinking at all but is best described as a cognitive state where people are using existing routines, paying little attention to the setting and not learning. The conditions that create mindfulness and are reflected in good interpretive practice are those that are novel, where the stimuli are impressive, colourful and changing, where individuals can exercise choice and control and where the subject matter is personally relevant and clear. Mindfulness is considered to be pre-conscious rather that under continuous conscious control. Mindfulness may be induced by effort on the part of the individual but more ordinarily it is not to be viewed as especially requiring more effort than mindlessness (Chanowitz & Langer, 1980). The conditions that set up mindlessness are familiar routine ones where personal interest is limited and the displays and settings are predictable and structured.

The concept of mindfulness was applied to tourism studies generally in a set of applications by the author and colleagues in the 1980s (Moscardo & Pearce, 1986b; Pearce, 1988; Pearce & Moscardo, 1985). Its specific detailed application to interpretation has been particularly developed by Moscardo (1996, 1999) and colleagues (Moscardo *et al.*, 1998) and it continues to flourish as a dominant organising model for understanding how visitors respond to information. The model is summarised in Figure 6.3, which is built on (but re-ordered from) the earlier work of Moscardo (1999).

The multiple tactics and pragmatic efforts to improve interpretation (Knudson *et al.*, 1995) can be understood from within the mindfulness model (Alt & Shaw, 1984; Bitgood *et al.*, 1988; Borun & Adams, 1991). There are recurring recommendations in the interpretive texts to attend to the communication factors and visitor factors cited in the model. In addition, its applicability can be seen as working in all types of interpretation, both personal and in settings where the visitor is supported by non-personal mechanisms.

Interpretation, particularly when it induces mindfulness and therefore promotes learning, satisfaction and understanding, is one of the dominant contemporary techniques for influencing sustainable visitor behaviour. It is sometimes seen as a special category of persuasive communication (Pearce, 1988) and indeed the mindfulness model is conceptually very similar to central and peripheral processing models used in the attitude-change literature. Persuasive communication is employed in a variety of tourist behaviour applications and can essentially be understood with the same parameters used in Figure 6.3 to explain interpretation effectiveness.

The concept of 'edutainment', a neologism often ascribed to the Disney planners, should also be seen as connected to interpretation. The marriage of education and entertainment which is the basis of the term is functionally equivalent to providing interpretation that is both informative and interesting with the specific difference between the terms being a more explicit recognition of sustainability dimensions in the interpretation framework. Nevertheless the spirit of edutainment, the view that education can be enjoyable and entertainment need not be without intellectual stimulation is highly consistent with quality interpretation.

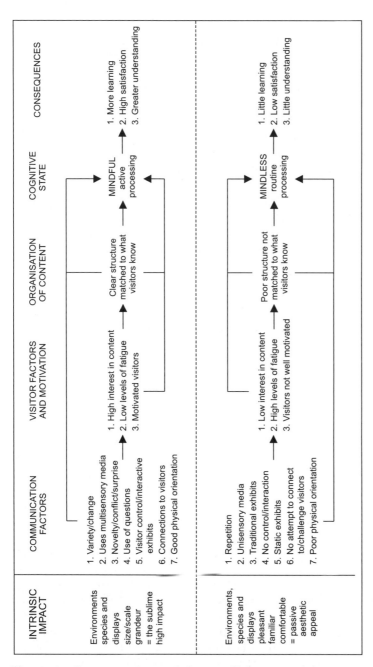

Figure 6.3 Interpretation and the mindfulness model

Sampling On-site Behaviour: Kangaroo Island

The themes explored in this chapter will be illustrated by some original work being conducted at one tourist site, that of Kangaroo Island located off the coast of South Australia at a latitude of 37° south. The island is approximately 150 kilometres long and up to 50 kilometres wide, and has just over 4000 residents, who mainly live in four settlements in the eastern, northern and central sections of the island (Jack, 2001). Visitor numbers are almost 200,000 per annum. The predominant reason for visiting is to see the diverse and abundant wildlife, although the island has marked scenic appeal with its rugged coastlines. There are also seasonal wildflowers, numerous shipwrecks, farming landscapes and a history of exploration of some note (Toft, 2002). Visitors are virtually guaranteed of seeing some wildlife on Kangaroo Island and while the whole island functions as a habitat for many species, the Flinders Chase National Park which occupies almost one quarter of the island at its western end is a major focus of visitor attention.

The southern coast of the island, which is particularly spectacular, has little settlement and often receives storms and gale force winds from the adjacent Southern Ocean. One site along the southern coast, Seal Bay, is promoted and managed as the key wildlife icon of the island. Australian Sea Lions are always present at Seal Bay and visitors are able to walk onto the beach in guided groups and manoeuvre among the resting animals.

The catalogue of wildlife species is impressive and important to under-standing the tourist experience. The island has over 180 resident bird species as well as additional migrants and a particularly rare species of cockatoo, the Glossy Black Cockatoo, is a conservation symbol and the focus of considerable management attention. Southern right whales are sometimes visible from island headlands. Tamar wallabies and Kangaroo Island kangaroos are abundant. The roadsides are well vegetated and vehicle-wildlife accidents are a recurring hazard. Other species of note include several types of possums, koalas, fairy penguins, short-beaked echidnas and Rosenburg goannas. The island is essentially promoted as a worldclass wildlife tourist destination.

Not surprisingly, given the number of visitors compared to the resident population, studies of tourism and tourism planning on Kangaroo Island have been intensifying as tourism has flourished. In 1970/71 there were 20,000 visitors, one tenth of current numbers. In 1984 the South Australian Department of Tourism published a Working Party Report on Tourism Development and Management, the first in a series of government manage-ment plans to foster sustainable growth (Jack, 2001; Manidis Roberts Consultants, 1997; South Australian Department of Tourism, 1984; Tourism South Australia, 1991a, 1991b).

Three sources of information will be used to illustrate and reflect on the site- based experiences of visitors reviewed in this chapter. One source of information comes from the author's periods of residence and several subsequent visits to the island. This interaction lasted over a 10-year period and included six months of living on the island with repeated visits to the key wildlife sites. These observational insights are supplemented by a major survey of 710 Kangaroo Island visitors undertaken by a 7-person team of researchers from the author's research group (Greenwood *et al.*, 2000; Saltzer, 2002; Woods, 2001). The management model being developed at Kangaroo Island, the Tourism Optimisation Management Model, also monitors some visitor experiential conditions as a part of its total package of management (Manidis Roberts Consultants, 1997; Newsome *et al.*, 2002). An awareness and knowledge base concerning Kangaroo Island tourism is being maintained through an ongoing evaluation of tourist responses to a newly constructed visitor centre at Flinders Chase. The interpretation in the new centre and at the attractions in the vicinity were designed in part as a response to the 1999 visitor survey.

Tourists visit Kangaroo Island either as self-drive independent travellers or as a part of a tour group. In the 1999 survey data both groups were systematically sampled, and data was obtained both before and after these visitors had experienced the key wildlife sites (Woods, 2001). The surveys were conducted in English only with an overall response rate of 97%. The sample breakdown is shown in Table 6.3.

Some 70% of the visitors had not been to Kangaroo Island before. The importance of wildlife in the travel decisions was confirmed by comparing responses to a five-part question on interest levels and contrasting the findings with other Australian wildlife settings.

A more detailed examination of the expected and desired features of the wildlife experiences is presented in Table 6.5 and a range of satisfaction measures from the post-visit sample are presented in Tables 6.6, 6.7 and 6.8.

Visitors were also asked to report on their on-site experiences using a more open-ended format (Tables 6.9 and 6.10). This material contrasts pre-visit and post-visit perspectives and begins to reveal the ways in which the

Table 6.3 Kangaroo Island visitor study samples

	Tour group visitors	*Independent visitors*	*Total*
Pre-sample	172	173	345
Post-sample	140	225	365
Total	312	398	710

Table 6.4 Importance of wildlife in travel decisions

	Kangaroo Island visitors		Northern Australia regional visitors (%) (n = 790)	Wildlife attraction in Queensland (%) (n = 800)
	Tour group visitors (%) (n = 312)	Independent visitors (%) (n = 398)		
I prefer to avoid wildlife while on holidays	0	2	3	0
I'm not interested in viewing wildlife while on holidays	1	2	1	1
Viewing wildlife is not a factor in my travel decisions, but I do enjoy it	17	18	57	37
The opportunity to view wildlife is included as part of my travel decisions	44	45	32	46
The opportunity to view wildlife is one of the most important factors in my travel decisions	38	33	7	16

experience has been constructed and affected the visitors' information and interpretation needs.

Some of the major themes in this chapter can be seen to be operating in this Kangaroo Island visitor experience data. First, there are some marked differences in the on-site behaviour of the tour group and the independent traveller. The tour group arrangements effectively provided a quota on the visitors' use of time at the wildlife sites. The tour groups expected to be shown rather than to seek out the wildlife, and they were a little less concerned with the environmental ambience than the independent travellers. The issue of skill in tourists' on-site experiences was manifest in the data. Visitors, both before and after the experience, recognised that skilled techniques for spotting wildlife were critical to their holiday experience on the island. Skill was also manifest in the identified need for a future visitor centre to tell visitors how to minimise their impact on the environment and on the wildlife they encountered. The group of visitors surveyed had both a strong interest in the wildlife and an interest in how to behave appropriately. These results confirm the view that intentionality and skill need to be married in promoting sustainable behaviours.

The wider context of experiencing a place, that is the influence of other juxtaposed features mentioned in the earlier sections of this chapter, was

Table 6.5 Importance of features of wildlife experiences

Feature	Kangaroo Island visitors	
	Tour group visitors (%)	Independent visitors (%)
Seeing wildlife in a natural environment	71	72
Seeing wildlife behaving naturally	67	72
Unique/unusual wildlife	57	55
Being able to get close to the wildlife	51	46
Seeing rare/endangered species*	**54**	**44**
A natural environment with little evidence of humans	45	48
Knowledgeable guides/staff are available*	**57**	**34**
Interesting information about the wildlife*	**44**	**38**
Pleasant environment	38	43
Feeling safe	41	37
Large variety of wildlife	38	38
Wildlife are easy to see	41	35
Large numbers of wildlife to see	35	31
Visitor numbers are limited	29	30
Being able to touch or feed the wildlife	17	12

Table 6.6 Responses to the Kangaroo Island wildlife experience: Satisfaction with features of the wildlife experience at Flinders Chase National Park

Feature	Tour group visitors %	Independent visitors (%)	Total post-visit sample (%)
Condition of the natural environment	69	62	65
How close I could get to the wildlife*	**52**	**58**	**56**
How easy wildlife were to see	45	48	47
Number of wildlife I saw	41	41	41
Variety of wildlife I saw*	**34**	**46**	**41**

In both tables above: * Indicates a statistically significant difference at the $p<0.05$ level between Flinders Chase tour group visitors and independent visitors (statistically

Table 6.7 Responses to the Kangaroo Island wildlife experience: Best features of respondents' wildlife experiences at Flinders Chase National Park

Best feature	Tour group visitors %	Independent visitors (%)	Total post-visit sample (%)
Wildlife in their natural environment	10	19	16
Fur seals	15	16	16
Able to see wildlife close-up	20	7	11
Numbers and/or variery of wildlife	10	11	10
Natural beauty of animal(s)	1	10	7
Admiral's Arch	**11**	4	**6**
Everything	5	4	4
Koalas	0	4	3
Sealed accessible road	**0**	3	**2**

Table 6.8 Responses to the Kangaroo Island wildlife experience: Suggested improvements to the wildlife experience at Flinders Chase National Park

Improvement	Tour group visitors %	Independent visitors (%)	Total post-visit sample (%)
To see/information on knowing where to see more wildlife	16	10	12
Visitor Centre – upgrade, provide more information	6	12	10
Seal roads	2	13	10
Better signage	10	8	8
Allow animal feeding	16	2	6
To see more kangaroos – encourage more interaction	6	3	4
To be able to see platypuses	2	5	4
More time with animals	12	0	4
More guided tours, presence of guides	2	4	4

Table 6.9 Information and interpretation needs expressed by Kangaroo Island visitors:Percentage of visitors rating topics for a new visitor centres as 'very interesting'

Topic	Pre-visit	Post-visit
1 Wildlife in FCNP	61	72
2 Interesting geographical features	52	61
3 Hints on how to see wildlife	52	54
4 How visitors can minimise impacts on FCNP environment	50	51
5 How visitors can minimise their impacts on wildlife	47	48
6 The giant animals that once roamed the area	41	41
7 Feral animal management	39	35
8 The plants of FCNP	36	44
9 Aboriginal occupation and connections	35	27
10 Ecosystems	32	32
11 Shipwrecks	31	32
12 Weed management	31	27
13 Fire management	30	26
14 Biodiversity	29	29
15 Lighthouses	25	28
16 Pastoral land use	14	14

also a notable part of the findings. Visitors reported a 10% rise, post-visit, in rating the geographical features of the area as very interesting. A strong case can be made from the personal observational data that several of the settings involved can be considered as sublime and awe-inspiring land-scapes. Admiral's Arch, Seal Bay and Remarkable Rocks, particularly when seen on stormy days with massive ocean waves and pounding seas, dwarf the human scale as represented by the few visitor facilities and boardwalks. The environmental conditions at these sites are also the basis for social interaction amongst visitors who frequently comment to strangers on the struggle to walk and endure the cold while witnessing the power of the sea and the adaptability of the sea lions, fur seals and other species. The condition of the natural environment as the satisfaction item with the highest rating in the overall set of response scales is, arguably, explained by the emotional and physical impact of these settings on the visitor.

Table 6.10 Information and interpretation needs expressed by Kangaroo Island visitors: Most popular questions respondents would like to ask about Flinders Chase National Park

Question pre-visit	Tour group visitors %	Independent visitors (%)	Total pre-visit sample (%)
Where do I find/see wildlife?	11	22	19
Are visitors careless?	14	17	16
Why was Flinders Chase selected for a National Park?	4	14	11
How much does it cost to maintain the Park?	2	8	6
What can I see/do there?	5	4	4
Question post-visit	Tour group visitors %	Independent visitors (%)	Total post-visit sample (%)
Where do I find the wildlife/ information on finding the wildlife?	27	16	19
When will the roads be sealed/ completed?	7	18	14
Will there be more guided tours/ presence of guides in the future?	2	10	7
How is wildlife/environment maintained with large visitor numbers?	7	5	5
Why was Flinders Chase selected for a National Park – history/geography of the Park?	2	6	5

The central theme of authenticity and its social negotiation has been pursued in this chapter mainly in relation to cultural settings. In this natural-environment example the quest for authenticity is transmuted into the experience and appreciation of naturalness. Wildlife in their natural environment, behaving naturally, were key responses of all post-visit tourists. The ability to observe wildlife at close quarters reiterates the theme that quality encounters matter. This line of thinking is consistent with the view expressed earlier in this chapter that authenticity is devolving into more specific and localised concepts in accounting for tourists' on-site experiences.

Interpretation as an augmenting aspect of experience as well as a management tool is evident throughout Kangaroo Island tourism and is a core part of the visitor responses. The guides who take visitors for the local walks at Seal

Bay keep their 10–20 person groups in tight clusters with specified distances from the resting sea lions. The quest for more information and interpretation is context-dependent and, while the visitors did not want more guides in the Flinders Chase National Park, they did want a range of information in the proposed visitor centre to enhance their control, develop their skills and permit their vision of the setting to be expanded. The data also suggested that the existing wildlife and natural-environment experiences induced mindfulness in the Kangaroo Island visitors. Mindfulness, it was suggested earlier, is a predisposition to respond in novel ways, to seek information and to develop and enhance cognitive categories for dealing with the world. The post-experience visitors studied in the major survey reported greater interest in the wildlife and in the geographical features and plants on the island; these are all solid indications that they had experienced the environmental mindfully and were receptive to new and additional information as foreshadowed in the outcomes section of Figure 6.2

In summary, Kangaroo Island is a place where the on-site experiences of visitors reflect the integration of the themes discussed in this chapter. It is a demonstration of the core elements of the place model proposed by Canter (1977) as it suggests that the conception of the setting, its physical properties and the activities of viewing and touring at the sites together function to make it a tourism success for the visitor. The wider issues of the total management of the island's sustainability are also partly served by the responsible and pro-environment attitude expressed by the Kangaroo Island tourists.

As reported in Chapter 1, issues of sustainability and regional development extend beyond tourist behaviour studies. There are a number of issues concerning the management of the commercial tour groups on Kangaroo Island, and a particular concern is the time such visitors have for appreciating sites and benefiting from new interpretive information. Further, the ability of the local community to benefit from tourism that is controlled by operators outside the region is a persistent concern for many locations and, while this issue is not immediately reflected in visitors' assessments of their experience, it can ultimately create a disenfranchised anti-tourist community.

There is, however, one powerful way in which the tourist behaviour data can be used to inform these large issues. Continued monitoring of visitor satisfaction and, further, establishing evidence of a widening gap in visitor experiences between commercial and independent travellers may signal the need for business operators to change itineraries and schedules to prevent the product becoming unattractive. The further value of outcome-oriented tourist behaviour research – studies that investigate satisfaction, enjoyment, learning and reflections on experience – are pursued in the next chapter.

Chapter 7

Tourists' Reflections on Experience

Introduction

A challenge is often mounted to those who participate in tourism, those who manage it and those who study it. The challenge to tourists (Pizam & Mansfield, 2001) is why they spend their money on travel and its associated activities when there are other appealing, and perhaps more tangible, socially-visible products to be consumed? Managers of tourism environments are faced with queries about why they seek to encourage more visitors if they are unsure of the long-term consequences of visitor activities. Tourism researchers, too, can be challenged. Here the perspective is offered that presumably talented well-educated researchers might more usefully contribute to their society by applying their social science skills to pressing issues such as those found in medicine and social welfare.

A comprehensive answer to these challenges can be found in the concept of *eudaimonia*, a Greek philosophical term that can be approximately translated as human flourishing (de Botton, 2002). Eudaimonia was a concern of Plato and Aristotle, and later of Socrates and his followers. In essence, the concept asserts that a valued purpose in human life is to include but go beyond survival and good health, to achieve more than standards of comfort and well-being and instead to thrive on all the possibilities of existence (cf. Armstrong, 2003). In a tourism context *eudaimonia* draws attention to the issue of what is sometimes termed 'the quality of life' with the additional meaning that this involves deep satisfaction and enjoyment of experiences, as well as learning, personal growth and skill development.

The outcomes and consequences of tourists' on-site experiences will be considered in this chapter under this broad rubric of eudaimonia. Initially, a consideration of satisfaction enjoyment and engagement will be pursued. There are several existing issues and traditions of research in the visitor-satisfaction arena and this topic will occupy an important and primary part of this chapter. In other areas, notably the learning, personal growth and skill development components of tourism, research work is just beginning and the legacy of existing studies is not as strong. These topics will be considered as part of the broad spectrum of why tourism matters to tourists, and why the people who manage and study it can see a value in its controlled development that includes, but lies beyond, simple profits for business.

As in Chapter 6, the focus of the studies and the conceptual schemes that help interpret them, lie centrally with the behaviour and experiences of the tourists themselves. It is the psychological effects and intragroup bonds rather than the societal consequences that constitute the foreground of attention.

Satisfaction

The literature on tourist satisfaction is replete with the challenges of operationalisation, measurement, elaboration and case studies (Noe, 1999). Nearly all of this literature ignores a fundamental starting point – satisfaction is simply a post-experience attitude, and attitudes are not fixed or tangible parameters. Typically satisfaction is viewed through a well-defined empirical lens, with respondents providing an assessment of their attitude on a Likert scale or a related rating scale format (Veal, 1997). Reporting on one's satisfaction with a product as diverse as 'a holiday in Hong Kong', involves complex issues of reactivity since the attitude may well be crystallised by the process of being asked and by who is inquiring. As Tunnell (1977) suggested some time ago, good research methods involve ensuring a naturalness in the responses being sought from people and condensing one's overview of a place to a point on a 10-point rating scale is less than totally natural. Nevertheless it has been established in several decades of leisure, recreation, tourism and business research that seeking empirical accounts of attitudes is useful, so how might this initial quibble about the starting point for attitude research be incorporated or assist in modifying satisfaction studies?

One approach consistent with the idea of eudaimonia is to seek travellers' best experiences as a kind of raw data on which satisfaction attitudes partly depend. Accounts of travellers' best experiences, either about episodes of interaction or facilities enjoyed, may begin the process of expanding the frame of empirically- oriented studies adding to their meaning and interpretation. The work of Small (2003), who has studied cohorts of older women travellers, illustrates the advantages of the approach. Detailed interviews with individual women travellers who were in post-child-rearing family roles were conducted. Small's respondents consistently reported that travel was deeply rewarding for them because it connected them to the world and expanded the scope of their life. This is surely satisfaction with travel, but it would require very high levels of psychometric skill to easily establish this perspective in a traditional empirical framework. The implication of this initial perspective is that researchers and managers who need to simplify the way satisfaction is assessed should still maintain an awareness that it is a socially-negotiated account of sometimes deeply felt attitudes that lie at the heart of the topic.

Key Issues

Expressive and instrumental attributes

There are several key issues that provide a useful preliminary perspective on tourist satisfaction research. The concept of enjoyment has already been cited in this chapter and treated initially as if it were synonymous with satisfaction. This is only partly correct as the term enjoyment, which is widely applied in the leisure literature, is typically used for the more fulfilling and psychological contributions deriving from experiences as opposed to the core facilitating and experience-enabling components. This distinction is usually referred to as the split between *expressive* and *instrumental* attributes (Swan & Combs, 1976). Instrumental components of satisfaction refer to the physical products or the means to the travellers' goals. By way of contrast, expressive attributes refer to the psychological meaning and experience attached to more holistic and less tangible setting features. In a National Park context assessing instrumental attributes involves obtaining scores or appraisals of the parking spaces, toilets, seating and signs. Assessing expressive attributes involves reactions to scenery, beauty, wildlife and achieving the goals of the visit. The distinction is illustrated by evaluations of toilet facilities. An instrumental attribute appraisal is appropriate with questions such as 'How satisfied were you with our Park's toilet facilities?' – possibly followed by further subquestions on cleanliness and location. An expressive appraisal is inappropriate with few respondents being able to make sense of a question such as 'How much did you enjoy our toilets?' or 'How much did the toilets contribute to your overall satisfaction with your visit to the park?'

The distinction between these forms of satisfaction is not trivial. It is central to tourist behaviour studies to emphasise that, along certain key dimensions, tourist behaviour is unlike other forms of consumer behaviour. This perspective was introduced in Chapter 1 but it is particularly appropriate to restate the distinction in satisfaction studies since models of consumer satisfaction are largely oriented toward instrumental attributes (Fuchs, 2002). This narrower focus has important implications when the conceptual models for understanding satisfaction are considered.

Purpose of satisfaction studies

The kind of work undertaken in tourist satisfaction research is shaped by some distinctively different goals. Researchers seeking to understand the phenomenon of tourism typically use satisfaction as a dependent variable linked to travellers' experience of sites, their activities and their social contexts. For this kind of work satisfaction studies may be empirical, but they may also be descriptive and thematic as researchers can value what tourists report in detail about their experience (Ryan, 1995a). Managerial approaches to tourist satisfaction, and researchers seeking to serve that tradition are typically concerned with competitive advantage and assessing performance targets (Noe, 1999; Payne, 1993; Ritchie *et al.*, 2000). At times some satisfaction appraisals may be functional for promoting organisations or individual concerns and may have political and intra-organisational consequences (Hockings *et al.*, 2000).

One of the particular consequences of the different purposes of satisfaction studies lies in what is assessed. For managerial purposes there is little point in determining satisfaction with fixed attributes, such as the location of a hotel, that cannot be changed. Similarly, collecting generic information about satisfaction or dissatisfaction with hotel staff is not useful if it is not specific and is unable to pinpoint problems at the individual or organisation level. Satisfaction studies, it can be suggested, are not a uniform body of work addressing the same set of coherent purposes. This diversity of effort needs to be considered when conceptual and methodological efforts to understand and enhance the existing traditions are reviewed.

The satisfaction trap

Satisfaction is certainly a commonly used outcome measure in tourist behaviour research. Yet it can also be a trap, since its importance is modified by other outcome appraisals. An expensive restaurant offering fine food and a desirable ambience may produce highly satisfied customers, yet fail on the all-important outcome dimension of profitability. In natural environments it is possible to envisage a scenario where visitors are again highly satisfied, yet their behaviour is destructive, and their enjoyment of the setting is built on the activities of lighting campfires, driving irresponsibly on sensitive trails and pursuing close encounters with wildlife that they manifestly disturb. In a more spiritual context, the early studies of English cathedrals as tourist attractions produced a response from the clergy which summarises the need to establish satisfaction as one but not the only success measure: '[Tourists matter] ... but we give complete priority to the sense of worship' (English Tourist Board, 1979: Foreword). The satisfaction trap is to view high levels of satisfaction as the sole or dominant indicator of performance. It is a trap more likely to ensnare students than industry analysts since the former may not always have business imperatives or other organisational goals in their frame of reference.

Positivity bias

This concept refers to the frequently-observed phenomenon in tourist satisfaction studies that very positive appraisals are given for a great variety of products and services. Is tourism really this good? Is everybody really so happy most of the time? On the surface, the empirical evidence would suggest they are, with many people giving a score of 6 or 7 on a

7–point rating scale. There is, however, an explanation for this kind of result. It is likely that a substantial amount of ego or self-esteem protection is operating with customers not wanting to admit that in the free-choice tourism situation they have selected badly. Tourism products and experiences reflect people's values and represent aspects of (and opportunities to enhance) their identity; it is therefore counterproductive and reflects poorly on personal credibility to be very dissatisfied with a situation that one has willingly entered and often paid handsomely to experience.

The positivity bias produces difficulties for managers and researchers. When all customers are providing scores of the order of 4 out of 5 or 6 out of 7, analysts are effectively working with a blunt instrument because it is difficult to detect the actual need for improvement or to measure the consequences of any innovative management.

It is noteworthy that cross-cultural perspectives, and sometimes industry-based cross-cultural myths about positivity and satisfaction also appear to exist. Asian visitors in particular are often seen as smiling and approving, yet there are suspicions that there is a grimace behind the smile (cf. Finney & Watson, 1975). Reisinger and Turner (2003) stress the importance of understanding cultural factors influencing satisfaction appraisal. They argue that interaction difficulties and styles may underwrite both satisfaction appraisals and complaints. Their argument may be extended a little further and applied to the method of collecting satisfaction data. Collecting satisfaction data with face-to-face interviews or with surveys handed out by tourism operators is a common form of industry appraisal. There is, however, a hidden interaction dimension in this process and individuals from cultural groups who value harmony consensus and smooth interaction are unwilling to assert strong negative opinions (cf. Hofstede, 1980; Triandis, 1994; Trompenaars & Hampden-Turner, 1984). It is particularly interesting to note that, when the assessment is carried out by individuals not associated with the business itself, and when the materials are fully translated and back-translated into the appropriate first language of the visitor, tourists from consensus cultures can be quite critical and less positive in their appraisals. As Turner and Reisinger (1999) report, when Japanese respondents to Hawaii and to Australia's Gold Coast were not required to express reactions directly to the interviewer, a sophisticated and demanding set of consumers may appear in the written appraisals and the positivity bias disappears.

There are heuristics for interpreting the apparently restricted range of information when highly positive appraisals occur in the researchers' data sets. One possible rule of thumb, at least for Western cultures, is reported by Hanan and Karp (1989), who suggest that a high level of satisfaction exists if the top categories add up to 85–90%. If the top categories amount to only 70–80%, satisfaction can be seen as moderate and if the cumulative figure is of the order of 60% satisfaction is low. There may be some important cross-cultural and tourism-context differences in the application of these percentages since Hanan and Karp were working with mostly instrumental attributes in National Park and natural environment settings. Nevertheless, the work begins to provide a context for interpreting the frequently positively-skewed measures reported in tourist satisfaction assessments.

There are a number of technical solutions to the problems of positivity bias. One path for enhancing satisfaction studies lies in using expanded scales, such as 0 to 10 rating scales rather than 1 to 5 scales. While the expanded scales are not normally used in attitude assessment the careful labelling of each scale point can offer a route for enhancing the discriminatory power of a single satisfaction item. Typical scale point labels for a 0 to 10 scale would read:

10 = extremely satisfied, 9 = very very satisfied, 8 = very satisfied, 7 = quite satisfied, 6 = somewhat satisfied, 5 = neither particularly satisfied nor dissatisfied, 4 = somewhat dissatisfied, 3 = quite dissatisfied, 2 = very dissatisfied, 1 = very very dissatisfied, 0 = extremely dissatisfied.

These verbal modifiers and labels help analysts to make sense of the mean values expressed by respondents. Additional approaches include the use of multiple items to assess component satisfaction scores and summing these to create an overall satisfaction index. There are some complexities with indices since it is necessary to weight the importance of the components rather than simply add them. This requirement demands that researchers collect both importance ratings and satisfaction ratings of the contributing elements.

Hazelrigg and Hardy (2000) have argued that particular attention should be given to the language of satisfaction, particularly the way individuals interpret the modifiers such as 'quite satisfied' and 'somewhat satisfied'. They also foreshadow the need to understand one's domain of research and highlight the need to develop a benchmark of the way respondents report satisfaction in specific facets of life. For example, it is suggested that satisfaction with one's health, one's financial well being, one's friends and one's holidays are treated as different kinds of entities with the modifiers operating differently in these domains. A further possibility exists that the modifiers may operate differently for different kinds of tourism products and experiences – it might be harder to get 'extremely satisfied' ratings for a 12-hour international flight than it is for a theme park ride or restaurant meal. A further but potentially important implication of this issue in the tourism domain is the adequacy of translated questionnaires in conveying the satisfaction modifiers to visitors from different market sources. There would appear to be some necessary psychometric work required in this area of tourism study, both in the use of expanded rating scales that flaunt much existing methodological advice and in the adequacy of the modifiers (Oppenheim, 1966).

Understanding satisfaction

There is one dominant tradition used to understand satisfaction and two emerging traditions that challenge its position. The established approach is called the *expectancy/confirmation/disconfirmation* or EDP model (Oliver, 1980). This adopts the position that customers compare the actual product and service performance with their expectations. The argument is that if customers' expectations are met or exceeded the customer is well satisfied. Dissatisfaction will ensue if the expectations are not met. This perspective is the orthodox one that derives from the vast literature in the wider field of consumer behaviour (cf. Schofield, 2000). In many tourism settings, businesses use some form of this EDP approach to shape their thinking and mission statements. Some examples include 'We aim to exceed our customers' expectations' and 'More than you can dream' (cf. Hanan & Karp, 1989). These views of business success in the satisfaction sphere are then often translated into assessment practices, such as shown in Figure 7.1.

The EDP approach is problematic. Expectations for tourism products and services can vary in clarity and relevance. For a hotel room there may be clear unambiguous expectations deriving from previous experiences. In other words guests have a normative standard and (as is with breakfast cereal, soap and other tangible products) a good basis for evaluation. Several researchers in tourism have pointed out that expectations are not so applicable or relevant when the goods or services vary substantially and when they are purchased only occasionally (Fornell *et al.*, 1996; Hughes, 1991). Additionally for certain kinds of tourism settings the operating business or destination is at the whim of a range of external, unexpected and uncontrollable forces likely to dominate satisfaction appraisals. Specific examples abound, but in the backpacker market, for example, the satisfaction with one's hostel might be much more about the friendships and relationships formed there than about its facilities. For reef tourism, the conditions at sea and ensuing nausea may dominate the day's trip but were unforeseen by the visitor, and for urban tourism large shopping discounts at all stores may be very welcome but not anticipated. Further, satisfaction may exist when tourists simply report that the location and facilities are simply not quite what was expected, but still very suitable and enjoyable (Hughes, 1991).

Measurement issues also undermine the adequacy of the EDP model in some circumstances. It has been noted by Teas (1993) that when interval level scales are used to assess expectations and satisfaction, a performance expectation discrepancy of, for example, -2 (minus 2) can be realised in a number of ways. Working with a 7- point scale -2 may result when expectations were

1. Please indicate your opinion of the following services and facilities supplied during your stay with us by filling in the appropriate response.			
	Exceeded expectations	Met expectations	Below expectations
Reservations			
Efficiency of our hotel's reservation service	O	O	O
Efficiency of Accor's central reservations service	O	O	O
Knowledge of reservation staff	O	O	O
Reservation requests being met	O	O	O
Hotel Overall			
Value for money	O	O	O
Consistency of standards	O	O	O
Check In and Check Out			
Speed and efficiency	O	O	O
Treatment as a valued guest	O	O	O
Availability of porters	O	O	O
Assistance through check in/check out	O	O	O
Readiness of room on check in	O	O	O
Accuracy of account/bill	O	O	O
Room			
Cleanliness and tidiness	O	O	O
Security and safety	O	O	O
Quietness	O	O	O
Noise of air conditioning	O	O	O
Provision of extras on request	O	O	O
Standard of maintenance	O	O	O
Suitability of lighting	O	O	O
Effectiveness of curtains	O	O	O
Food & Beverage			
Value of restaurant meals	O	O	O
Speed of service	O	O	O
Choice of breakfast styles	O	O	O
Temperature of room service meals on arrival	O	O	O
Fairness of Room service charges	O	O	O

Figure 7.1 Customer feedback form: Accor Hotels Australia

Staff			
Courtesy and friendliness	O	O	O
Competence and professionalism	O	O	O
Neatness and tidiness	O	O	O
Ability to make you feel important	O	O	O
Helpfulness	O	O	O
Understanding your needs	O	O	O
Contribution to enjoyment of your stay	O	O	O
Hotel Facilities and Services (*if provided*)			
Luggage minding	O	O	O
Timeliness of wake up calls	O	O	O
Pool and recreational facilities	O	O	O

Figure 7.1 *continued*

very high (7) and the performance was judged as 5. The -2 score may also be obtained when the expectation was 4 and the performance was quite bad, a value of 2. The equivalence of these 2 scores of -2 is at issue. Is it likely that customers with the higher expectations and moderate outcomes are as satisfied as those with modest expectations and quite inferior outcomes? A plausible answer is that many travellers would be more content in the former than the latter situation, but the arithmetic of the EDP model asserts equivalence.

Distortions of several other kinds exist because of the logic of the EDP model and the likely behavioural responses to measuring expectations and satisfaction in the way it prescribes. Babakus and Boller (1992) report that expectations are generally rated very highly. As suggested earlier in the chapter, self-esteem and ego-protection can operate in the way that respondents view holiday choices. High expectation scores may be driven by a desire to be seen as a discriminating and sophisticated consumer, and by a vision of oneself as an experienced, competent decision maker. The more honest answer to many expectations questions is less self-aggrandising and amounts to a 'I don't know what to expect as I haven't really prepared myself for this situation or thought about it too much'.

Expectations

The reactivity of expectation assessment has been noted for some time (Pearce, 1988; Ryan, 1995a). In turning attention to expectations researchers may be clarifying or creating them. Additionally once expectations have been produced in response to the assessment they may shape the individual's view of his or her travel experience as attention is now crystallised around features perhaps not previously considered. For example, alerting travellers to their own expectations about congestion at a summer resort might sensitise them to the presence of others and create its own self-fulfilling appraisal. Such issues of reactivity are particularly relevant when people report that they have no expectations or where expectations are initially described as vague, superficial and uncertain (Crompton & Love, 1995; Mazursky, 1989). In particular, expectations for the expressive element of the experience, such as the aesthetic, the sublime and the engaging, may be less appropriate for an EDP approach than for the instrumental attributes.

The issue of timing – when to measure expectations – is also a concern. The pragmatic issues of convenience and expense often prompt researchers to measure expectations and satisfaction together. For example questions of the type illustrated in Figure 7.1, effectively ask people to reflect on the expectations they once held. Respondents may indeed answer these questions out of courtesy to the researcher or the business. Nevertheless it is likely that the experience itself has re-organised earlier thoughts and mutated previous anticipatory responses. The helpful visitors are in fact likely to be 'telling more than they can know' (Nisbett & Wilson, 1977).

The practice of extending theories and conceptual schemes to their logical conclusion is one form of incisive analysis for testing their adequacy. A slightly odd implication for practice arises from extending EDP approaches. If companies and destination managers could reduce expectations by under-promising (such as suggesting their product is adequate rather than the more florid description of fantastic), then consumers' expectations could be more easily surpassed, thus guaranteeing outstanding satisfaction results. It is highly questionable whether the EDP approach is helpful here.

The EDP approach is not specifically associated with one researcher, although it has been heavily used in one subdomain of tourist satisfaction – that of appraising service quality and staff–visitor interaction (Parasuraman *et al.*, 1985, 1994b). Kozak (2001) contributes the observation that the expectation performance approach is really a family of mini theories and conceptual schemes. Some of the family members are labelled a little differently and include contrast theory, aspiration theory, gap analysis, adaptation level, disconformation approach and the importance-performance approach. The importance-performance system is worth highlighting. In many of the EDP approaches in academic work and even more so in industry practice in assessing satisfaction, insufficient attention is given to the value or significance of specific components of satisfaction in contributing to a total outcome. This point was noted briefly in referring to index construction as a resolution of the positivity bias. The contribution made by Martin Fishbein to attitude theory and to researchers working in the line of work broadly referred to as 'reasoned action' and 'expectancy value' models of attitudes, is particularly important in this context (Bagozzi *et al.*, 2002; Barsky, 1992; Fishbein, 1967; Fishbein & Ajzen, 1975). The relative significance of each component attribute needs to be assessed and then the satisfaction with that component should be separately measured. There is a larger argument here of whether the EDP approach should be used (or at least when it should be used), but the reasoned-action and expectancy-value approaches reinforce the view that evaluating and weighting the importance of attributes is informative for analysis and action (Lunt, 1995).

There are other approaches to understanding satisfaction that avoid an expectancy emphasis. Kozak labels these approaches the Nordic School, and this can again be seen as a family of linked and like schemes. At core, Nordic School approaches to satisfaction are pragmatic and consistent with the definition of satisfaction as a *post hoc* attitude. They are performance-only appraisals of customer satisfaction and offer the view that travellers' perception of the quality of the performance, the product or the experience is what really matters in satisfaction research. Crompton and Love (1995) established that a performance-only approach was superior to expectations-based analysis in assessing visitor satisfaction at festivals. Earlier Prakash (1984) had noted the superiority of performance-only measures for predicting future behaviour. Numerous examples of performance-only approaches consistent with the Nordic School definition of satisfaction exist and are illustrated by work on rural travellers (Black & Rutledge, 1996), birdwatchers (Applegate & Clarke, 1987), campgrounds (Foster & Jackson, 1979) marine tourists (Greenwood & Moscardo, 1999), and participants on guided tours (Hughes, 1991).

The basic Nordic School approach, that of assessing satisfaction with a cross-section survey or appraisal raises one important dilemma. A criticism of the approach is that, when analysts and stakeholders obtain a set of scores, they may have difficulty in understanding their meaning and lack a context of interpretation. This issue is at the core of the charge made by Parasuraman and colleagues that the expectations approach is superior because it offers valuable contextual information (Parasuraman *et al.*, 1985, 1994b). There are, however, three kinds of extensions to the basic Nordic School system that can augment the value of the *post hoc* only appraisals.

Benchmarking

The expression 'benchmarking' is widely used in the management literature as a system to establish meaning and context for individual units and businesses. Benchmarking in tourist satisfaction can take three forms; two of which involve collecting and assembling comparative data and one which integrates a benchmarking appraisal into the design of the satisfaction question. These three forms of benchmarking can be referred to as *internal* benchmarking, *external* benchmarking and *inquiry* benchmarking. Internal benchmarking applies when satisfaction scores are retained by a business or organisation, and is used as a basis for comparison over time, across departments or across-market segments. The material is entirely held and collected in-house and can be used with confidence for monitoring and management purposes since its quality and collection parameters are known and trusted. External benchmarking applies when the performance scores of competitors are obtained and used to constitute a wider inter-business or inter-organisation frame of reference. In the commercial context, such information is often closely guarded and unavailable, but in public management agencies and arenas external benchmarking, for example, national park to national park or among world heritage areas, can be accessed and purposefully employed (Hockings *et al.*, 2000).

Inquiry benchmarking is a variant of internal benchmarking where the question asked has an inbuilt comparative statement. For example, the satisfaction question can be phrased as follows: 'Compared to other hotels of this type, how satisfied were you overall with our hotel?' In using the inquiry benchmarking approach, it can be valuable to ascertain how much experience the travellers have with other comparable properties.

Synthesising Satisfaction

Reviews of major topic areas in tourism often conclude with cautious and indeterminate remarks as well as frequent calls for further understanding. There is still much to be done to develop satisfaction studies specifically in the tourism context and some suggestions for this kind of work have already been offered. To repeat these emphases: there is potential for study in the area of less-quantitative appraisals of satisfaction; there is work in the psychometric realm with modifiers and the use of scales; there are issues for translating and understanding cross-cultural response styles; and there are new opportunities to build databases for benchmarking appraisals. Importantly some of the larger and more ambitious destination-management schemes view visitor satisfaction as a pivotal measure of regional performance, and the further use of Nordic School benchmark-enhanced approaches for these management systems offers a rich vein of development (Fuchs, 2002; Hockings *et al.*, 2000; McCarthur, 2000; Ritchie *et al.*, 2000; WTO, 1999).

It is possible, however, to be a little more definitive in synthesising satisfaction rather than simply noting new research opportunities. Both the EDP tradition and the Nordic School approaches can be applicable in tourist studies. The EDP family of approaches will be best applied to frequently purchased, standardised products that are familiar to the consumer. Much of the content being appraised will be of an instrumental rather than an expressive nature. The measurement of the expectation is best done prior to the experience since reflective questions are particularly problematic. Additionally the opportunity for respondents to indicate that they have unclear or few expectations should be built into the question format rather than forcing or structuring the travellers' anticipatory view. There may also be advantages for research logistics to use matched samples of respondents in the pre- and post-test phases of the design since such an approach not only attends to reactivity issues but is simpler to implement and avoids difficulties in pursuing the same individuals in natural settings. The study of tourists to Kangaroo Island, used as an illustration of visitor reactions on site in Chapter 6, was conducted with exactly this kind of large sample independent but matched pre-post design (Woods, 2000). A final but central part of the EDP style assessments should be the rating of attribute importance in relation to expectations and performance.

For the more expressive aspects of tourism experience, particularly those where the expectations are likely to be poorly defined, unfamiliar or non-existent, a Nordic School performance only approach can be recommended. Some of the strengths of this approach lie in the clarity of its task for the traveller. The researcher too benefits from the *post hoc* assessment if both importance ratings and any one of the benchmarking approaches reviewed are employed to facilitate data interpretation.

Tourist Knowledge Acquisition

While education and knowledge acquisition have long been themes guiding tourism, the assessment of travellers' experiences in this realm is quite limited. How much travellers learn about the visited environments and the cultures they visit is of little commercial interest, so a strong push to pursue such a topic has not arisen from industry personnel. Additionally, learning about the world and re-arranging one's views and attitudes do not apply to consumers' experiences and their purchases of most everyday products. Consequently, there is not a well-developed consumer-behaviour literature detailing how one's knowledge is stimulated and affected by the purchase of white goods, food products or bars of chocolate. A closer analogy lies with learning from television which, like learning from travel involves the sharing of experiences and the discussion of their meaning in a social context (Howe, 1983).

Initially, however, it is perhaps appropriate to heed the cautionary statement offered by Huxley:

> Reading and travelling, they say, broaden the mind, stimulate imagination, are a liberal education. And so on. These are specious arguments ... For though it may be quite true that for certain people

> desultory reading and aimless tavelling are richly educative, it is not
> for that reason that most true readers and travellers born indulge their
> tastes. We read and travel, not that we may broaden and enrich our
> minds but that we may pleasantly forget they exist (Huxley, 1948: 12).

Huxley's remarks repay close attention. There is a weak acknowledge-
ment here that some travellers do actively seek learning and educational
experiences. This view is consistent with the emphasis in earlier chapters
that specialists and experienced travellers have travel career patterns
where learning matters and is likely to occur. More generally, however,
Huxley is emphasising that travel is frequently desultory. Here, Huxley is
anticipating Benjamin's concept of the *flaneur*, the somewhat empty-
headed idling consumer seeking diversion rather than engagement in his
or her search for satisfaction (Benjamin, 1973; Edwards, 2000). As discussed
previously, broad generalisations about types of tourists need to be treated
with caution, but a succinct summary that knowledge acquisition is
unlikely to be important to all kinds of travellers is an appropriate caution.

In assessing some of the existing literature on visitor learning and
knowledge acquisition a recurring theme in this volume is again operating.
Only a sample of the full set of references can be reviewed. Nevertheless the
sampling serves the purpose of highlighting dominant themes, and the
material discussed can then be set in the context of an organising conceptual scheme. The existing studies on visitor learning derive almost exclusively from the analysis of the effectiveness of interpretation (Light, 1995).
As such, tourist behaviour and knowledge acquisition are treated largely
within museums, visitor centres, zoos and natural environment settings.
Broader considerations of learning about a whole destination are almost
non-existent.

The studies reported are presented in an ascending order of complexity
and sophistication in treating forms of visitor learning. For example, Cole *et
al.* (1997) working in a wilderness area in Montana established that visitor
knowledge of low impact behaviours was improved by messages organised by the researchers on trailside bulletin boards. They evaluated the
learning with a quiz on the recommended practices. The findings do
however reveal a limited amount of visitor learning. Cole *et al.* report:

> Our research found that few visitors were willing to spend more than
> 25 seconds to read low-impact messages and that posting more than
> two messages had no positive effect on knowledge of recommended
> practices (Cole *et al.*, 1997: 69).

The Montana findings do not offer a very auspicious account of how
much visitors learn and how much effort they are prepared to commit to the
education process.

Tan *et al.* (1992) used a pre–post design with nearly 300 respondents to study visitor knowledge of river-based issues in the Lower Salmon River recreation area in Idaho. They investigated the impact of specialist guide training on communicating river information to visitors. Visitors whose guides had received training were contrasted with visitors whose guides had not. The assessment of visitor knowledge consisted of 25 multiple choice questions, 20 of which were repeated post-test. Three questionnaire versions were used to randomise question order and reduce test sensitisation. Visitors with the guides who had received training obtained significantly higher scores on the content areas of river history, ecology, geology, low-impact camping, wildlife, grazing, mining and related management topics. This study begins to indicate that thorough investigative efforts and comprehensive educational programmes can reveal some specific factual knowledge gains. Importantly the enduring nature of the knowledge gain remains untested.

In another interpretive evaluation study, this time conducted in Great Smoky Mountains National Park, the researchers constructed their own signs and placed them at 270-metre intervals along a 1.5 kilometre trail (Hammitt, 1998). Nine hundred trail users were studied. The signs, which consisted of 2–3 sentences as well as a sketch, provided localised information specific to the site. The inclusion of highly-localised information was a tactic used by the researcher to control prior information that visitors might hold. The technique for assessing knowledge gained from the signs was to provide photos of the 8 sites to act as memory aids and then ask the subjects to choose from three statements the actual information they might have acquired from the sign. Hammitt reports that 73% of the sample were able to recognise more than 70% of the information.

The mounting complexity of these studies can be highlighted. Hammitt's work attests to the importance of two distinctions: prior knowledge versus new knowledge, and recognition of information as a form of learning as opposed to recall of information (Prince, 1982). It appears that how much visitors learn might depend on how much they already know and how they are asked to respond. As well as recognition of information and recall of information, another approach to visitor learning lies in assessing how much visitors think they have learned – a category of response termed subjective knowledge. Evans (1999) reporting on tourists visiting Wonambi Fossil Centre, a World Heritage site at Naracoorte in South Australia, noted that 95% of visitors felt that they had learned something from the information at the interpretive centre. The visitor site employs robotic displays to depict extinct Australian megafauna. Visitors also recognised their own limited information gains, reporting that they were unable to take in very much interpretive commentary because of the overwhelming noise, scale and style of the display. The purchase of educational material, another broad indicator of at least an interest in learning, was also quite high at this site with over 40% of visitors opting to purchase a mix of souvenir and information-based products. The broader one's definition of learning and knowledge acquisition, including subjective knowledge, the more it appears that there are some modest learning effects at these kinds of tourist sites.

Some further attention to methodological and assessment issues assists in understanding these results and their wider meaning. Figures 7.2 and 7.3 contrasts three styles of assessing learning derived from information brochures, displays and pictorial signs. The testing materials are drawn from Woods and Moscardo (1998) and Heffernan (1998).

The kinds of data collected on visitor learning in Figures 7.2 and 7.3 are all focused and factual. The styles assess increasing levels of cognitive processing – the recitation and recall of facts in the first case, the judgement of appropriateness in the second and the ability to recognise the behaviours in a larger context in the third. Together with the subjective knowledge appraisals these approaches represent a first level in assessing visitor learning.

A more complex account of what visitors learn is accessed by exploring how the relationships among concepts and attitudes alter owing to site visits. Here the attention is on how visitors reorganise their overall understanding of the topic and mindfully restructure their social representation. The full definition and meaning of this term will be developed in the next few pages.

Two examples involving visitors' reorganisation of their everyday knowledge systems can be cited. Lee and Uzzell (1980) explored the effect on visitor learning of participating in farm open days. They showed that, for a high percentage of the visitors, the bucolic and pleasant images of a productive farm with appealing animals and upright farm workers was restructured in the minds of those attending the open days. The new social representation could be better described as viewing farms as rational technical production systems, a less favourable image but one built on the realities of economics, efficient animal management practices and rural realities.

Working in New Zealand, Stewart *et al.* (1998) studied how the use of interpretive sources shaped visitor understanding of Mount Cook as a special place. They argue that qualitative techniques, in their case detailed interviews, can shift the evaluation of interpretation and the assessment of learning beyond the simple kinds of questions that have typified previous research. The mental reorganisation that they identify in relation to visiting Mount Cook was quite consistent across different kinds of visitors and indeed across visitors who used the interpretation with different degrees of enthusiasm. Stewart and colleagues report that the initial representation of

Please check the answer that you think is correct. Choose only one.

1 The Great Bay is best described as a(n):
   a _____ rocky shore
   b _____ forested wetland
   c _____ estuarine system
   d _____ salt marsh
   e _____ none of the above

2 Which river of the Great Bay Estuary connects directly with the Atlantic Ocean?
   a _____ Piscataqua
   b _____ Oyster
   c _____ Lamprey
   d _____ Squamscott
   e _____ Winnicut

3 Which of the following contributes to tidal action (high tide/low tide)?
   a _____ rain
   b _____ moon
   c _____ animals
   d _____ land
   e _____ none of the above

4 Where are soft-shelled clams found?
   a _____ mud flats
   b _____ rocky shore
   c _____ eelgrass beds
   d _____ freshwater ponds
   e _____ uplands

5 Food chains are made up of plants and animals. Plants can make their own food while animals get their energy from eating plants or other animals. Which item listed is best described as the 'beginning of the food chain' in the Great Bay?
   a _____ fish
   b _____ shellfish
   c _____ plankton
   d _____ insects
   e _____ worms

6 Which item(s) are considered a change or challenge that Great Bay animals face?
   a _____ tidal action
   b _____ temperature
   c _____ salty water
   d _____ all of the above
   e _____ none of the above

7 Which animal is not found in the Great Bay?
   a _____ bald eagle
   b _____ humpbacked whale
   c _____ horseshoe crab
   d _____ lobster
   e _____ harbour seal

8 Which type of pollution can be found in Great Bay?
   a _____ fertilizers from lawns
   b _____ dirt & debris from construction sites
   c _____ plastics
   d _____ all of the above
   e _____ none of the above

9 There have been no successful attempts to restore salt marshes or eelgrass beds that have been degraded by pollution
   a _____ true
   b _____ false

10 The Great Bay Reserve's parent agency is:
   a _____ Environmental Protection Agency
   b _____ National Oceanic and Atmospheric Administration
   c _____ Army Corps of Engineers
   d _____ Department of the Interio
   e _____ U.S. Department of Health and Human Services

Figure 7.2 Approaches to assessing visitor learning: Multiple choice questions (Heffernan, 1998)

True/False Questions about Appropriate Visitor Behaviour

Which of the following statements are true, and which are false?

1 Coral is alive.

2 You should not take home any pieces of coral.

3 Feeding fish bread is okay, but other sorts of food can make them sick.

4 Collecting shells from islands is okay.

5 When you are swimming you should never try and chase or touch fish.

6 Taking photographs of the reef and fish is a good thing to do.

7 You should remember to put on sunscreen.

8 Touching corals very gently is a good way to better understand the reef.

9 You should never put litter in the sea.

10 Standing on coral can kill it.

11 Big fish don't mind being touched, but little ones can get stressed.

12 You should not collect shells from the reef.

Underlining Inappropriate Behaviour from a Reef Behaviour Story

In the following passage, please underline anything that shows Kate or John doing something that would be harmful to the coral reef.

John and Kate were visiting the Great Barrier Reef for the first time. When their boat arrived at the reef they decided to go snorkelling straight away so they could see what the reef was really like. Kate was not as strong a swimmer as John and got tired. She found a place on the reef where she could stand on the coral and have a rest. John was a strong swimmer and he found a place where there were many different types of coral. He very carefully touched some to see if they were as different as they looked. After a while both Kate and John went back to the boat for lunch. They threw their orange peels into the ocean.

After lunch John went diving and saw many different fish and other marine creatures. It was such a great experience that he collected a very small shell to take home so that he would not forget the day. Kate went snorkelling again and this time fed some bread from her lunch to the fish to get them to come close to her. She took some photographs of the fish by resting the camera on some coral and she was able to touch some of the fish. John and Kate had a great day on the reef.

Figure 7.3 Approaches to assessing visitor learning: True/false questions and underlining inappropriate behaviour (Woods & Moscardo, 1998)

Mount Cook is one of undifferentiated space. Following their on-site experiences people move towards an organised mapping of subplace experiences that are symbolically connected to a deepening sense of appreciation and care for the environment.

A sophisticated treatment of tourist learning and knowledge gain needs to deal adequately with the visitors' existing meanings and belief systems. The small accumulation of facts is likely to disappear in a relatively short time period unless it is connected to enduring knowledge systems held by the traveller. As a major conceptual scheme for understanding the complexity of tourist learning, or lack of learning, the social-representations framework offers a substantial new direction for tourism researchers. It has been used sparingly in tourism analysis (Crick, 1989; Pearce *et al.*, 1996), but is developing into a core account for understanding how people respond to information in other arenas – their responses to the mass media, for example, or to the effects of technology or in studies of deviance (Joffe, 2003; Verkuyten *et al.*, 1994; Wagner *et al.*, 2002).

Social Representation Theory

The concept of social representations developed by Moscovici (1972, 1973) has been mentioned earlier in this volume in summarising tourist stereotypes, but will be treated more extensively here. At core, *social representations* are mini-theories or branches of knowledge in their own right with a characteristic kind of discourse. They are held by individuals and shared by social groups. Moscovici proposed that the term social representations should be applied to knowledge and belief systems that exist in ordinary communication rather than to specialist knowledge realms that have their own structure (such as science or religion). Importantly, Moscovici argued that social representations should be seen as dynamic and responsive to change over time, space and cultures. Social representations are particularly sensitive to the influence of others. Jaspars and Fraser (1984) noted that social representations are social in at least three senses: they originate socially, they describe or represent an aspect of the social world, and they are shared with others.

Several authors have noted that there is an ambiguity or residual unease about what social representations actually are, how they are defined and indeed how useful they are (Eiser, 1986; McGuire, 1986; McKinley *et al.*, 1993). One approach to clarifying the multiple meanings lies in itemising the features of social representations (cf. Pearce *et al.*, 1996). Table 7.1 highlights the nature of social representations by adopting this itemising approach, but adds to earlier similar efforts by incorporating recent developments and elaborations of the theory.

The multiple intersecting features of social representations theory as an

Table 7.1 Social representations: Key features

Defining ideas for social representations	Explanatory statement
Systems of knowledge	Social representations are complex meta-systems of everyday knowledge and include values, beliefs and attitudes. They are mini theories or branches of knowledge in their own right.
Content and structure	Both content and structure of the knowledge system are important.
Central and peripheral elements	Central elements are seen as irrefutable, core ideas which are very difficult to change. Peripheral elements are the operational parts of social representations; they are conditional guides to action.
Reality organisation	Social representations assist in organising and defining reality, but they are not merely cognitive summaries but contain guides to action and response.
Applicable to conflict settings	Social representations help understand conflict by contrasting group knowledge systems and recognising power.
Centrality of communication	Social representations are not individual beliefs but are public and shared with communication being central to their continuity.
Uncertainty	Social representations make the unfamiliar familiar.
Metaphor as process	Through analysis, metaphors and comparisons social representations fit and synthesise new information into existing or extended understanding.
Image	Social representations usually have an image and a visual component.
External visibility	Social representations can be 'seen' in social and cultural artefacts and forms.
Identity	Sharing social representations is central to identity group formation and behaviour.
Dynamic	Social representations are changing systems of knowledge. Individuals influence and create changes in social representations but so do larger communication processes such as the media.
Social connection	Social representations provide a commonality for discourse and interaction connecting people to each other.
Other knowledge realms	Social representations can be influenced by other knowledge systems such as science or religion but in turn influence these systems.
Culturally bound – culturally shared	Social representations can differ across and within cultures but attention to shared representations amongst cultures and group can exist and should be studied.

Sources of information: Breakwell and Canter (1993), Crick (1989), Doise (1993), Farr and Moscovici (1984), Halfacree (1993), Huguet and Latane (1996), Jaspars and Fraser (1984), Joffe (2003), Moliner (1995), Moscovici (1972, 1973, 1981, 1984, 1988), Pearce, Moscardo and Ross (1996), Wagner *et al.* (2002)

account of dynamic, socially-dependent systems of knowledge held by individuals and groups enhances the discussion of learning already considered in this chapter. The social representations approach confirms the importance of identifying the existing knowledge base in assessing learning in tourism settings (cf. Hammitt, 1998). It also draws attention to the structure of information and how central and peripheral beliefs may affect the incorporation of new material (Cole *et al.*, 1997).

Additionally a social representation account is allied to the discursive tourist. The ways in which tourists communicate with one another, with reference groups, or with service personnel are all central to social representations. Halfacree (1993) notes that Potter and Wetherell (1987) have criticised social representations theory as still being too cognitive and feel that defining a satisfactory degree of consensus in the knowledge systems is a problem. Instead Potter and Wetherell prefer to emphasise a:

> lexicon or register of terms and metaphors drawn upon to characterise and evaluate actions and events. (Potter & Wetherell, 1987: 138)

This criticism loses the image element of social representations which, at least for tourists experiencing places and destinations, as argued in Chapter 4, needs to be retained and strengthened to account for tourist-related behaviours. The visitor accounts of Mount Cook provided by Stewart *et al.* (1998) and of farm visits by Lee and Uzzell (1980) are strongly visual in the ways visitors reflect on and record their experiences. For visitor learning in tourism settings, the social representations approach blends language and imagery in a highly suitable conceptual fusion.

Another strength of the social representations approach lies in identifying the issue that seeking changes in visitor attitudes and knowledge may only partially account for the effects of travel experience. Social representations may indeed simply be strengthened and consolidated by the on-site experiences. There is evidence from the vast literature on attitude that direct contact with objects and settings provides respondents with a greatly-enhanced confidence in their beliefs, values and knowledge systems. Travel, too, may be affecting social representations in this powerful confirmatory style. The possibility of empirically investigating the strength with which place images, attitudes and beliefs are held as a consequence of tourists' experiences flows directly from this expansive view of people's knowledge systems.

The concept of *eudaimonia* was employed at the start of this chapter to promote a wide view of the outcomes of travel experience for the traveller. The focus of attention has been on satisfaction, conceived broadly in both its instrumental and its expressive forms. Additionally, a wide view of learning and knowledge acquisition has been advanced with factual gains being noted, but broader systems of knowledge accounts being highlighted. There are other consequences of travelling that benefit human flourishing as encoded in *eudaimonia*. Travellers may develop life-related skills as well as benefit in terms of fitness and health. Identifying these travel-based skills (such as managing finances, dealing with novelty and confronting one's own limitations) is a subject that has just started to be investigated in the tourism literature (Foster, 2003; Kuilboer, 2003). The direction of this work can be positively shaped by experiences in the satisfaction and learning fields. It is desirable to conceptualise these new studies that seek to determine the wide benefits of tourism with an expansive conceptual framework where language, discourse and imagery are all considered in the full treatment of the topics.

Social representations theory promises to be a major conceptual pathway in building the next generation of studies that explore tourists' reflections on, and the further outcomes of, their experiences.

Chapter 8

Synthesis and Further Analysis

Introduction

The amount of information on tourism topics flowing through the world's multiple communication channels is daunting to the researcher, the student and the practitioner. Lew *et al.* (2004) observe that there are more than 80 tourism journals, each of which produces at least 100 pages of text annually. As well as scholarly journals, there are rising numbers of monographs, edited books, technical reports, website publications and conference proceedings. Tourism is studied and reported in many languages and the work of analysts in Spanish, Korean, French, Mandarin, Dutch, Turkish and Croatian constitutes a long and continuing contribution to global analysis.

For the author and readers of a book such as this, the information-flow problem is an acute one, since the advent of 'the latest' literature might be seen to prompt any author into a never-ending cycle of revisions and, further, to prompt readers to doubt if the work reported is indeed 'up to date' or still useful. As noted in Chapter 1, Wurman (1989) suggested that an intelligent response to such deluges of information is to be guided by a map or system, thus avoiding totally time-dependent limitations. In brief, this volume has attempted to provide an overall outline and a set of conceptual schemes to guide readers in, through and around enduring topics in tourist behaviour. These achievements will be summarised in this final chapter, and then placed in an even broader framework of tourism studies and their purpose. Using this larger framework, suggestions for the continuing conceptual and methodological development of tourist behaviour studies will then be outlined.

Conceptual Schemes and Tourist Behaviour

The early pages of this volume raised the question of who is interested or concerned with tourist behaviour. The answers provided identified an array of interested parties: tourists themselves, tourist business operators, public management agency personnel, tourism researchers and analysts and, occasionally, media figures and politicians. This kind of broad answer to such a basic question has shaped the range of topics and studies discussed. Further, it allowed the presentation of key topics to vary and hence meet some different kinds of needs likely to be expressed by interested parties. For example, integral or internal benchmarking approaches to satisfaction were presented, and these are likely to be of direct interest to tourist managers. By way of contrast, few people in the tourist business are likely to be overly concerned with how much tourists learn, or what skills they develop during travelling, whereas interpretive officers working in public management agencies might find this to be core information that helps them appraise their own performance. In a less functional mode, tourists themselves may be quite interested in their own ability to cope in a cross-cultural encounter, and find it rewarding to analyse their experiences and read about and compare them with the adventures and misadventures of others.

A brief return to the problem of information flow and a tourism-derived metaphor might help to clarify the purpose and consequence of approaching tourist behaviour by developing and enhancing a set of conceptual schemes. The great waterfalls of the world – Niagara, Victoria, Iguazu – are all characterised by rushing and apparently ceaseless torrents of water. Any analyst of tourist behaviour occupies a position akin to a thirsty traveller standing at the base of such waterfalls endeavouring to drink. As reported already in this chapter, the flow of information is torrential, so simply being a passive recipient is unlikely to be effective. Our would-be analyst, like our thirsty traveller, needs ways of imposing some order on at least subsections of the torrent. The conceptual schemes developed in and deduced from the tourist behaviour studies reported here may not last for a long time; they may be first approximations in our ability to catch some of the core information flow but they represent convenient containers for personal and shared synthesis and survival.

Table 8.1 summarises many of the themes and schemes highlighted in this volume. It is not a complete rendering of all the concepts discussed but it does serve as a marker of areas of attention and achievement.

Two topics are slightly hidden from view in Table 8.1. First, the variety of topics and schemes obscures the issue of how the tourist has been seen and considered throughout this volume. The challenge here is to articulate clearly the overarching view of the tourist developed in previous chapters in order to examine the consistency and utility of the approach. A second topic is also lurking within Table 8.1 and is manifested at times in previous chapters. This is the style of research undertaken and its usefulness to the larger tourism world. This concern is informed by broader sociological and epistemological accounts of the overall purpose of tourism research. While the two topics are ultimately connected, since how one views the tourist is usually linked to the purpose of the research, the two covert issues can be addressed in separate ways. The first concern will be examined by drawing together comments made in previous chapters on how tourists behave and how the tourist can be viewed. The larger yet interconnected issue of the

Table 8.1 A thematic and conceptual scheme summary of tourist behaviour

Themes	*Concepts and conceptual schemes*
Social roles of the tourist How tourists are viewed, what tourists do, distinctive features of being a tourist, implications of travelling to other places	• Stereotype analysis • Social representations • Role theory, including role distance, altercasting, role conflict, role prescriptions • The outsider and flaneur roles • Liminality and liminoid space
Tourist demographics and product classifications How observable characteristics account for tourist behaviour, understudied groups of tourists, tourists with focused interests, naming of tourist groups	• Phase and stage models • Cultural differences, classifications • Muted voices, gender analysis • Specialisation • Experience outcomes
Motivation and tourist behaviour: What psychological needs shape travel behaviour, how these motives might change over time and form a pattern for understanding tourist motivation	• Travel career pattern • Life cycle • Travel experience levels
Destination choice What forces are at work when people choose a destination, how destinations are imagined and imaged, how these images are built and how they are acted upon in selecting holiday places	• Multi-attribute destination schema • Cognitive maps and image analysis • Attitude theory • Choice set models • Activity augmented destination choice model
Tourist-tourist relationships What do tourists think of the presence of others and under what circumstances are these co-actors seen as contributors to or detractors from the travel experience?	• Goal interference hypotheses • Tourist gaze • In group-out group scheme • Familiar strangers, the flaneur • Social situations analysis
Travellers, hosts and others How do tourists interact with other cultural groups? What are the difficulties and how can these be understood in a framework which directs attention to improving cultural interaction?	• Culture shock components • Co-ordinated management of meaning
Travellers' on-site experiences How travellers appraise and value on-site experiences. What techniques manage and shape tourists' on-site experiences? How do tourists use and respond to the information and interpretation to fulfil their motives and social goals?	• Sustainability enhanced place model • Authenticity and performance • The concept • Skilled performance • Mindfulness
Reflections on experience: Satisfaction and learning What is the totality of human flourishing or growth achieved by travelling? How can satisfaction and enjoyment be understood and assessed for multiple stakeholder purposes? How much do tourists learn and how do different kinds of learning fit with existing knowledge? What other subtle benefits adhere to the travel experience?	• *Eudaimonia* • Expectancy/confirmation/ disconfirmation paradigm • Nordic School of *post hoc* assessment • Benchmarking approaches • Knowledge structures and • Social representations

style of tourism research requires its own treatment and a model of contemporary tourism study.

Studying the Tourist

It was noted in Chapter 1 that the present treatment of tourist behaviour is enriched by, but not very dependent on, a distillation of personal experiences. It relies much more on the empirical work and conceptual contributions of an immediate and extended research circle with valuable and numerous contributions from a wider college of authors. This approach sees observable activities and mental processes guiding and resulting from social life as the content area of tourist behaviour study. It recognises the role of the human body and its physical characteristics as worthy of some attention in appraising how people deal with and respond to new settings. Tourist behaviour is seen as distinct from consumer behaviour partly because tourism has distinctive phases of experience and partly because tourists have the power to transform their ongoing product experiences. Consumer behaviour research is seen to be an inexact and imperfect match in studying large sections of tourist behaviour. There are multiple extensions and links between tourists and other terms of interest, including customers, clients, users, visitors and, at times, consumers. Tourist behaviour is arguably important to many parties and stakeholders; it is a foundation for much tourism study but is certainly not core to all tourism topics and research concerns.

Chapter 2 identified the value of seeing some broad commonalities in tourist behaviour while remaining aware of the sin of homogenisation – the tendency to be overly simplistic or overgeneralise about tourists. It reviewed some stereotypes about tourists and offered the insight that such stereotypes revealed much about the values and needs of the commentators presenting them. It introduced the value of a social representations framework, as a way of describing not just how tourists themselves view the world, but also how analysts view tourists viewing the world. Tourists were depicted as filling roles, but an active view of the older versions of role theory was portrayed, with role performances being variously embraced or modified or against which rebellion was sought. The basic role responsibilities of the tourist as externally defined by some commentators were considered, particularly as these formulations apply to the important topic of promoting sustainable tourist behaviour. The implicit ability of tourists to control their world in these prescriptive statements effectively reinforces earlier emphases on the socially active and self-determining experience view of tourists. The tourist as an outsider, a person who moves through a community and has a privileged viewing and interaction status was considered. The mobility of the tourist was further emphasised in frameworks where transition phases in the travel journey were noted as tourists move from ordinary profane states of being through liminoid or threshold modes where life's possibilities are expanded before once again returning them to the profane. There is a structured inevitability to these liminoid views of the tourists' journey, but it is not incompatible with the sub-text view that the tourist still has to work at the encounters and learn how to manage new people in new settings.

The consistent theme that the tourist has agency (power to influence how his or her experience is formed) was reinforced by an account of culture shock, where mental and physical preparations were seen as the allies of effective performance as judged by reduced stress on the inter-acting parties. Tourist behaviour in the cross-cultural context, it was argued, differs from that of diplomats, business persons and migrants owing to the stimulation associated with achieving short-term goals in novel settings. Tourists exist in three cultures (a tourist culture, the host culture and residual elements of their accompanying home culture), and a portrayal of their behaviour can be conceptualised in the interaction of these tri-cultural frameworks. Tripographics, unlike demographics, repre-sents a set of variables that uniquely portray tourist behaviour in external, etic classificatory frameworks. These variables include activity profiles, trip purpose, travel arrangements, length of stay and destination visit patterns. Tourists are also often understood and cast within the framework of their product choices. In particular, tourists classified as generalists or specialists or variants along such a continuum represent another researcher-derived scheme for organising visitor segments. Chapter 2 concluded with a model classifying tourists according to pre-travel experience commit-ment, the on-site style of interacting with the setting and post-experience outcomes. The tourist role in summary was seen as ambiguous, open to restructuring and requiring physical and psychological work and adjust-ment.

Chapters 3 and 4 offered more specific tailored understandings of tour-ists' mental processes and cognitive states. In Chapter 3 where the concern was with developing one specific approach to tourist motivation, it was argued, and evidence was provided to support the view, that travellers exhibit changing motivational patterns over life stages and with mounting levels of travel experience. The pattern of motives is dynamic, reflecting both individual and larger social change. Tourist behaviour is accounted for by more than one single motive. The framework for examining the tourist here mixes emic and etic accounts. The perspective of the tourist as assessed with standardised response scales is built on an emic measure that comprehensively appraises tourists' range of motives. In the material reviewed on destination-image, the tourist is depicted as both a passive collector of information and an active seeker of destination-based material.

The phasing of these two tourist styles depends on the would-be traveller's position in a destination choice process, with the more purposeful and continuing information collection occurring when the choices are becoming more emphatic. Social processes and relationships are heavily implicated in collecting information and guaranteeing its quality. Additionally social dynamics frequently operate to situate the tourist in a travel party where compromise and the promise of mutual fulfilment guide the tourist's choice behaviour.

In Chapter 5, which reviewed how tourists deal with other people while travelling, travellers were frequently described as building their experiences and managing their relationships. They do this building and constructing as a part of their everyday activities in a preconscious state. That is, they do not habitually or explicitly decide to act in certain ways to shape their experience but rather express these constructions in mundane behaviours including conversation, activity participation and day-to-day living. While travellers are not explicitly aware of the managed social construction of some of their experiences, if attention is drawn to their role they report that it is understandable and consistent with reflecting on their own experiences. Even those occupying more casual roles, such as the flaneur, are still observers of the world engaged in synthesising information using other people as reference points and mentally summarising their encounters with people and places. Some limited attention was given in Chapter 5 to teleological perspectives, where tourists' present actions are largely determined by anticipated future outcomes. It was also noted that tourists invent and reinvent themselves in discourse – at times they play with the role of being a tourist – and these actions can serve their larger motivational purposes.

In Chapters 6 and 7 further active participatory, performance-based accounts of tourist experiences were highlighted. Chapter 6 stressed the way in which contemporary post-modern tourists evaluate on-site experiences, including their appreciation of sincerity and effort. Multisensory immersion in experiences, it was reported, makes a difference in the evaluation and credibility of cultural and natural settings. Spontaneity and naturalness as two dimensions of experience were seen to reflect tourists' own participation and immersion in the setting and to support the judged human effort or qualities of the sites visited. The foreground of attention in Chapter 7 was the communication amongst tourists, their friends and contacts. This was viewed as a core mechanism, not just to strengthen intragroup bonds but as a mechanism for understanding oneself and what has been achieved in enjoyment, satisfaction, learning and skill development. It was proposed that tourists can be mindfully or mindlessly engaged in their experiences: when mindful they are likely to be learning and reorganising their social representations of the world.

In all of these traditions and accounts, a consistent view of the tourist as an active socially embedded individual manipulating and managing experience according to motivational patterns and within a context of social representations that frame the phenomenon encountered was repeatedly emphasised. There is more work to be done and more cases to be considered, and integration among the perspectives could be pursued further in new studies. To mount such investigations, both in methodological and theoretical terms, it is useful to turn initially to the second of the two issues seen as covert but related to Table 8.1 – the understanding of tourism research styles and goals.

The Purposes of Tourism Research

The approach taken here to understand and explicate the purposes of tourism research is an interpretive one and is an attempt to provide a purposeful structure to locate and inform the future study of tourist behaviour. To restate the style being adopted, this analysis of the goals of tourism research is qualitative rather than quantitative; it is an approach that begins with the author's personal immersion in the activity.

These personal insights are informed and supported in the following analysis by four key sources of information and inspiration. These include academic treatment of whole areas of scholarship (Becher, 1989; Burrell & Morgan, 1979; Fuchs, 1992; Outhwaite, 2000; Rosnow, 1981; Schon, 1987). A second source of information resides in the appraisals of the specific disciplinary contributions to tourism (Graburn & Jafari, 1991; Jafari, 2000; Jafari & Ritchie, 1981; Tribe, 2004). In addition, the debates that have arisen in fostering a qualitative research tradition in tourism are influential in helping to characterise the purposes of tourism research (Jamal & Hollinshead, 2001; Phillimore & Goodson, 2004; Riley & Love, 2000; Walle, 1997). A fourth and central source of information includes the close analysis of tourism study developed specifically by tourism scholars (Aramberri, 2001; Cooper, 2003; Dann, 1996a; Echtner, 1999; Faulkner *et al.*, 1995; Gunn, 1994b; Leiper, 1995; Pearce, 1993a, 2004; Ryan, 1997b; Seaton, 1996; Tribe, 1997).

From the author's immersion experiences as well as the wide ambit of issues discussed in the research literature, several frames of analysis can be identified. First, the focus of attention is on academic tourism research and its purposes. This kind of research can be distinguished from government and industry-based research efforts that have some different overall agendas (Jafari, 1990; Pearce, 1993a). The agendas for government-based studies are much more directed towards market analysis, statistics collection schemes that inform policy and provide classifications of activity. The consultancy-based work conducted for industry organisations and businesses has an immediate and applied focus often for local profit motives and occasionally to support advocacy in relation to rebutting or antici- pating government policy. By way of contrast the focus on academic tourism research is knowledge-oriented and represents attempts to meet the needs of the multiple stakeholder with accessible, quality-controlled information. Rapport among these different research cultures has been seen as increasingly valuable, but major institutional forces continue to support the separate cultures of analysis (Cooper, 2003).

A multi-dimensional space can be proposed here as defining specifically academic tourism research. There are three dimensions, each of which has two poles that characterise and define the space. These dimensions are the interpretive–functional dimension, the macro–micro scale of analysis and the emancipatory–regulatory dimension. These dimensions can be con- ceived as related to one another in different ways, with a closer link among the interpretive–emancipatory poles and the regulatory and functional poles. It needs to be restated that the approach taken here is itself interpre- tive; it is an informed and subjective appraisal, but the kind of spatial portrayal of tourism research being presented is similar to the multi-dimen- sional scaling analysis outputs obtained from quantitative studies (cf. Pearce & Fenton, 1994). The relationships among the dimensions in the tourism studies space are presented in Figure 8.1.

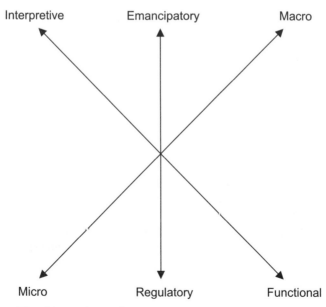

Figure 8.1 The dimensions of tourism study

The dimensions portrayed in Figure 8.1 follow some of the earlier writing of Burrell and Morgan (1979) with select influences deriving from Becher (1989), Farrell and Twining-Ward (2004), Rojek and Urry (1997a) and Tribe (2004).

The *emancipatory–regulatory* dimension classifies the space along a continuum which, at the emancipatory end, emphasises new and revolutionary initiatives in tourism system thinking. Studies at the other regulatory pole effectively preserve power relations and promote efficient business practices.

The *interpretive–functional* dimension classifies the space according to studies which, at the interpretive pole, are qualitative, emic and directed at a subjective understanding of tourism. Analyses at the functional end are quantitative, etic in character, and seek generalisations from empirical relationships.

The *macro–micro* dimension organises the space according to the scale of tourism being considered, with the macro pole referring to studies of large systems and whole regions. By way of contrast, the micro scale applies to sites as well as to more individual and small group analyses.

It is possible to locate, in broad terms, the contributions of disciplinary areas to the study of the specialism of tourism. The term specialism is used deliberately to indicate an emerging applied field of study having only some of the features of long-established coherent study fields usually referred to as disciplines (cf. Pearce, 1993a; Rojek & Urry, 1997a; Tribe, 1997). It is important to note that the disciplines considered, such as geography and economics, are included because they have been particularly applied to the specialism of tourism. The sources of this kind of appraisal derive from the accounts provided about each discipline in Jafari (2000) as well as earlier discipline-based reviews in the *Annals of Tourism Research* in 1991. The assessment of the disciplines provided in the *Encyclopedia of Tourism* as well as in the major review work presented in the *Annals of Tourism Research* is presented in Table 8.2. The year 2000 references are to the entries in the *Encyclopedia of Tourism*. Importantly these specific references are supplemented in a major way by the numerous discipline-linked references employed to inform previous chapters of this book.

Figure 8.2 shows how the disciplines considered have been employed in tourism. But it is certainly not meant to be suggested in Figure 8.2 that all psychology, for example, contributes to the space to which it is allocated in the figure; rather it is the kind of psychology that has appeared in tourism study that is being depicted.

An important principle, that of intelligent eclecticism, underlies the territory of tourism graphic presented in Figure 8.2. It is valuable to see the synthesis of methods and concepts arising from underlying disciplinary contributions as a useful medley of effort rather than incompatible and

Table 8.2 Sources of information about the disciplines of tourism

Psychology	Pearce (2000: 471–472); Pearce and Stringer (1991); Ross (1994); Stringer (1984)
Planning	Cooper (2000: 440–441); Mohamad (2000: 441–442); Wall (2000b: 438–440); Morrison (2000: 463–464)
Marketing	Calantone (2000: 381–383); Calantone and Mazanec (1991); Mazanec (2000: 375–378); Middleton (2000: 378–379)
Business	Allcock and Przeclawiki (1990); Pizam (2000: 367–369); Roper (2000: 63); van Raaij (1986)
Ecology	Brah (2000: 198–199); Ding (2000: 195–196); Dowling (2000: 160); Farrell and Runyan (1991); Pigram (2000a: 143–195); Pigram (2000b: 198)
Management	Calantone and Mazanec (1991); Pizam (2000: 367–369); Roper (2000: 370–371)
Economics	Eadington and Redman (1991); Fayos-Sola and Pedro (2000: 164–165); Fletcher (2000: 161–163).
Law	Hartshorne (2000: 353–354); Wahab (2000a: 349–350); Wahab (2000b: 352–353)
Philosophy	Barnett (2000: 443–444; de Botton (2002); Hollinshead (2000a: 425–426); Hollinshead (2000b: 435–436)
Political science	Enloe (2000: 453); Hall (2000: 445–448); Matthews and Richter (1991); Richter (2000: 450–452)
History	Ashworth (2000: 277–278); Towner (2000: 278–280); Towner and Wall (1991)
Geography	Mitchell (2000: 251); Mitchell and Murphy (1991); Wall (2000a: 248–251).
Sociology	Cohen (2000: 544–547); Dann (2000: 543–544); Dann and Cohen (1991); Swain (1995); Wang (2000: 43–45)
Gender studies	Harrison (2000: 530–531); Kinnard (2000a: 225); Kinnard (2000b: 246–248)
Anthropology	Nash and Smith (1991); Selwyn (2000: 286–288); Smith (1992); Swain (2000: 23–26)
Recreation	Fedler and Ahola (1987); Payne (2000: 492); Simmons (2000: 488–490); Smith and Goodbey (1991).
Leisure	Fedler and Ahola (1987); Smith and Godbey (1991); Smith and Mannell (2000: 354–356)

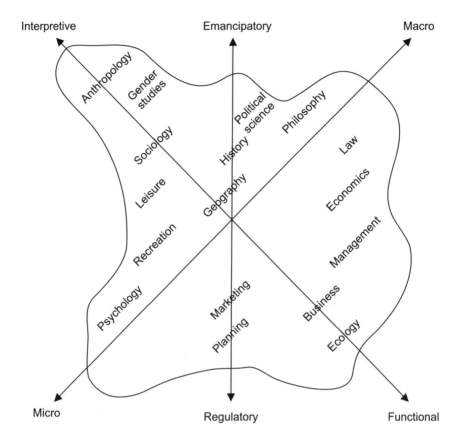

Figure 8.2 The territory of tourism: Underlying disciplines as they have been used in tourism study

competing approaches to analysis. The spirit of recent writing about fields of study and the expansion of tourism analysis reinforces the view that complex systems in tourism need the full array of styles. As Farrell and Twining-Ward observe:

> a restricted approach to research, governed by disciplinary priorities and researchers' educational backgrounds is an impairment to integration, unity and sustainability. (Farrell & Twining-Ward, 2004: 277)

Intelligent eclecticism, then, lies neither in denigrating specific realms of the tourism space nor in simply tolerating all research styles. Instead, it sees the contribution of approaches as multi-faceted and capable of being interconnected in myriad ways to tackle diverse problems. For example, if a visitor centre is being evaluated in a holistic framework then contributions from the tourism-derived components of psychology, ecology, management and economics are all likely contributors to a total appraisal. On this occasion geography, health and law may have a lesser or even non-existent role.

From the appraisal of tourism research space identified in Figure 8.2, it is now possible to describe the multiple purposes of tourism research. Some tourism research, principally that described in the upper wedge of Figure 8.2 and represented by the fields of anthropology, gender studies, sociology, political science and philosophy, rate highly in the domains of understanding and influencing change in the tourism world, often at a more macro societal scale. Other disciplinary contributions, notably ecology, business, planning and marketing, are concerned with supporting and extending existing tourism businesses and systems. These disciplinary contributions are largely etic, and have the core purpose of establishing generalisations and principles for enhancing system performance. There are similarities here to Tribe's (2004) T_1 and T_2 areas of tourism research, although some of the disciplinary classifications are cast a little differently. Importantly the present system portrays a number of disciplines (notably psychology, recreation, geography and law) as having some different and previously poorly identified roles in tourism research. For the present volume on tourist behaviour, the role of psychology and its margins with other disciplines is particularly instructive.

Some parts of psychology as applied to tourism are in close proximity to the regulatory and functional area of Figure 8.2. Examples drawn from the material already considered in this volume are motivation, decision making and the management of crowding.

At other times the field of tourist behaviour has a different purpose, approaching the margins of sociology and offering more interpretive qualitative and micro-scale insights into the phenomenon of tourism. The examples drawn from the material already considered in this volume include the role of the tourist, cross-cultural interaction and the expressive components of satisfaction study.

Tourist behaviour researchers may well be amongst the most flexible in the territory of tourism study. Psychology, a core background discipline to the study of tourist behaviour, can be applied and extended in multiple ways to meet either interpretive and emancipatory purposes or regulatory and functional roles. In schemes such as that depicted in Figure 8.2, there will always be outliers, examples of studies from disciplinary areas that break the rules and generic patterns. Nevertheless the studies that lie midway on the interpretive–functional dimension (geography, recreation, sociology, psychology, marketing) are also able to draw on a wide range of methodologies to meet the varied purposes of research. Again this flexibility offers the promise that tourist behaviour studies, which if not conceived within psychology are usually framed within one of the other disciplines in the mid-range, can be developed in the future using multiple methods and benefiting from substantial efforts in the area of methodological innovation.

Pearce and Yagi (2004) suggest that there are four particular sources of methodological innovation in tourism research, some of which can be applied directly to tourist behaviour study. The four sources of innovation derive from:

- opportunities to use new technologies;
- the growing acceptance of qualitative research;
- extending studies into as-yet-underexplored cultures with much potential for comparative work;
- commercial imperatives requiring research to be timely and resource efficient.

The four sources of methodological innovation, and some of the examples deriving from them, are depicted in Table 8.3.

Employing any one or even triangulating the methods reported in Table 8.3 is unlikely to be effective unless linked to the expansion and further development of the conceptual schemes for understanding tourist behaviour that have already been reviewed. One can also suggest some innovative ways to augment the stock of theoretical and conceptual knowledge in tourism, or more accurately, ways to trial new conceptual schemes and insights. Pearce (2004) following creativity and theory construction approaches suggested by Gergen (1983) and de Bono (1992) has argued that tourism can benefit from four sources of conceptual innovation. These innovations derive from greater attention to the metaphors underlying tourist behaviour and a trialling of new metaphors. The existing metaphors such as gaze, thresholds, balance and patterns of behaviour could well be supplemented by other views such as Rojek and Urry's (1997a) use of computer filing and indexing or Clarke and Clegg's notions of transformation, organic systems and elasticity of tolerance (1998).

Additional methods for stimulating and extending conceptual schemes include the full extension of current behaviours and circumstances to logical extremes. An example here might be studying the behaviour of those who travel for years at a time as well as those who never leave an area and refuse to participate in any form of tourism. Attention to the forgotten and muted voices in tourism markets (such as the disabled, the very rich and the deeply critical) might also repay attention, with the possibility of increasing the number of ways in which some kinds of tourist behaviour are considered. For those with a strong interest in cross-cultural topics and experiences, the unique and special relationship concepts that exist in some

Table 8.3 Sources and examples of methodological innovation in tourism research

Source	Technique	Research example
Technology	Internet surveys	Tierney (2000); Schonland and William (1996); Yuan *et al.* (2003)
	Internet as data source: • marketing/businesses	Connell and Reynolds (1999); Law and Leung (2000); Preitz (2000); Wan (2002); Wober (2003)
	• travellers' accounts	Yagi (2001)
	• tourism plans/policies	Sharma *et al.* (2000)
	Computer-assisted questionnaire coding	Anderson and Shaw (1999); Andsager and Drzewiecka (2002)
	Digital photography for quasi experiments	Inglis *et al.* (1999); Pearce and Hyvonen (2003); Yagi and Pearce (2002)
Qualitative research tolerance	Conversational interviews	Klemm (2002); Loker-Murphy, Pearce (1995); Murphy (2001); Pearce (1990b); Ryan (1995b); Sorensen (2003)
	Behavioural observation: • tracking/timing	Bowen (2002); Getz, O'Neill and Carlsen (2001); Moscardo (1999); Seaton (1997)
	• immersion	Weber (2001); Bowen (2002); Pearce (1980); Stewart and Hull (1996)
	Expanded focus groups	Ap and Wong (2001); Hovinen (2002); Ray and Ryder (2003); Waller and Lea (1999), Williams and Lawson (2001); Yagi (2003)
	Future wheels	Benckendorff (2004)
	Mental maps	Guy, Curtis and Crotts (1990); Young (1999)
Cross-cultural emphasis	Critical incidents	Callan (1998); Callan and Lefebve (1997); Jackson *et al.* (1996); Pearce and Greenwood (1999); Woods (2000)
	Culture assimilators	Pearce *et al.* (1998), Bhawuk and Brislin (2000)
	Comparative analyses	Enoch (1996); Gursoy and Chen (2000); Kim and Prideaux (2003); Pearce, D. (1993); Pizam and Sussmann (1995)
Commercialisation agendas	Rapid assessment techniques	Hampton (1998); Louisiana Recreation and Tourism Assessment Team (1987)
	Benchmarking archives	Kozak (2002)
	Environmental audits	Carter and O'Reilly (1999)

cultures deserve sustained attention. Researchers from Western cultural traditions are at the beginning of understanding how both domestic and international tourists are affected by such human arrangements and views of life as those embodied in *guanxi* (the Chinese term for the web of relationships and their reciprocity), *kwarm sanuk* (the Thai term for the intrinsic pleasure of participating), *akogare* (the Japanese term for the respect for Western styles), and *kibun* and *nunchi* (the paired Korean terms for the importance of assessing other people's moods and the skill to assess those moods). Theoretical innovation and topic selection in tourism may require all of the new methods already presented, as well as traditional social science techniques, to advance an international understanding of tourist behaviour.

Concluding Remarks

The study of tourist behaviour looks set for an assured future in the territory of tourism research. As outlined in detail in this volume, there are numerous themes to explore, a developing array of conceptual schemes to inform these topics and both traditional and innovative approaches to undertake that exploration. The purposes of tourism research are varied, and significant achievements can be recorded and proposed in two realms: the functional regulatory style of work and the interpretive emancipatory sector of tourism study. Extensive documentation justifying achievements and progress in both sectors can be cited and the numerous studies reviewed throughout previous chapters attest to the enthusiasm for progressing understanding and action in these different areas.

This monograph commenced with the observation that the author, like many readers, has been fortunate to experience a range of tourism locations, activities and challenges. During the final stages of writing this book one of the research staff of the James Cook University tourism team concluded her contract and set forth on a European travel schedule. The concerns, aspirations and comments of this traveller in communicating these experiences to friends and colleagues reflect much of what has been discussed in these chapters. An understanding of the demographics and multiple motives of travellers, the decisions made and the on-site experiences enjoyed are all displayed in the following communication. Importantly, the significance of relaying experiences to others, that is the self-aware discursive and reflective role that has been seen as central to the tourist experience is also revealed in the communication. The effort at managing oneself and one's social relationships is also core to the expressive processes. The email, an entirely unsolicited account of the individual's first experience in Italy, is reproduced unabridged (but with permission) and embodies the raw material of experience that preceding chapters have reviewed:

Hello from Italia!

Would you believe I just spent ages writing an email and thensomehow lost it! I am so annoyed – now I have to remember what I wrote. Here I go again ...

Well I'm now in a little town called Manarola in a region called the Cinque Terre – five coastal towns in hiking distance from each other. The scenery here is really amazing – colourful little houses built into the Cliffside. I'm loving it here because it is so much quieter away from the bigger cities, and the food (which has been delicious everywhere) is much cheaper.

I spent last week in Florence and felt much safer here than in Napoli. The first few days I did my own thing including getting a dose of culture by visiting the Uffizi Gallery. The works by Botticelli were my favourites, particularly the 'Birth of Venus' and 'Primavera (Spring)'. Mamma Mia for all you women who love to shop (Sandra, Marissa, Lauren, May ...) Florence (Firenze) is the place for you! I could have gone berserk here if I had the money and the room in my backpack, but I had to settle for a few token souvenirs.

On Thursday and Friday last week I teamed up with some other women at my hostel to do some day trips from Firenze to Siena and a small town called Lucca. Jacqueline from Mexico and Melanie from Germany. I am really enjoying all the discussions with other travellers.

Just one last thing – did I tell you about my visit to the Pompeii ruins near Napoli the other week? Weren't they an erotic bunch back then! Many of the mosaics they recovered from the ruins, which are now housed in the Naples Archeological museum, were very sexual. As an example, one famous one is called 'Do it slowly' – you get the picture! I was also intrigued by the collection of penis sculptures. One standout was the penis with wings that had a smaller penis for a tail and two penis's (what is the plural for penis!) for horns. Very weird ...

Okay, I'm think I'll go now before I lose this again. This is gonna cost me a fortune because I've now been connected for over an hour. At 4.50 euro ($8) or so an hour, quite a costly exercise!!

Ciao for now

It is indeed 'Ciao for now' in the study of tourist behaviour but like this and other travellers' experiences there is undoubtedly much more to come in the near future.

References

Ahmed, Z. and Kron, F. (1992) Understanding the unique consumer behaviour of Japanese tourists. *Journal of Travel and Tourism Marketing* 1 (3), 73–86.

Ahmed, Z.U. (1991) The influence of the components of a state's tourist image on product positioning strategy. *Tourism Management* 12, 331–340.

Allcock, J. and Przeclawiki, K. (1990) Tourism in centrally planned economies. *Annals of Tourism Research* 17 (1), whole issue.

Alt, M.B. and Shaw, K.M. (1984) Characteristics of ideal museum exhibits. *British Journal of Psychology* 75, 25–36.

Altman, J. and Finlayson, J. (1993) Aborigines, tourism and sustainable development. *Journal of Tourism Studies* 4 (1), 38–50.

Anderson, M.J. and Shaw, R.N. (1999) A comparative evaluation of qualitative data analytic technique in identifying volunteer motivation in tourism. *Tourism Management* 20 (1), 99–106.

Andsager, J.L. and Drzewiecka, J.A. (2002) Desirability of differences in destinations. *Annals of Tourism Research* 29 (2), 401–421.

Ap, J. and Wong, K.K.F. (2001) Case study on tour guiding: Professionalism, issues and problems. *Tourism Management* 22 (5), 551–563.

Applegate, J.F. and Clarke, K.E. (1987) Satisfaction levels of birdwatchers: An observation on the consumptive–nonconsumptive continuum. *Leisure Sciences* 21, 81–102.

Aramberri, J. (2001) The host should get lost: Paradigms in the tourism theory. *Annals of Tourism Research* 28 (3), 738–761.

Argyle, M., Furnham, A. and Graham, J. (1981) *Social Situations*. Cambridge: Cambridge University Press.

Armstrong, J. (2003) *Conditions of Love: The Philosophy of Intimacy.* London: Penguin.

Ashcroft, F. (2001) *Life at the Extremes: The Science of Survival*. London: Flamingo.

Ashworth, G. (2000) Historical tourism. In J. Jafari (ed.) *Encyclopedia of Tourism* (pp. 277–278). London: Routledge.

Ashworth, G. (2003) Heritage, identity and places: For tourists and host communities. In S. Singh, D. Timothy and R.K. Dowling (eds) *Tourism in Destination Communities* (pp. 79–99). Wallingford: CABI Publishing.

Ashworth, G.J. (1992) Is there an urban tourism? *Tourism Recreation Research* 17 (2), 3–8.

Ashworth, G.J. (2003) Urban tourism: Still an imbalance in attention? In C. Cooper (ed.) *Classic Reviews in Tourism* (pp. 143–163). Clevedon: Channel View Publications.

Babakus, E. and Boller, G.W. (1992) An empirical assessment of SERVQUAL. *Journal of Business Research* 24 (3), 253–268.

Bagozzi, R.P. and Warshaw, P.R. (1992) An examination of the etiology of the attitude–behaviour relation for goal-directed behaviours. *Multivariate Behavioral Research* 27, 601–634.

Bagozzi, R.P., Gruhan-Canli, Z. and Priester, J.R. (2002) *The Social Psychology of Consumer Behaviour*. Buckingham: Open University Press.

Bail, M. (1980) *Homesickness*. Harmondsworth: Penguin.

Bales, R.F. (1950) *Interaction Process Analysis*. Cambridge, MA: Addison-Wesley.

Bales, R.F. and Slater, P.E. (eds) (1955) Role differentiation in small decision-making groups. In T. Parsons and R.F. Bales (eds) *Family Socialization and Interaction Process* (pp. 259–306). Glencoe, IL: Free Press.

Ballantyne, R., Packer, J. and Beckman, F. (1998) Targeted interpretation: Exploring relationships among visitors' motivations, activities, attitudes, information needs and preferences. *Journal of Tourism Studies* 9 (2), 14–25.

Baloglu, S. and Brinberg, D. (1997) Affective images of tourism destinations. *Journal of Travel Research* 35 (4), 11–15.

Baloglu, S. and McCleary, K.W. (1999) A model of destination image formation. *Annals of Tourism Research* 26 (4), 868–97.

Bammel, G. and Bammel, L. (1992) *Leisure and Human Behaviour* (2nd edn). Dubuque, IA: WCB Group.

Barnett, L. (2000) Play. In J. Jafari (ed.) *Encyclopedia of Tourism* (pp. 443–444). London: Routledge.

Baron, R. and Byrne, D. (1997) *Social Psychology* (8th edn). Boston: Allyn and Bacon.

Barsky, J.D. (1992) Customer satisfaction in the hotel industry: Meaning and management. *Hospitality Research Journal* 16 (1), 51–73.

Bauer, T. and McKercher, R. (eds) (2003) *Sex and Tourism: Journeys of Romance, Love and Lust*. Binghampton, NY: Haworth.

Baum, T. and Lundtorp, S. (eds) (2001) *Seasonality in Tourism*. Oxford: Pergamon.

Beames, G. (2003) The rock, the reef and the grape: The challenges of developing wine tourism in Australia. *Journal of Vacation Marketing* 9 (3), 205–212.

Beard, J. and Ragheb, M. (1983) Measuring leisure motivation. *Journal of Leisure Research* 15 (3), 219–28.

Becher, T. (1989) *Academic Tribes and Territories*. Milton Keynes: The Society for Research into Higher Education and the Open University Press.

Bello, D.C. and Etzel, M.J. (1985) The role of novelty in pleasure travel experience. *Journal of Travel Research* 24 (Summer), 20–26.

Benckendorff, P. (2004) Planning for the future: A profile of Australian tourist attractions. Unpublished doctoral dissertation, James Cook University, Townsville.

Benjamin, W. (1973) *Illuminations*. Glasgow: Fontana.

Bernstein, I.H., Teng, G.K. and Garbin, C.D. (1988) *Applied Multivariate Analysis*. New York: Springer-Verlag.

Berry, J. (1969) The stereotypes of Australian states. *Australian Journal of Psychology* 21, 227–233.

Bhawuk, D.P.S. and Brislin, R.W. (2000) Cross-cultural training: A review. Applied psychology. *An International Review* 49 (1), 162–191.

Biddle, B. and Thomas, E.J. (eds) (1966) *Role Theory: Concepts and Research*. New York: Wiley.

Biglan, A. (1973) The characteristics of subject matter in different scientific areas. *Journal of Applied Psychology* 57 (3), 195–203.

Bitgood, S., Patterson, D. and Benefield, A. (1988) Exhibit design and visitor behavior: Empirical relationships. *Environment and Behavior* 20, 474–491.

Bitner, M.J. (1990) Evaluating service encounters: The effect of physical surroundings and employee responses. *Journal of Marketing* 54, 69–82.

Bitner, M.J. (1992) Servicescapes: The impact of physical surroundings on customers and employees. *Journal of Marketing* 56, 57–71.

Black, N. and Clark, A. (1998) *Tourism in North West Queensland: 1996. Tourist Characteristics, Numbers and Travel Flows*. Townsville: Tropical Savannas CRC.

Black, N. and Rutledge, J. (1996) *Outback Tourism*. Townsville: JCU Tourism.

Blalock, H. (1969) *Theory Construction from Verbal to Mathematical Formulations*. New Jersey: Prentice Hall.

Blamey, R. and Hatch, D. (1998) *Profiles and Motivations of Nature-Based Tourists Visiting Australia: Occasional Paper No. 25*. Canberra: Bureau of Tourism Research.

Blazey, M.A. (1992) Travel and retirement status. *Annals of Tourism Research* 19, 771–783.

Bonder, B. and Wagner, M. (2001) *Functional Performance in Older Adults* (2nd edn). Philadelphia: FA Davis Company.

Boniface, B.G. and Cooper, C.P. (1987) *The Geography of Travel and Tourism*. London: Heinemann.

Borun, M. and Adams, K.A. (1991) From hands on to minds on. *Visitor Studies: Theory, Research and Practice* 4, 115–120.

Bosong, Z.R.L. (2002) Roundup: Cambodia says 'no' to sex tourism. *Xinhua News Agency*, August 31. On WWW at http://80-web6.infotrac.galegroup.com. elibrary.jcu.edu.au/itw/infomark/267/769/49265035w6/purl=rc1_EAIM_0_A909 48327&dyn=3!xrn_1_0_A90948327?sw_aep=james_cook. Accessed 07.02.04.

Bowen, D. (2002) Research through participant observation in tourism: A creative solution to the measurement of consumer satisfaction/dissatisfaction (CS/D) among tourists. *Journal of Travel Research* 41 (1), 4–14.

Boxall, P. and McFarlane, B. (1993) Human dimensions of Christmas bird counts: Implications for non-consumptive wildlife recreation programs. *Wildlife Society Bulletin* 21 (4), 390–396.

Brah, N. (2000) Environmental management systems. In J. Jafari (ed.) *Encyclopedia of Tourism* (pp. 198–199). London: Routledge.

Breakwell, G.M. and Canter, D.V. (1993) Aspects of methodology and their implications for the study of social representations. In G.M. Breakwell and D.V. Canter (eds) *Empirical Approaches to Social Representations* (pp. 1–12). Oxford: Clarendon Press.

Broad, S. and Weiler, B. (1998) Captive animals and interpretation: A tale of two tiger exhibits. *Journal of Tourism Studies* 9 (1), 14–27.

Bruner, E.M. (1994) Innocents abroad. *Annals of Tourism Research* 21 (4), 889–891.

Bryan, H. (1977) Leisure value system and recreational specialization: The case of trout fishermen. *Journal of Leisure Research* 9, 174–187.

Buchanan, I. and Rosetto, A. (1997) With my swag upon my shoulder. *Occasional Paper No 24*. Canberra: Bureau of Tourism Research.

Burman, J. (2002) Gender/Tourism/Fun(?). *Annals of Tourism Research* 29 (4), 1205–1207.

Burr, S.W. (1991) Review and evaluation of the theoretical approaches to community as employed in travel and tourism impact research on rural community organisation and change. In A.J. Veal, P. Jonson and G. Cushman *Leisure and Tourism: Social and Environmental Changes* (pp. 540–553). Papers from the World Leisure and Recreation Association Congress, Sydney, 1991.

Burrell, G. and Morgan, G. (1979) *Sociological Paradigms and Organisational Analysis*. London: Heinemann.

Butler, R. (1998) Tartan mythology. The traditional tourist image of Scotland. In G. Ringer (ed.) *Destinations* (pp. 121–139). London: Routledge.

Calantone, R. (2000) Marketing research. In J. Jafari (ed.) *Encyclopedia of Tourism* (pp. 381–383). London: Routledge.

Calantone, R.J. and Johar, J.S. (1984) Seasonal segmentation using benefit segmentation framework. *Journal of Travel Research* 23 (2), 14–24.

Calantone, R.J. and Mazanec, J.A. (1991) Marketing management and tourism. *Annals of Tourism Research* 18, 103–119.

Calhoun, C. (2000) Social theory and the public sphere. In B. Turner (ed.) *The Blackwell Companion to Social Theory* (2nd edn; pp. 505–544). Oxford: Blackwell.

Callan, R. and Lefebve, C. (1997) Classification and grading of UK lodges: Do they equate to managers' and customers' perception? *Tourism Management* 18 (7), 417–428.

Callan, R.J. (1998) The critical incident technique in hospitality research: An illustration from the UK lodge sector. *Tourism Management* 19 (1), 93–98.

Canter, D. (1977) *The Psychology of Place*. London: The Architectural Press.

Carter, R.W. and O'Reilly, P. (1999) A rapid appraisal methodology for environmental auditing. *Journal of Tourism Studies* 10 (2), 14–22.

Cha, S., McCleary, K. and Uysal, M. (1995) Travel motivations of Japanese overseas travelers: A factor–cluster segmentation approach. *Journal of Travel Research* 34 (1), 33–39.

Chadee, D. and Mattson, J. (1996) Measuring customer satisfaction with tourist service encounters. *Journal of Travel and Tourism Marketing* 4 (4), 97–107.

Chanowitz, B. and Langer, E. (1980) Knowing more (or less) than you can show: Understanding control through the mindlessness/mindfulness distinction. In M. E.P. Seligman and J. Garber (eds) *Human Helplessness*. New York: Academic Press.

Charters, S. and Ali-Knight, J. (2002) Who is the wine tourist? *Tourism Management* 23, 311–319.

Chesney-Lind, M. and Lind, I.Y. (1986) Visitors as victims: Crimes against tourists in two Hawaii counties. *Annals of Tourism Research* 13, 167–191.

Child, D. (1972) *The Essentials of Factor Analysis*. London: Holt, Rinehart & Winston Ltd.

Chipman, B. and Helfrich, L. (1988) Recreation specialisations and motivations of Virginia River anglers. *North American Journal of Fisheries Management* 8, 390–98.

Clarke, T. and Clegg, S. (1998) *Changing Paradigms*. London: Harper Collins.

Classen, C., Howes, D. and Synott, A. (1994) *Aroma: The Cultural History of Smell*. New York: Routledge.

Clawson, M. and Knetsch, J.L. (1966) *Economics of Outdoor Recreation*. Baltimore: John Hopkins Press.

Cleaver, M., Muller, T.E., Ruys, H.F.M. and Wei, S. (1999) Tourism product development for the senior market, based on travel-motive research. *Tourism Recreation Research* 24 (1), 5–11.

Clift, S., Callister, C. and Luongo, M. (2002) Gay man, holidays and sex: Surveys of gay men visiting the London Freedom Fairs. In S. Clift, M. Luongo and C. Callister (eds) *Gay Tourism Culture, Identity and Sex* (pp. 231–249). London: Continuum.

Clift, S. and Forrest, S. (1999) Gay men and tourism: Destinations and holiday motivations. *Tourism Management* 20 (5), 615–625.

Clift, S., Luongo, M. and Callister, C. (eds) (2002) *Gay Tourism Culture, Identity and Sex*. London: Continuum.

Coakes, S.J. and Steed, L.G. (1999) *SPSS: Analysis Without Anguish: Versions 7.0, 7.5, 8.0 for Windows*. Brisbane: John Wiley.

Coday, B. (2000) Trial draws attention to child sex tourism. *National Catholic Reporter* 37 (3), 10. On WWW at http://80-web6.infotrac.galegroup.com.elibrary.jcu.edu. au/itw/infomark/267/769/49265035w6/purl=rc1_EAIM_0_A67374311&dyn =7!xrn_1_0_A67374311?sw_aep=james_cook. Accessed: 12.02.04.

Cohen, E. (1972) Toward a sociology of international tourism. *Social Research* 39 (1), 164–182.

Cohen, E. (1974) Who is a tourist? A conceptual clarification. *The Sociological Review* 22 (4), 527–555.

Cohen, E. (1979) Rethinking the sociology of tourism. *Annals of Tourism Research* 6 (1), 18–35.

Cohen, E. (1982) Thai girls and Farong men: The edge of ambiguity. *Annals of Tourism Research* 9, 403–428.

Cohen, E. (1988) Authenticity and commoditization. *Annals of Tourism Research* 15 (3), 371–386.

Cohen, E. (2000) Sociology. In J. Jafari (ed.) *Encyclopedia of Tourism* (pp. 544–547). London: Routledge.

Cohen, E. (2003) Transnational marriage in Thailand: The dynamics of extreme heterogamy. In T. Bauer and R. McKercher (eds) *Sex and Tourism: Journeys of Romance, Love and Lust* (pp. 57–77). Binghampton, NY: Haworth.

Cole, D.N., Hammond, T.P. and McCool, S.F. (1997) Information quantity and communication effectiveness: Low-impact messages on wilderness trailside bulletin boards. *Leisure Sciences* 19 (1), 59–72.

Cole, J.C. and Scott, D. (2000) Segmenting participation in wildlife watching. A comparison of casual wildlife watchers and serious birders. *Human Dimensions of Wildlife* 4 (4), 44–61.

Connell, J. and Reynolds, P. (1999) The implication of technological development on tourist centers. *Tourism Management* 20 (4), 501–509.

Cooper, C. (2003) Progress in tourism. In C. Cooper (ed.) *Classic Reviews in Tourism* (pp. 1–8). Clevedon: Channel View Publications.

Cooper, C. (ed.) (2003) *Classic Reviews in Tourism*. Clevedon: Channel View Publications.

Cooper, M. (2000) Planning. In J. Jafari (ed.) *Encyclopedia of Tourism* (pp. 440–441). London: Routledge.

Cox, L.J. and Fox, M. (1991) Agriculturally based leisure attractions. *Journal of Tourism Studies* 2 (2), 18–27.

Craik, J. (1997) The culture of tourism. In C. Rojek and J. Urry (eds) *Touring Cultures* (pp. 113–136). London: Routledge.

Crandall, R. (1980) Motivations for leisure. *Journal of Leisure Research* 12 (1), 45–54.

Crang, P. (1997) Performing the tourist product. In C. Rojek and J. Urry (eds) *Touring Cultures* (pp. 137–154). London: Routledge.

Crawford, J., Kippax, S., Onyx, J., Gault, U. and Benton, P. (1992) *Emotion and Gender*. London: Sage.

Crawshaw, C. and Urry, J. (1997) Tourism and the photographic eye. In C. Rojek and J. Urry (eds) *Touring Cultures* (pp. 176–195). London: Routledge.

Crick, M. (1989) Representations of international tourism in the social sciences: Sun, sex, sights, savings, and servility. *Annual Review of Anthropology* 18, 307–344.

Crompton, J. and Love, L.L. (1995) The predictive validity of alternate approaches to evaluating quality of a festival. *Journal of Travel Research* 34 (1), 11–25.

Crompton, J.L. (1979) Motivations for pleasure vacation. *Annals of Tourism Research* 6 (1), 408–424.

Crompton, J.L. and Ankomah, P.K. (1993) Choice set propositions in destination decisions. *Annals of Tourism Research* 20, 461–476.

Cronen, V. and Shuter, R. (1983) Forming intercultural bonds. In W. Gudykunst (ed.) *Intercultural Communication Theory: Current Perspectives* (pp. 89–118). Beverley Hills, CA: Sage Publications.

Crouch, G.I. (1993) Currency exchange rates and the demand for international tourism. *Journal of Tourism Studies* 4 (2), 45–53.

Csikszentmihalyi, M. (1990) *Flow: The Psychology of Optimal Experience.* New York: Harper Perennial.

Dahles, H. and Bras, K. (1999) *Tourism and Small Entrepreneurs: Development, National Policy, and Entrepreneurial Culture: Indonesian Cases.* Sydney: Cognizant Communication Corporation.

Daniel, Y.P. (1996) Tourism dance performances: Authenticity and creativity. *Annals of Tourism Research* 23 (4), 780–797.

Dann, G. (1993) Limitations in the use of 'nationality' and country of residence variables. In D. Pearce and R. Butler (eds) *Tourism Research: Critiques and Challenges* (pp. 88–112). London: Routledge and Kegan Paul.

Dann, G. (2000) Sociolinguistics. In J. Jafari (ed.) *Encyclopedia of Tourism* (pp. 543–544). London: Routledge.

Dann, G. and Cohen, E. (1991) Sociology and tourism. *Annals of Tourism Research* 18 (1), 155–169.

Dann, G. and Cohen, E. (1996) Sociology and tourism. In Y. Apostolopoulos, S. Leivadi and A. Yiannakis (eds) *The Sociology of Tourism* (pp. 301–314). New York: Routledge.

Dann, G. and Jacobsen, J.K. (2002) Leading the tourist by the nose. In G. Dann (ed.) *The Tourist as a Metaphor of the Social World* (pp. 209–236). New York: CABI Publishing.

Dann, G.M.S. (1977) Anomie, ego-enhancement and tourism. *Annals of Tourism Research* 4 (4), 184–94.

Dann, G.M.S. (1981) Tourist motivation: An appraisal. *Annals of Tourism Research* 8 (2), 187–219.

Dann, G.M.S. (1996a) *The Language of Tourism: A Sociolinguistic Perspective.* Wallingford: CABI International.

Dann, G.M.S. (1996b) Tourists' image of destination: An alternative analysis. *Journal of Travel and Tourism Marketing* 5 (1), 41–55.

Dann, G.M.S. (ed.) (2002) *The Tourist as a Metaphor of the Social World.* Wallingford: CABI.

Dann, G.M.S. and Seaton, A.V. (eds) (2001) *Slavery, Contested Heritage and Thanatourism.* New York: Haworth.

Davis, D., Birtles, A., Valentine, P., Cuthill, M. and Banks, S. (1997) Whale sharks in Ningaloo Marine Park. *Tourism Management* 18 (5), 259–271.

de Albuquerque, K. (1998) Sex, beach boys and female tourists in the Caribbean. *Sexuality and Culture* 2, 87–111.

de Albuquerque, K.D. and McElroy, J. (2001) Tourist harassment: Barbados survey results. *Annals of Tourism Research* 28 (2), 477–492.

de Bono, E. (1992) *Serious Creativity.* London: Harper Collins.

de Botton, A. (2002) *The Art of Travel.* New York: Pantheon.

Dichter, E. (1985) What is in an image? *Journal of Consumer Marketing* 2, 39–52.

Dickinson, B. and Vladimir, A. (1997) *Setting The Sea: An Inside Look at The Cruise Industry* New York: John Wiley & Sons.

Diekhoff, G. (1992) *Statistics for the Social and Behavioral Sciences: Univariated, Bivariate, Multivariate.* Dubuque: Wm C. Brown Publishers.

Dinçer, F.I. and Ertugral, S.M. (2003) Economic impact of heritage tourism hotels in Istanbul. *Journal of Tourism Studies* 14 (2), 23–34.

Ding, P. (2000) Environmental auditing. In J. Jafari (ed.) *Encyclopedia of Tourism* (pp. 195–196). London: Routledge.

Doise, W. (1993) Debating social representations. In G.M. Breakwell and D.V. Canter (eds) *Empirical Approaches to Social Representations* (pp. 157–170). Oxford: Clarendon Press.

Douglas, N. (1997) The fearful and the fanciful: Early tourists' perceptions of Western Melanesia. *Journal of Tourism Studies* 8 (1), 52–61.

Dowling, R. (2000) Ecology. In J. Jafari (ed.) *Encyclopedia of Tourism* (p. 160). London: Routledge.

Downs, R. and Stea, D. (1977) *Maps in Minds.* New York: Harper & Row.

Driver B.L. and Manfredo, M.J. (1996) Measuring leisure motivation: A meta analysis of the recreation experience preference scales. *Journal of Leisure Research* 28 (3), 188–213.

Driver, B., Brown, P. and Peterson, G. (eds) (1991) *Benefits of Leisure.* Pennsylvania: Venture Publishing.

du Cros, H. and du Cros, D. (2003) Romance, retsina and reality in Crete. In T. Bauer and R. McKercher (eds) *Sex and Tourism: Journeys of Romance, Love and Lust* (pp. 43–53). Binghampton, NY: Haworth.

Duffus, D.A. and Dearden, P. (1990) Non-consumptive wildlife-orientated recreation: A conceptual framework. *Biological Conservation* 53, 213–231.

Eadington, W. and Redman, M. (1991) Economics and tourism. *Annals of Tourism Research* 18 (1), 41–56.

Echtner, C. (1999) The semiotic paradigm: Implications for tourism research. *Tourism Management* 20 (1), 47–57.

Echtner, C.M. and Ritchie, J.R.B. (1991) The meaning and measurement of destination image. *Journal of Tourism Studies* 2 (2), 2–12.

Edwards, T. (2000) *Contradictions of Consumption: Concepts, Practices and Politics in Consumer Society.* Buckingham: Open University Press.

Ehrentraut, A. (1993) Heritage authenticity and domestic tourism in Japan. *Annals of Tourism Research* 20 (2), 262–278.

Eiser, J.R. (1986) *Social Psychology: Attitudes, Cognition and Social Behaviour.* Cambridge: Cambridge University Press.

English Tourist Board (1979) *English Cathedrals and Tourism.* London: English Tourist Board.

Enloe, C. (2000) Political stability. In J. Jafari (ed.) *Encyclopedia of Tourism* (p. 453). London: Routledge.

Enoch, Y. (1996) Contents of tour packages : A cross-cultural comparison. *Annals of Tourism Research* 23 (3), 599–616.

Etzel, M.J. and Woodside, A.G. (1982) Segmenting vacation markets: The case of the distant and near-home travelers. *Journal of Travel Research* 21 (spring), 10–24.

Evans, L.U. (1999) Measuring the benefits of multi-media interpretive centres in natural environments. In *Interpretation: The Human Factor* (pp. 51–59). Proceedings of Interpretation Australia Association National Conference, Hobart, September, 1999.

Fallon, L.D. and Kriwoken, L.K. (2003) Community involvement in tourism infrastructure: The case of the Strahan Visitor Centre. *Tasmania Tourism Management* 24, 289–308.

Fan, J. (1994) Household budget allocation patterns of Asian-Americans: Are they different from other ethnic groups. *Consumer Interests Annuals* 40, 81–88.

Farr, R. (1990) Social representations as widespread beliefs. In C. Fraser and G. Gaskell (eds) *The Social Psychological Study of Widespread Beliefs* (pp. 47–64).

Farr, R.M. (1987) Social representations: A French tradition of research. *Journal for the Theory of Social Behaviour* 17 (4), 343–369.

Farr, R.M. (1993) Common sense, science and social representations. *Public Understanding of Science* 2, 289–304.

Farr, R.M. and Moscovici, S. (1984) *Social Representations*. Cambridge: Cambridge University Press.

Farrell, B. and Runyan, D. (1991) Ecology and tourism. *Annals of Tourism Research* 18 (1), 26–40.

Farrell, B. and Twining-Ward, L. (2004) Reconceptualising tourism. *Annals of Tourism Research* 31 (2), 274–295.

Faulkner, B. and Russell, R. (1997) Chaos and complexity in tourism: In search of a new perspective. *Pacific Tourism Review* 1, 93–102.

Faulkner, B., Pearce, P., Shaw, R. and Weiler, B. (1995) Tourism research in Australia: Confronting the challenges of the 1990s and beyond. In *Tourism Research and Education in Australia* (pp. 3–25). Proceedings from the Tourism and Educators Conference, Gold Coast (1994). Canberra: Bureau of Tourism Research.

Fayos-Sola, E. and Pedro, A. (2000) Economics of scale. In J. Jafari (ed.) *Encyclopedia of Tourism* (pp. 164–165). London: Routledge.

Fedler, A.J. and Ahola, S.E. (eds) (1987) Interrelationships of leisure, recreation, and tourism. *Annals of Tourism Research* (special issue)14, 3.

Fesenmaier, D., Vogt, C. and Stewart, W.P. (1993) Investigating the influence of the welcome centre information on travel behaviour. *Journal of Travel Research* 31 (3), 47–52.

Figler, M.H., Weinstein, A.R., Sollers, J.J. and Devan, B.D. (1992) Pleasure travel (tourist) motivation: A factor analytic approach. *Bulletin of the Psychonomic Society* 30, 113–116.

Findlay, K.P. (1997) Attitudes and expenditures of whale watchers in Hermanus, South Africa. *South African Journal of Wildlife Research* 27 (2), 57–62.

Finney, B.R. and Watson, A. (eds) (1975) *A New Kind of Sugar: Tourism in the Pacific*. Honolulu: East-West Center.

Fishbein, M. (1967) A behavior theory approach to the relations between beliefs about an object and the attitude towards the object. In M. Fishbein (ed.) *Readings in Attitude Theory and Measurement* (pp. 289–400). New York: Wiley.

Fishbein, M. and Ajzen, I. (1975) *Belief, Attitude, Intention and Behavior*. Reading, MA: Addison-Wesley.

Fisher, R.J. and Price, L.L. (1991) International pleasure travel motivations and post vacation cultural attitude change. *Journal of Leisure Research* 23 (3), 193–208.

Fletcher, J. (2000) Economics. In J. Jafari (ed.) *Encyclopedia of Tourism* (pp. 161–163). London: Routledge.

Fodness, D. (1992) The impact of family life cycle on the vacation decision making process. *Journal of Travel Research* (Fall), 8–13.

Fodness, D. (1994) Measuring tourist motivation. *Annals of Tourism Research* 21 (3), 555–81.

Font, X. and Tribe, J. (eds) (2000) *Forest Tourism and Recreation. Case Studies in Environmental Management*. Wallingford: CABI Publishing.

Foo, J., McGuiggan, R. and Yiannakis, A. (2004) Roles tourists play: An Australian perspective. *Annals of Tourism Research* 31 (2), 408–427.

Fornell, C., Johnson, M.D., Anderson, E.W., Cha, J. and Bryant, B. (1996) The American Customer Satisfaction Index: Description, findings, and implications. *Journal of Marketing* 60 (4), 7–18.

Foster, F.A. (2003) The 'University of Travel': Backpackers and the development of generic skills. Unpublished honours thesis, James Cook University, Townsville.

Foster, R.J. and Jackson, E.L. (1979) Factors associated with camping satisfaction in Alberta Provincial Park campgrounds. *Journal of Leisure Research* 11 (4), 292–306.

French, C.N., Craig-Smith, S.J. and Collier, A. (1995) *Principles of Tourism.* Melbourne: Longman.

Frigden, J. (1987) Use of cognitive maps to determine perceived tourism regions. *Leisure Sciences* 9 (2), 101–117.

Fuchs, M. (2002) Benchmarking indicator systems and their potential for tracking guest satisfaction. *Tourism* 50 (2), 141–155.

Fuchs, S. (1992) *The Professional Quest for Truth: A Social Theory of Science and Knowledge.* New York: State University of New York.

Furnham, A. and Bochner, S. (1986) *Culture Shock.* London: Methuen.

Galani-Moutafi, V. (1999) The self and the other. *Annals of Tourism Research* 27 (2), 203–224.

Gale, F. and Jacobs, J. (1987) *Tourists and the National Estate.* Canberra: Australian Government Publishing Service.

Galloway, G. (1998) Motivations for leisure. In W. Faulkner, C. Tidswell and D. Weaver (eds) *Progress in Tourism and Hospitality Research 1998 Part 1* (pp. 99–108). Proceedings of the Eighth Australian Tourism and Hospitality Research Conference, Gold Coast. Canberra: Bureau of Tourism Research.

Gampbell, J. (1999) Getting your kicks without kidding around. *Time International* 153 (21), 8. On WWW at http://80-web6.infotrac.galegroup.com.elibrary.jcu. edu.au/itw/infomark/499/737/49309634w6/purl=rc1_EAIM_0_A54910448& dyn=20!xrn_1_0_A54910448?sw_aep=james_cook. Accessed 12.02.03.

Garfinkel, H. (1967) *Studies in Ethnomethodology.* Englewood Cliffs, NJ: Prentice-Hall.

Gartner, W. (1993) Image formation process. *Journal of Travel and Tourism Marketing* 2 (2/3), 191–216.

Gartner, W. and Shen, J. (1992) The impact of Tiananmen Square on China's tourism image. *Journal of Travel Research* 30 (4), 47–52.

Gee, C. and Fayos-Sola, E. (1997) *International Tourism: A Global Perspective.* Madrid: World Tourism Organisation.

Gee, C.Y., Choy, D.J.L. and Makens, J.C. (1984) *The Travel Industry.* Westport: AVI.

Gergen, K. (1978) Toward generative theory. *Journal of Personality and Social Psychology* 36 (11), 1344–60.

Gergen, K. (1983) *Toward Transformation in Social Psychology.* New York: Springer Verlag.

Gergen, K.J. (1997) The place of the psyche in a constructed world. *Theory and Psychology* 7/6, 723–746.

Getz, D. (2000) *Explore Wine Tourism: Management, Development and Destinations.* New York: Cognizant Communication Corporation.

Getz, D., O'Neill, M. and Carlson, J. (2001) Service quality evaluation at events through service mapping. *Journal of Travel Research* 39 (4), 380–390.

Gibbons, S. and Ruddell, E.J. (1995) The effect of goal orientation and place dependence on select goal interferences among winter backcountry users. *Leisure Sciences* 17, 171–183.

Gibson, H. and Yiannakis, A. (2002) Tourist roles: Needs and the life course. *Annals of Tourism Research* 29 (2), 358–383.

Gitelson, R.J. and Kerstetter, D.L. (1990) The relationship between sociodemographic variables, benefits sought and subsequent vacation behavior: A case study. *Journal of Travel Research* 28 (3), 24–29.

Glaser, B. (1992) *Basics of Grounded Theory Analysis.* Mill Valley, CA: Sociology Press.

Glaser, B. and Strauss, A. (1967) *The Discovery of Grounded Theory.* Chicago: Aldine.

Glasson, J., Godfrey, K. and Goodey, B. (1995) *Towards Visitor Impact Management: Visitor Impacts, Carrying Capacity, and Management Responses in Europe's Historic Towns and Cities.* Aldershot: Avebury.

Goffman, E. (1959) *The Presentation of Self in Everyday Life.* New York: Doubleday.

Goffman, E. (1961) *Asylums: Essays on the Social Situation of Mental Patients and Other Inmates.* New York: Doubleday Anchor.

Goffman, E. (1971) *Relations in Public.* London: Allen Lane.

Goodrich, J.N. (1977) Benefits bundle analysis: An empirical study of international travellers. *Journal of Travel Research* 16 (2), 6–9.

Gould, S.J. (1997) *Life's Grandeur. The Spread of Excellence from Plato To Darwin.* London: Vintage.

Gould, S.J. (2004) *The Hedgehog, the Fox and the Magister's Pox: Mending and Minding the Misconceived Gap Between Science and the Humanities.* London: Vintage.

Graburn, N.H. (1989) Tourism: The sacred journey. In V. Smith (ed.) *Hosts and Guests: The Anthropology of Tourism* (2nd edn; pp. 21–36). Philadelphia: University of Pennsylvania Press.

Graburn, N.H.H. and Jafari, J. (1991) Introduction: Tourism social science. *Annals of Tourism Research* 18 (1), 1–11.

Graefe, A.R. and Vaske, J.J. (1987) A framework for managing quality in the tourist experience. *Annals of Tourism Research* 14 (3), 390–404.

Greene, J.O. (1994) What sort of terms ought theories of human action incorporate? *Communication Studies* 45 (2), 187–211.

Greenwood, T. and Moscardo, G. (1999) Australian and North American coastal and marine tourists: What do they want? In N. Saxena (ed.) *Recent Advances in Marine Science and Technology, 98* (pp. 253–260). Seoul: Korea Ocean Research and Development Institute.

Greenwood, T., Moscardo, G., Woods, B., Johnstone, S., Richards, F. and Pearce, P. (2000) *Flinders Chase National Park: The Visitor Experience.* Townsville: Tourism Program, James Cook University.

Gross, R. (2001) *Psychology: The Science of Mind and Behaviour* (4th edn). London: Hodder and Stoughton.

Gudykunst, W. and Kim, Y.Y. (1997) *Communication with Strangers: An Approach to Intercultural Communication.* New York: McGraw-Hill.

Gudykunst, W. and Shapiro, R.B. (1996) Communication in everyday interpersonal and intergroup encounters. *International Journal of Intercultural Relations* 20, 19–45.

Gudykunst, W.B., Gao, G., Schmidt, K.L., Nishida, T., Bond, H.M., Leung, K., Wang, G. and Barraclough, R.A. (1992) The influence of individualism–collectivism, self-monitoring, and predicted-outcome value on communication in ingroup and outgroup relationships. *Journal of Cross-Cultural Psychology* 23 (2), 196–214.

Gullahorn, J.E. and Gullahorn, J.T. (1963) An extension of the U-curve hypothesis. *Journal of Social Issues* 19, 33–47.

Gunn, C. (1972) *Vacationscape: Designing Tourist Regions.* Austin: University of Texas.

Gunn, C.A. (1988) *Tourism Planning* (2nd edn). New York: Taylor and Francis.

Gunn, C.A. (1994a) *Tourism Planning: Basic, Concepts, Cases* (3rd edn). New York: Taylor and Francis.

Gunn, C.A. (1994b) A perspective on the purpose and nature of tourism research methods. In J.R. Brent Ritchie and C.R. Goeldner *Travel, Tourism, and Hospitality Research* (2nd edn; pp. 3–11). New York: John Wiley & Sons.

Gursoy, D. and Chen, J.S. (2000) Competitive analysis of cross cultural information search behavior. *Tourism Management* 21 (6), 583–590.

Guy, B.S., Curtis, W.W. and Crotts, J.C. (1990) Environmental learning of first-time travelers. *Annals of Tourism Research* 17 (3), 419–431.

Halfacree, K.H. (1993) Locality and social representation: Space, discourse and alternative definitions of the rural. *Journal of Rural Studies* 9 (1) 23–37.

Hall, C.M. (1994) Gender and economic interests in tourism prostitution: The nature, development and implications of sex tourism in South-East Asia. In V. Kinnaird and D. Hall (eds) *Tourism: A Gender Analysis*. Chichester: John Wiley & Sons.

Hall, C.M. (2000) Policy. In J. Jafari (ed.) *Encyclopedia of Tourism* (pp. 445–448). London: Routledge.

Hall, E.T. (1976) *Beyond Culture*. New York: Doubleday.

Hall, E.T. (2000) Context and meaning. In L. Samovar and R. Porter (eds) *Intercultural Communication* (pp. 45–60). Belmont, CA: Wadsworth.

Ham, S. (1992) *Environmental Interpretation: A Practical Guide for People with Big Ideas and Small Budgets*. Golden, CO: North American Press.

Hammitt, W.E. (1998) Cognitive processes involved in environmental interpretation. *Journal of Environmental Education* 29 (1), 11–15.

Hammitt, W.E. and Cole, D.N. (1998) *Wildlife Recreation: Ecology and Management* (2nd edn). New York: Wiley.

Hampton, M.P. (1998) Backpacker tourism and economic development. *Annals of Tourism Research* 25 (3), 639–660.

Hanan, M. and Karp, P. (1989) *Customer Satisfaction*. New York: Amacom.

Hardy, A. (2003) An investigation into the key factors necessary for the development of iconic touring routes. *Journal of Vacation Marketing* 9 (4), 314–330.

Harper, D.W. Jr (2000) Planning in tourist robbery. *Annals of Tourism Research* 27, 517–520.

Harré, R. and Secord, P. (1972) *The Explanation of Social Behaviour*. Oxford: Blackwell.

Harrison, D. (2000) Sex tourism. In J. Jafari (ed.) *Encyclopedia of Tourism* (pp. 530–531). London: Routledge.

Hartshorne, D. (2000) Legislation. In J. Jafari (ed.) *Encyclopedia of Tourism* (pp. 353–354). London: Routledge.

Hatt, J. (1982) *The Tropical Traveller*. London: Pan.

Hazelrigg, L.E. and Hardy, M.A. (2000) Scaling the semantics of satisfaction. *Social Indicators Research* 49, 147–180.

Heffernan, B.M. (1998) Evaluation techniques for the Sandy Point Discovery Center, Great Bay National Estuarine Research Reserve. *The Journal of Environmental Education* 30 (1), 25–33.

Heidegger, M. (1962) *Being and Time*. Oxford: Blackwells (first published 1927).

Herold, E., Garcia, R. and de Moya, T. (2001) Female tourists and beach boys: Romance or sex tourism? *Annals of Tourism Research* 28 (4), 978–997.

Hibbert, C. (1969) *The Grand Tour*. London: Weidenfeld & Nicolson.

Hockings, M., Stoltson, S. and Dudley, N. (2000) *Evaluating Effectiveness: A Framework for Assessing the Management of Protected Areas*. Cambridge: IUCN, The World Conservation Union.

Hofstede, G. (1980) *Culture's Consequences: Comparing Values, Behaviours, Institutions and Organizations Across Nations*. Thousand Oaks, CA: Sage Publications.

Hofstede, G. (1984) *Culture's Consequences: International Differences in Work-related Values*. Beverly Hills, CA: Sage.

Hofstede, G. (1997) *Cultures and Organisations: Software of the Mind*. New York: McGraw-Hill.

Hollender, J.W. (1977) Motivational dimensions of the camping experience. *Journal of Leisure Research* 9 (2), 111–41.

Hollinshead, K. (1999) Myth and the discourse of Texas: Heritage tourism and the suppression of instinctual life. In M. Robinson and P. Boniface (eds) *Tourism and Cultural Conflicts* (pp. 47–94). Wallingford: CABI.

Hollinshead, K. (2000a) Paradigms. In J. Jafari (ed.) *Encyclopedia of Tourism* (pp. 425–426). London: Routledge.

Hollinshead, K. (2000b) Philosophy. In J. Jafari (ed.) *Encyclopedia of Tourism* (pp. 435–436). London: Routledge.

Holt, D.B. (1995) How consumers consume: A typology of consumption practices. *Journal of Consumer Research* 22, 1–16.

Hong Kong Tourist Association (1995) *Visitor and Tourism Study for Hong Kong: Strategy Report.* Hong Kong: Hong Kong Tourist Association.

Hong, G., Kim, S.Y. and Lee, J. (1999) Travel expenditure patterns of elderly households in the US. *Tourism Recreation Research* 24 (1), 43–52.

Horne, D. (1984) *The Great Museum: The Re-presentation of History.* London: Pluto Press.

Horne, D. (1992) *The Intelligent Tourist.* McMahons Point: Margaret Gee.

Hottola, P. (2004) Culture confusions: Intercultural adaptation in tourism. *Annals of Tourism Research* 31 (2), 447–466.

Hovinen, G.R. (2002) Revising the destination lifestyle model. *Annals of Tourism Research* 29 (1), 209–230.

Howard, P. (2003) *Heritage Management, Interpretation, Identity.* London: Continuum.

Howe, M.J.A. (ed.) (1983) *Learning From Television.* London: Academic Press.

Hsieh, S., O'Leary, J.T. and Morrison, A.M. (1992) Segmenting the international travel market by activity. *Tourism Management* 13 (2), 209–223.

Hu, B. and Morrison, A. (2002) Tripography: Can destination use patterns enhance understanding of the VFR market? *Journal of Vacation Marketing* 8 (3), 201–220.

Hughes, E.C. (1937) Institutional office and the person. *American Journal of Sociology* 43, 404–13.

Hughes, G. (1995) The cultural construction of sustainable tourism. *Tourism Management* 16 (1), 49–59.

Hughes, H. (1987) Culture as a tourist resource: A theoretical consideration. *Tourism Management* 8, 205–216.

Hughes, H. (1998) Theatre in London and the inter-relationship with tourism. *Tourism Management* 19 (5), 445–452.

Hughes, K. (1991) Tourist satisfaction: A guided cultural tour in North Queensland. *Australian Psychologist* 26 (3), 166–171.

Huguet, P. and Latane, B. (1996) Social representations as dynamic social impact. *Journal of Communication* 46, 57–63.

Hunt, J.D. (1975) Image as a factor in tourism development. *Journal of Travel Research* 13 (3), 1–7.

Huxley, A. (1948) *Along the Road.* London: Chatto and Windus.

Inglis, G.J., Johnson, V.L. and Ponte, F. (1999) Crowding norms in marine settings: A case study of snorkeling on the Great Barrier Reef. *Environmental Management* 24 (3), 369–381.

Iso-Ahola, S.E. (1982) Towards a social psychological theory of tourism motivation: A rejoinder. *Annals of Tourism Research* 9 (2), 256–62.

Iso-Ahola, S.E. and Allen, J. (1982) The dynamics of leisure motivation: The effects of outcome on leisure needs. *Research Quarterly for Exercise & Sport* 53, 141–49.

Jack, L. (2001) Development and application of the Kangaroo Island TOMM (Tourism Optimisation Management Model). On WWW at http://www. regional.org.au/au/countrytowns/options/jack.htm. Accessed 12.04.04.

Jackson, E.L. and Wong, R.A.G. (1982) Perceived conflict between urban cross-country skiers and snowmobilers in Alberta. *Journal of Leisure Research* 14 (1), 47–62

Jackson, M.S., White, G.N. and Schmiere, C.L. (1996) Tourism experiences within an attributional framework. *Annals of Tourism Research* 23 (4), 798–810.

Jackson, R.T. (1990) VFR Tourism: Is it underestimated? *Journal of Tourism Studies* 1 (2), 10–17.

Jacob, G.R. and Schreyer, R. (1980) Conflict in outdoor recreation: A theoretical perspective. *Journal of Leisure Research* 12 (4), 368–380.

Jafari, J. (1987) Tourism models: The sociocultural aspects. *Tourism Management* 8 (2), 151–159.

Jafari, J. (1990) Research and scholarship: The basis of tourism education. *Journal of Tourism Studies* 1 (1), 33–41.

Jafari, J. (ed.) (2000) *The Encyclopedia of Tourism*. Oxford: Pergamon.

Jafari, J. and Ritchie, J.R.B. (1981) Towards a framework for tourism education. *Annals of Tourism Research* VIII (I), 13–34.

Jakobs, P. (1996) The true north strong and free. *Ecodecision* (Spring), 70–72.

Jamal, T. and Hollinshead, K. (2001) Tourism and the forbidden zone: The underserved power of qualitative inquiry. *Tourism Management* 22, 63–82.

Jansen-Verbeke, M. and Van Rekom, J. (1996) Scanning museum visitors: Urban tourism marketing. *Annals of Tourism Research* 23 (2), 364–375.

Jaspars, J. and Fraser, C. (1984) Attitudes and social representations. In R.M. Farr and S. Moscovici (eds) *Social Representation* (pp. 101–123). Cambridge: Cambridge University Press.

Javalgi, R.G., Thomas, E.G. and Rao, S.R. (1992) Consumer behaviour in the U.S. pleasure travel marketplace: An analysis of senior and non senior travellers. *Journal of Travel Research* 27 (3), 14–21.

Joffe, H. (2003) Risk: From perception to social representation. *British Journal of Social Psychology* 42, 55–73.

Jokinen, E. and Veijola, S. (1997) The disoriented tourist: The figuration of the tourist in contemporary cultural critique. In C. Rojek and J. Urry (eds) *Touring Culture* (pp. 23–51). London: Routledge.

Josiam, B.M., Hobson, J.S.P., Dietrich, V.C. and Smeaton, G. (1998) An analysis of the sexual, alcohol and drug-related behavioural patterns of students on spring break. *Tourism Management* 19 (6), 501–513.

Kagitcibasi, C. and Berry, J.W. (1989) Cross-cultural psychology: Current research and trends. *Annual Review of Psychology* 40, 493–531.

Kandampully, J., Mok, C. and Sparks, B. (2001) *Service Quality Management in Hospitality, Tourism, and Leisure*. London: Haworth Press.

Katz, D. and Brady, K. (1933) Racial stereotypes in one hundred college students. *Journal of Abnormal and Social Psychology* 28, 280–290.

Kellert, S. and Berry, J. (1980) American attitudes, knowledge and behaviors toward wildlife and natural habitats. Yale University, CT: US Fish and Wildlife Service.

Kim, C. and Lee, S. (2000a) Understanding the cultural difference in tourist motivation between Anglo-American and Japanese tourists. *Journal of Travel and Tourism Marketing* 9 (1/2), 153–170.

Kim, C. and Lee, S. (2000b) Japanese tourists' experiences of the natural environments in North Queensland Region Great Barrier Reef Experience. *Journal of Travel and Tourism Marketing* 9 (1/2), 93–114.

Kim, S.S. and Prideaux, B. (2003) A cross-cultural study of airline passengers. *Annals of Tourism Research* 30 (2), 489–492.

Kim, Y.J. (1997) Korean inbound tourism in Australia: An analysis of motivation and cross-cultural contact. Unpublished doctoral dissertation, James Cook University, Townsville.

Kim, Y.J., Pearce, P.L., Morrison, A.M and O'Leary, J.T. (1996) Mature vs. Youth travellers: The Korean market. *Asia Pacific Journal of Tourism Research* 1 (1), 102–12.

Kinnard, U. (2000a) Feminism. In J. Jafari (ed.) *Encyclopedia of Tourism* (p. 225). London: Routledge.

Kinnard, U. (2000b) Gender. In J. Jafari (ed.) *Encyclopedia of Tourism* (p. 246–248). London: Routledge.

Klemm, M.S. (2002) Tourism and ethnic minorities in Bradford: The invisible segment. *Journal of Travel Research* 41 (1), 85–91.

Klenosky, D., Frauman, E., Norman, W.C. and Gengler, C.W. (1998) Nature based tourists' use of interpretive services: A means–end investigation. *Journal of Tourism Studies* 9 (2), 26–36.

Knorr-Cetina, K.D. (1983) The ethnographic study of scientific work. Towards a constructivist interpretation of science. In K.D. Knorr-Cetina and M. Mulkay (eds) *Science Observed* (pp. 115–140). London: Sage.

Knudson, D.M., Cable, T.T. and Beck, L. (1995) *Interpretation of Cultural and Natural Resources*. State College, PA: Venture.

Kotler, P. (1994) *Marketing Management: Analysis, Planning, Implementation and Control*. Paramus, NJ: Prentice Hall International.

Kozak, M. (2001) A critical review of approaches to measure satisfaction with tourist destinations. In J.A. Mazanec, G. Crouch, J.R. Brent Ritchie and A. Woodside (eds) *Consumer Psychology of Tourism Hospitality and Leisure* (Vol. 2; pp. 303–320). Wallingford: CABI Publishing.

Kozak, M. (2002) Destination benchmarking. *Annals of Tourism Research* 29 (2), 497–519.

Kozak, M. and Neild, K. (1998) Importance-performance analysis and cultural perspectives in Romanian Black Sea resorts. *Anatolia: An International Journal of Tourism and Hospitality Research* 9 (2), 99–116.

Krippendorf, J. (1987) *The Holiday Makers: Understanding the Impact of Leisure and Travel*. London: William Heinemann.

Krueger, R. A. (1994) *Focus Groups: A Practical Guide for Applied Research*. Thousand Oaks, CA: Sage

Kuentzel, W. and McDonald, C. (1992) Differential effects of past experience, commitment, and lifestyle dimensions on river use specialization. *Journal of Leisure Research* 24 (3), 269–87.

Kuhn, T.S. (1970) *The Structure of Scientific Revolutions* (2nd edn). Chicago: University of Chicago Press.

Kuilboer, A. (2003) The health and well being of senior travellers. Unpublished Honours thesis, James Cook University, Townsville.

Kushner, K.E. and Moriow, R. (2003) Grounded theory, feminist theory, critical theory: Toward theoretical triangulation. *Advances in Nursing Science* 26 (1), 30–46.

Langer, E.J. (1989) *Mindfulness*. Reading, MA: Addison-Wesley.

Law, C.M. (2002) *Urban Tourism: The Visitor Economy and the Growth of Large Cities* (2nd edn). London: Continuum.

Law, R. and Leung, R. (2000) A study of airline's online reservation services on the Internet. *Journal of Travel Research* 39 (2), 202–211.

Lawson, F. and Baud-Bovy, M. (1977) *Tourism and Recreational Development*. London: The Architectural Press.

Lee, C.K.C. and Beatty, S.E. (2002) Family structure and influence in family decision making. *Journal of Consumer Marketing* 19 (1), 24–44.

Lee, D. and Pearce, P.L. (2002) Community attitudes to the acceptability of user fees in natural settings. *Tourism and Hospitality Research* 4 (2), 158–173.

Lee, M.H. (2002) Male Taiwanese attitudes to sex tourism. In *Asia Pacific Tourism Association Conference: APTA*. Conference proceedings. Dalian, China.

Lee, T. (1976) *Psychology and the Environment*. London: Methuen.

Lee, T. and Crompton, J. (1992) Measuring novelty seeking in tourism. *Annals of Tourims Research* 19 (4), 732–52.

Lee, T. and Uzzell, D. (1980) *The Educational Effectiveness of the Farm Open Day*. Perth: Countryside Commission for Scotland.

Lee, U-I. (1998) International tourist behaviour: A comparative study of Japanese and United Kingdom tourists in Cairns. Unpublished honours thesis. James Cook University, Townsville.

Lee, U-I. and Pearce, P. (2002) Travel motivation and travel career patterns. In *Proceedings of First Asia Pacific Forum for Graduate Students Research in Tourism, 22 May, Macao* (pp. 17–35). Hong Kong: The Hong Kong Polytechnic University.

Lee, W-H. (2002) Visitors' Experiences of Environmental Management Practices in Ecotourism Accommodation. Unpublished doctoral dissertation, James Cook University, Townsville.

Lee-Ross, D. (2001) Understanding the role of the service encounter in tourism, hospitality and leisure services. In J. Kandampully, C. Mok and B. Sparks (eds) *Service Quality Management in Hospitality, Tourism, and Leisure* (pp. 85–95). London: Haworth Press.

Lehto, X., Morrison, A. and O'Leary, J.T. (2001) Does the visiting friends and relatives' typology make a difference? A study of the international VFR market to the US. *Journal of Travel Research* 40 (2), 201–212.

Leiper, N. (1979) The framework of tourism: Towards definitions of tourism, tourists and the tourism industry. *Annals of Tourism Research* 6, 309–407.

Leiper, N. (1989) Tourism and tourism systems. *Occasional Paper No.1*. Department of Management Systems, Palmerston, North: Massey University.

Leiper, N. (1995) *Tourism Management*. Melbourne: TAFE Publications Ltd.

Lew, A.A., Hall, C.M. and Williams, A.M. (2004) *A Companion to Tourism*. Oxford: Blackwell Publishing.

Lewin, K. (1951) *Field Theory in Social Science: Selected Theoretical Papers*. D. Cartwright (ed.). New York: Harper & Row.

Liddle, M. (1997) *Recreation Ecology*. London: Chapman and Hall.

Loker, L.E. and Perdue, R.R. (1992) A benefit-based segmentation of a non-resident summer travel market. *Journal of Travel Research* 31 (Summer), 30–35.

Loker-Murphy, L. and Pearce, P.L. (1995) Young budget travelers: Backpackers in Australia. *Annals of Tourism Research* 22 (4), 819–843.

Loker-Murphy, L.E. (1995) Backpackers in Australia: A motivation-based segmentation study. In B. Faulkner, M. Fagence, M. Davison and C. Craig-Smith (eds) *Proceedings from the Tourism Research and Education Conference* (pp. 115–28). Canberra: Bureau of Tourism Research.

Louisiana Recreation and Tourism Assessment Team (1987) *An Assessment of Recreation and Tourism Development Opportunities*. Baton Rouge, LA: Louisiana Sea Grant College Programme, Center for Wetland Resources, Louisiana State University.

Lounsbury, J.W. and Hoopes, L.L. (1985) An investigation of factors associated with vacation satisfaction. *Journal of Leisure Research* 17 (1), 1–13.

Lue, C., Crompton, J.L. and Fesenmaier, D. (1993) Conceptualisation of multi-destination pleasure trips. *Annals of Tourism Analysis* 20 (2), 289–301.

Lunt, P. (1995) Psychological approaches to consumption. In D. Miller (ed.) *Acknowledging Consumption* (pp. 238–263). London: Routledge.

Lynch, K. (1960) *The Image of the City.* Cambridge, MA: MIT Press.

MacCannell, D. (1973) Staged authenticity: Arrangements of social space in tourist settings. *The American Journal of Sociology* 79 (3), 589–603.

MacCannell, D. (1976) *The Tourist: A New Theory of the Leisure Class.* New York: Schocken Books.

McCarthur, S. (2000) Beyond carrying capacity: Introducing a model to monitor and manage visitor activity in forests. In X. Font and J. Tribe (eds) *Forest Tourism and Recreation: Case Studies in Environmental Management* (pp. 259–278). Wallingford: CABI Publishing.

McCarthy, P. (2000) *McCarthy's Bar: A Journey of Discovery in Ireland.* London: Hodder and Stoughton

McCormick, N. (1994) *Female Salvation: Affirming Women's Sexual Rights and Pleasures.* Westport, CT: Praeger.

McCulloch, J. (1992) The Youth Hostels Association: Precursors and contemporary achievements. *Journal of Tourism Studies* 3 (1), 22–27.

McFarlane, B.L. (1994) Specialization and motivations of birdwatchers. *Wildlife Society Bulletin* 22, 361–370.

McFeely, T. (1996) From peacekeeper to vice cop: Ottawa's international sex-tourism crack-down probably won't work. *Alberta Report* 23 (20), 7. On WWW at http://80-web6.infotrac.galegroup.com.elibrary.jcu.edu.au/itw/infomark/499/737 /49309634w6purl=rc1_EAIM_0_A30291136&dyn=23!xrn_1_0_A30291136?sw_aep= james_cook. Accessed 07.02.04.

McGehee, N.G., Loker-Murphy, L. and Uysal, M. (1996) The Australian international pleasure travel market: Motivations from a gendered perspective. *Journal of Tourism Studies* 7 (1), 45–57.

McGuire, W.J. (1986) The vicissitudes of attitudes and similar representational constructs in twentieth century psychology. *European Journal of Social Psychology* 16 (2), 89–130.

McHugh, K.E. and Mings, R.C. (1991) On the road again: Seasonal migration to a sunbelt metropolis. *Urban Geography* 12, 1–18.

McHugh, K.E. and Mings, R.C. (1992) Canadian snowbirds in Arizona. *Journal of Applied Recreation Research* 17, 255–277.

McIntosh, R.W. and Goeldner, C.R. (1986) *Tourism: Principles, Practices, Philosophies* (5th edn). New York: John Wiley & Sons, Inc.

Mack, J.A. and Thompson, J.A. (1991) Visitor centre planning: Using visitor interests and available time. In G. Moscardo and K. Hughes (eds) *Visitor Centres: Exploring New Territory* (pp. 113–120). Townsville: James Cook University.

McKercher, B. (1999) A chaos approach to tourism. *Tourism Management* 20, 425–434.

McKercher, R. and Bauer, T. (2003) Conceptual framework of the nexus between tourism, romance and sex. In T. Bauer and R. McKercher (eds) *Sex and Tourism: Journeys of Romance, Love and Lust* (pp. 3–16). Binghampton, NY: Haworth.

McKinley, A., Potter, J. and Wetherell, M. (1993) Discourse analysis and social representations. In G.M. Breakwell and D.V. Canter (eds) *Empirical Approaches to Social Representations* (pp. 134–156). Oxford: Clarendon Press.

MacNeil, R.D. (1987) *Ageing and Leisure.* New Jersey: Prentice Hall.

Madrigal, R., Havitz, M. and Howard, R. (1992) Married couples involvement with family vacations. *Leisure Sciences* 14, 287–301.

Malloy, D.C. and Fennell, D.A. (1998) Codes of ethics and tourism: An exploratory content analysis. *Tourism Management* 19 (5), 453–461.

Manfredo, M.J., Driver, B.L. and Brown, P.J. (1983) A test of concepts inherent in experience based setting management for outdoor recreation areas. *Journal of Leisure Research* 15 (3), 263–283.

Manidis Roberts Consultants (1997) *The Tourism Optimisation Management Model for Kangaroo Island*. On WWW at http://www.tomm.info/background/files/ TOMM_Report.pdf+Manidis+Roberts+1997+Tourism+Optimisation&hl=en&ie= UTF-8. Accessed 02.03.05.

Mannell, R.C. and Iso-Ahola, S.E. (1987) Psychological nature of leisure and tourism experience. *Annals of Tourism Research* 14, 314–331.

Mannell, R.C. and Kleiber, D. (1997) *A Social Psychology of Leisure*. State College, PA: Venture Publishing.

Mansfeld, Y. (1992) From motivation to actual travel. *Annals of Tourism Studies* 19 (3), 399–419.

March, R. (2000) The Japanese travel life cycle. *Journal of Travel and Tourism Marketing* 9 (1/2), 185–200.

Marsh, P., Rosser, E. and Harre, R. (1978) *The Rules of Disorder*. London: Routledge and Kegan Paul.

Martin, S. (1997) Specialization and differences in setting preferences among wildlife viewers. *Human Dimensions of Wildlife* 2 (1), 1–18.

Masberg, B.A. (1998) Defining the tourist: Is it possible? A view from the convention and visitors bureau. *Journal of Travel Research* 37 (1), 67–70.

Maslow, A.H. (1970) *Motivation and Personality*. New York: Harper & Row.

Mason, P. and Mowforth, M. (1996) Codes of conduct in tourism. *Progress in Tourism and Hospitality Research* 2 (2), 151–164.

Mathieson, A. and Wall, G. (1982) *Tourism: Economic, Physical and Social Impacts*. London: Longman.

Matthews, H. and Richter, L. (1991) Political science and tourism. *Annals of Tourism Research* 18 (1), 120–135.

Mazanec, J. (2000) Marketing. In J. Jafari (ed.) *Encyclopedia of Tourism* (pp. 375–378). London: Routledge.

Mazursky, D. (1989) Past experience and future tourism decisions. *Annals of Tourism Research* 16, 333–344.

Meikle, S. (2003) Who calls the shots? Travel decision making within families. Unpublished Honours thesis, James Cook University, Townsville.

Middleton, V. (1998) *Sustainable Tourism: A Marketing Perspective*. Oxford: Butterworth Heinermann.

Middleton, V. (2000) Marketing, destination. In J. Jafari (ed.) *Encyclopedia of Tourism* (pp. 378–379). London: Routledge.

Miles, R.S., Alt, M.B., Gosling, D.C., Lewis, B.N. and Tout, A.F. (1982) *The Design of Educational Exhibits*. London: George, Allen & Unwin.

Mill, R.C. and Morrison, A.M. (1985) *The Tourism System: An Introductory Text*. Englewood Cliffs, NJ: Prentice-Hall.

Mill, R.C. and Morrison, A.M. (1992) *The Tourism System: An Introductory Text* (2nd edn). Englewood Cliffs, NJ: Prentice-Hall.

Miller, A.R. and Grazer, W.F. (2002) The North American cruise market and Australian tourism. *Journal of Vacation Marketing* 8 (3), 221–234.

Mills, A.S. (1985) Participation motivation for outdoor recreation: A test of Maslow's theory. *Journal of Leisure Research* 17, 184–99.

Mings, R.C. and McHugh, K.E. (1996) Wintering in the American sunbelt: Linking place and behaviour. *Journal of Tourism Studies* 6 (2), 56–62.

Miniard, P.W., Bhatla, S., Randall, L. and Rose, R.L. (1990) On the formation and relationship of ad and brand attitudes: An experimental and causal analysis. *Journal of Marketing Research* 27, 290–303.

Minichiello, V., Alexander, L. and Jones, D. (eds) (1992) *Gerontology: A Multi-disciplinary Approach*. Sydney: Prentice Hall.

Mitchell, L. (2000) Geography, recreational. In J. Jafari (ed.) *Encyclopedia of Tourism* (p. 251). London: Routledge.

Mitchell, L. and Murphy, P. (1991) Geography and tourism. *Annals of Tourism Research* 18 (1), 57–70.

Mohamad, S. (2000) Planning, recreation. In J. Jafari (ed.) *Encyclopedia of Tourism* (pp. 441–442). London: Routledge.

Moliner, P. (1995) A two-dimensional model of social representations. *European Journal of Social Psychology* 25, 27–40.

Moore, K. (2002) The discursive tourist. In G.M.S. Dann (ed.) *The Tourist as Metaphor of the Social World* (pp. 41–60). Wallingford: CABI.

Morley, C.L. (1994) Experimental destination choice analysis. *Annals of Tourism Research* 21 (4), 780–791.

Morrison, A. (2000) Product planning. In J. Jafari (ed.) *Encyclopedia of Tourism* (pp. 463–464). London: Routledge.

Morrison, A.M. (1996) *Hospitality and Travel Marketing* (2nd edn). New York: Delmar.

Morrison, A.M., Hsieh, S. and O'Leary, J.T. (1995) Segmenting the visiting friends and relatives market by holiday activity participation. *Journal of Tourism Studies* 6 (1), 48–63.

Morrison, A.M., Yang, C-H., O'Leary, J.T. and Nadkarni, N. (1996) Comparative profiles of travellers on cruises and land-based resort vacations. *Journal of Tourism Studies* 7 (2), 15–27.

Moscardo, G. (1996) Mindful visitors: Heritage and tourism. *Annals of Tourism Research* 23 (2), 376–397.

Moscardo, G. (1998) Interpretation and sustainable tourism: Functions, examples and principles. *Journal of Tourism Studies* 9 (1), 2–13.

Moscardo, G. (1999) *Making Visitors Mindful: Principles for Creating Quality Sustainable Visitor Experiences Through Effective Communication*. Champaign, IL: Sagamore Publishing.

Moscardo, G. (2000) Understanding wildlife tourism market segments: An Australian marine study. *Human Dimensions of Wildlife* 5 (2), 36–53.

Moscardo, G. and Green, D. (1999) Age and activity participation on the Great Barrier Reef. *Tourism Recreation Research* 24 (1), 57–68.

Moscardo, G., Morrison, A.M., Pearce, P.L., Lang, C-T. and O'Leary, J.T. (1996) Understanding destination vacation choice through travel motivation and activities. *Journal of Vacation Marketing* 2 (2), 109–122.

Moscardo, G. and Pearce, P.L. (1986a) Historical theme parks: An Australian experience in authenticity. *Annals of Tourism Research* 13 (3), 467–79.

Moscardo, G. and Pearce, P.L. (1986b) Visitor centres and environmental interpretations; and exploration of the relationships among visitor enjoyment, understanding and mindfulness. *Journal of Environmental Psychology* 6, 89–108.

Moscardo, G. and Pearce, P.L. (1999) Understanding ethnic tourists. *Annals of Tourism Research* 26 (2), 416–434.

Moscardo, G. and Pearce, P.L. (2003) Presenting destinations: Marketing host communities. In S. Singh, D. Timothy and R.K. Dowling (eds) *Tourism in Destination Communities* (pp. 253–272). Cambridge: CAB International.

Moscardo, G. and Pearce, P.L. (2004) Life cycle, tourist motivation and transport: Some consequences for the tourist experience. In L. Lumsdon and S.J. Page (eds) *Tourism and Transport: Issues and Agenda for the New Millennium* (pp. 29–43). Oxford: Elsevier.

Moscardo, G., Pearce, P. and Morrison, A. (1996) Evaluating different bases for market segmentation: A comparison of geographic origin versus activity participation for generating tourist market segments. In M. Opperman (ed.) *Pacific Rim Tourism 2000* (pp. 242–252). Conference proceedings, November 1996, Rotorua. Rotorua: Centre for Tourism Studies, Waiariki Polytechnic.

Moscardo, G., Pearce, P. and Morrison, A. (2001) Evaluating different bases for market segmentation: A comparison of geographic origin versus activity participation for generating tourist market segments. *Journal of Travel & Tourism Marketing* 10 (1), 29–49

Moscardo, G., Pearce, P.L., Morrison, A.M., Green, D. and O'Leary, J.T. (2000) Developing a typology for understanding visiting friends and relative markets. *Journal of Travel Research* 38 (3), 251–259.

Moscardo, G., Verbeek, M. and Woods, B. (1998) Effective interpretation and sustainable tourism. In *The Role of Tourism: National and Regional Perspectives Series B* (pp. 148–155). Proceedings of the Fourth Asia Pacific Tourism Association Conference. Pusan: Asia Pacific Tourism Association.

Moschis, G.P. (1996) *Gerontographics: Life Stage Segmentation for Marketing Strategy Development*. Westport, CT: Quorum.

Moscovici, S. (1972) Society and theory in social psychology. In J. Israel and H. Tajfel (eds) *The Context of Social Psychology* (pp. 17–68). London: Academic Press.

Moscovici, S. (1973) Foreword. In C. Herzlich (D. Graham, trans.) *Health and Illness* (pp. ix–xiv). London: Academic Press.

Moscovici, S. (1981) On social representations. In J.P. Forgas (ed.) *Social Cognition: Perspectives on Everyday Understanding* (pp. 181–209). London: Academic Press.

Moscovici, S. (1984) The phenomenon of social representations. In R.M. Farr and S. Moscovici (eds) *Social Representations* (pp.3–70). Cambridge: Cambridge University Press.

Moscovici, S. (1988) Notes towards a description of social representations. *European Journal of Social Psychology* 18 (3), 211–250.

Muller, T.E. and Cleaver, M. (2000) Targeting the CANZUS baby boomer explorer and adventure segments. *Journal of Vacation Marketing* 6 (2), 154–169.

Murphy, L. (2001) Exploring social interactions of backpackers. *Annals of Tourism Research* 28 (1), 50–67.

Murphy, L.E. (1997) Young budget travellers: A marketing and decision making analysis. Unpublished doctoral dissertation, James Cook University, Townsville.

Murphy, P.E. (1985) *Tourism: A Community Approach*. New York: Methuen.

Nash, D. (2001) On travellers, ethnographers and tourists. *Annals of Tourism Research* 28 (2), 493–495.

Nash, D. and Smith, V. (1991) Anthropology and tourism. *Annals of Tourism Research* 18 (1), 12–25.

Newsome, D., Moore, S.A. and Dowling, R.K. (2002) *Natural Area Tourism: Ecology, Impacts and Management*. Clevedon: Channel View Publications.

Nicholson, M. (1972) Planned expansion of tourism to bring in new areas and fresh fields of interest. *Tourism and the Environment* (pp. 48–51). London: British Tourist Authority.

Nisbett, R.E. and Wilson, T.D. (1977) Telling more than we can know: Verbal reports on mental processes. *Psychological Review* 84, 231–259.

Nishiyama, K. (1996) *Welcoming the Japanese Visitor: Insights, Tips, Tactics.* Honolulu: University of Hawai'i Press.

Noe, F.P. (1999) *Tourism Service Satisfaction.* Champaign, IL: Sagamore.

Oakes, M. (1986) *Statistical Inference: A Commentary for the Social and Behavioural Sciences.* Chichester: John Wiley & Sons.

Oberg, K. (1960) Culture shock: Adjustment to neo-cultural environments. *Practical Anthropology* 17, 177–182.

O'Hara, R. (2003) Jungle fever. *Weekend Australian,* August 23–24, p. R24–25.

Oliver, R.L. (1980, November) A cognitive model of the antecedents and consequences of satisfaction decisions. *Journal of Marketing Research* 17, 460–469.

Oliver, T. (2001) The consumption of tour routes in cultural landscapes. In J.A. Mazanec, G.I. Crouch, J. Brent Ritchie and A.G. Woodside (eds) *Consumer Psychology of Tourism, Hospitality and Leisure* (pp. 273–284). Wallingford: CABI.

O'Meara, K.P. (2003) Bush taking battle to the sex trade: President George W. Bush has appealed to the world's governments for help in combating human trafficking and shutting down the grim 'underground of brutality'. *Insight on the News,* 10 November, p. 24. On WWW at http://80-web6.infotrac.galegroup.com. elibrary.jcu.edu.au/itw/infomark/499/737/49309634w6/purl=rc1_EAIM_0_A10 9871303&dyn=26!xrn_1_0_A109871303?sw_aep=james_cook. Accessed 12.02.04.

Oppenheim, A.N. (1966) *Questionnaire Design and Attitude Measurement.* London: Heinemann.

Orams, M. (2002) Feeding wildlife as a tourism attraction: A review of issues and impacts. *Tourism Management* 23, 281–293.

Outhwaite, W. (2000) The philosophy of social science. In B.S. Turner (ed.) *The Blackwell Companion to Social Theory* (2nd edn; pp. 47–70). Oxford: Blackwell.

Page S. (1995) *Urban Tourism.* London: Routledge.

Page, S. and Dowling, R. (2002) *Ecotourism.* London: Prentice-Hall/Pearson Education Ltd.

Parasuraman, A., Zeithmal, V.A. and Berry, L.L. (1985) A conceptual model of service quality and its implications for future research. *Journal of Marketing* 49, 41–50.

Parasuraman, A., Zeithmal, V.A. and Berry, L.L. (1994a) Alternative scales for measuring service quality: A comparative assessment based on psychometric and diagnostic criteria. *Journal of Retailing* 70 (3), 201–230.

Parasuraman, A., Zeithmal, V.A. and Berry, L.L. (1994b) Reassessment of expectations as a comparison standard in measuring service quality: Implications for further research. *Journal of Marketing* 58, 111–124.

Park, M. (2000) Social and cultural factors influencing tourists' souvenir purchasing behavior: A comparative study on Japanese 'Omiyage' and Korean 'Sunmul'. *Journal of Travel and Tourism Marketing* 9 (1/2), 81–92.

Parker, S. (1992) Volunteering as serious leisure. *Journal of Applied Recreation Research* 17 (1), 1–11.

Parsons, T. (1951) *The Social System.* Glencoe, IL: Free Press.

Payne, R. (1993) Sustainable tourism: Suggested indicators and monitoring techniques. In J.G. Nelson, R. Butler and G. Wall (eds) *Tourism and Sustainable Development: Monitoring, Planning, Managing* (pp. 249–253). London, Ontario: University of Waterloo.

Payne, R.J. (2000) Research opportunity spectrum. In J. Jafari (ed.) *Encyclopedia of Tourism* (p. 492). London: Routledge.

Pearce, D. (1998) Tourism development in Paris: Public intervention. *Annals of Tourism Research* 25 (2), 457–476.

Pearce, D. (2001) An integrative framework for urban tourism research. *Annals of Tourism Research* 28 (4), 926–946.

Pearce, D.G. (1993) Comparative studies in tourism research. In D.G. Pearce and R. Butler (eds) *Tourism Research, Critiques and Challenges*. London: Routledge.

Pearce, P. and Fenton, M. (1994) Multidimensional scaling and tourism research. In J.R. Brent Richie and C.R. Goeldner (eds) *Travel, Tourism, and Hospitality Research: A Handbook for Managers and Researchers* (pp. 523–532) New York: John Wiley & Sons, Inc.

Pearce, P. and Greenwood, T. (1999) And then her snorkel filled with water: Analysing critical Reef tourism situations. In J. Molloy and J. Davies (eds) *Tourism and Hospitality: Delighting the Senses, 1999, Part 1* (pp. 222–234). Proceedings of 9th Australian Tourism and Hospitality Research Conference (CAUTHE), 10–13 February, Adelaide. Canberra: Bureau of Tourism Research.

Pearce, P., Kim, E. and Lussa, S. (1998) Facilitating tourist–host social interaction: An overview and assessment of the culture assimilator. In E. Laws, B. Faulkner and G. Moscardo (eds) *Embracing and Managing Changes in Tourism: International Case studies* (pp. 347–364). London: Routledge.

Pearce, P.L. (1977) Mental souvenirs: A study of tourists and their city maps. *Australian Journal of Psychology* 29, 203–210.

Pearce, P.L. (1980) Strangers, travellers, and greyhound terminals: A study of small-scale helping behaviour. *Journal of Personality and Social Psychology* 38 (6), 935–940.

Pearce, P.L. (1981a) Environmental shock: A study of tourists' reactions to two tropical islands. *Journal of Applied Social Psychology* 11 (3), 268–280.

Pearce, P.L. (1981b) Route maps: A study of travellers' perception of a section of countryside. *Journal of Environmental Psychology* 1, 141–155.

Pearce, P.L. (1982) *The Social Psychology of Tourist Behaviour*. Oxford: Pergamon Press.

Pearce, P.L. (1988) *The Ulysses Factor: Evaluating Visitors in Tourist Settings*. New York: Springer-Verlag.

Pearce, P.L. (1989) Towards the better management of tourist queues. *Tourism Management* 10 (4), 279–284.

Pearce, P.L. (1990a) *The Backpacker Phenomenon: Preliminary Answers to Basic Questions*. Townsville: James Cook University.

Pearce, P.L. (1990b) Farm tourism in New Zealand: A social situation analysis. *Annals of Tourism Research* 17 (3), 337–352.

Pearce, P.L. (1991a) Travel stories: An analysis of self-disclosure in terms of story structure, valence, and audience characteristics. *Australian Psychologist* 26 (3), 172–174.

Pearce, P.L. (1991b) Dreamworld: A report on public reactions to Dreamworld and proposed developments at Dreamworld. Unpublished report to Ernst and Young on behalf of the IOOF in conjunction with Brian Dermott and Associates.

Pearce, P.L. (1991c) Analysing tourist attractions. *Journal of Tourism Studies* 2 (1), 46–55.

Pearce, P.L. (1993a) Defining tourism study as a specialism: A justification and implications. *Teoros International* 1 (1), 25–32.

Pearce, P.L. (1993b) Fundamentals of tourist motivation. In D. Pearce and R. Butler (eds) *Tourism Research: Critiques and Challenges* (pp. 85–105). London: Routledge and Kegan Paul.

Pearce, P.L. (1998) Marketing and management trends in tourist attractions. *Asia Pacific Journal of Tourism Research* 3 (1), 1–8.

Pearce, P.L. (1999a) Touring for pleasure: Studies of the senior self-drive travel market. *Tourism Recreation Research* 24 (1), 35–42.

Pearce, P.L. (1999b) *Tourism Recreation Review* 24 (1), special issue on aging and tourism.

Pearce, P.L. (2000) Psychology. In J. Jafari (ed.) *Encyclopedia of Tourism* (pp. 471–472). London: Routledge.

Pearce, P.L. (2004) Theoretical innovation in Asia Pacific tourism research. *Asia Pacific Journal of Tourism Research* 9 (1), 57–70.

Pearce, P.L. (2005) The role of relationships in the tourist experience. In W. Theobald (ed.) *Global Tourism* (3rd edn; pp. 103–122). Oxford: Butterworth Heinemann.

Pearce, P.L. and Caltabiano, M.L. (1983) Inferring travel motivation from travellers' experiences. *Journal of Travel Research* 22 (2), 16–20.

Pearce, P.L. and Fagence, M. (1996) The legacy of Kevin Lynch: Research implications. *Annals of Tourism Research* 23 (3), 576–598.

Pearce, P.L. and Hyvonen, T. (2003) Litter in the city: Visitor perceptions and sustainable practices for urban tourism. *Tourism* 51 (2), 193–204.

Pearce, P.L., Innes, J.M. O'Driscoll, P. and Morse, S.J. (1981) Stereotyped images of Australian cities. *Australian Journal of Psychology* 33, 29–39.

Pearce, P.L. and Lee, U. (2005) Developing the travel career approach to tourist motivation. *Journal of Travel Research* 43, 226–237.

Pearce, P.L., Morrison, A., and Rutledge, J. (1998) *Tourism: Bridges Across Continents.* Sydney: McGraw-Hill.

Pearce, P.L., Morrison, A., Scott, N., O'Leary, J., Nadkarni, N. and Moscardo, G. (1996) The holiday market in Queensland: Building an understanding of visitors staying in commercial accommodation. In G. Prosser (ed.) *Tourism and Hospitality Research* (pp. 427–442). Canberra: Bureau of Tourism Research.

Pearce, P.L. and Moscardo, G. (1985) Tourist theme parks: Research practices and possibilities. *Australian Psychologist* 20, 3, 303–312.

Pearce, P.L. and Moscardo, G. (2004) Assessing market convergence and divergence: Studies of visitors to Australia's Great Barrier Reef. Paper prepared for Tourism State of the Art II Conference, University of Strathclyde, Glasgow, 27–30 June.

Pearce, P.L., Moscardo, G. and Ross, G.F. (1996) *Tourism Community Relationships.* Oxford: Elsevier

Pearce, P.L. and Rutledge, J.L. (1994) Architectural design and planning of tourist facilities: Theme park planning and design. In W. S. Roehl (ed.) *Proceedings of the Environments for Tourism Conference* (pp. 320–350). Las Vegas, NV: William F. Harrah College of Hotel Administration, University of Nevada, Las Vegas.

Pearce, P.L. and Singh, S. (eds) (1999) Senior tourism. *Tourism Recreation Research* 24 (1), 1–4.

Pearce, P.L. and Stringer, P. (1991) Psychology and tourism. *Annals of Tourism Research* 18 (1), 136–154.

Pearce, P.L. and Yagi, C. (2004) Methodological innovation in Asia Pacific tourism research. In K. Chon, C. Hsu and N. Okamoto (eds) *Globalisation and Tourism Research: East Meets West.* Proceedings of the Asia Pacific Tourism Association Tenth Annual Conference, Nagasaki, Japan, 4–7 July. Hong Kong: Hong Kong Polytechnic.

Pennington-Gray, L. (2003) Understanding the domestic VFR drive market in Florida. *Journal of Vacation Marketing* 9 (4), 354–367.

Phelps, A. (1986) Holiday destination image: The problem of assessment. *Tourism Management* 7 (3), 168–180.

Phillimore, J. and Goodson, L. (eds) (2004) *Qualitative Research in Tourism*. London: Routledge.

Pigram, J. (2000a) Environment. In J. Jafari (ed.) *Encyclopedia of Tourism* (pp. 143–195). London: Routledge.

Pigram, J. (2000b) Environmental management, best practice. In J. Jafari (ed.) *Encyclopedia of Tourism* (p. 198). London: Routledge.

Pike, K.L. (1966) *Language in Relation To a Unified Theory of the Structure of Human Behavior*. The Hague: Mouton.

Pimlott, J.A.R. (1947) *The Englishman's Holiday: A Social History*. London: Faber and Faber.

Pine II, B.J. and Gilmour, J. (1999) *The Experience Economy*. Boston: Harvard Business School Press.

Pizam, A. (1994) Planning a tourism research investigation. In J.R. Brent Ritchie and C.R. Goeldner (eds) *Travel Tourism and Hospitality Research* (pp. 91–104). New York: John Wiley.

Pizam, A. (1999a) The American group tourist as viewed by British, Israeli, Korean and Dutch tour guides. *The Journal of Travel Research* 38, 119–126.

Pizam, A. (1999b) Cross-cultural tourist behavior. In A. Pizam and Y. Manfeld (eds) (pp. 393–412). New York: Haworth Press.

Pizam, A. (2000) Management. In J. Jafari (ed.) *Encyclopedia of Tourism* (pp. 367–369). London: Routledge.

Pizam, A. and Jeong, G-H. (1966) Cross-cultural tourist behaviour: Perceptions of Korean tour-guides. *Tourism Management* 17 (4), 227–286.

Pizam, A. and Mansfield, J. (2000) *Consumer Behaviour in Travel and Tourism*. New York: The Haworth Hospitality Press.

Pizam, A. and Reichel, A. (1996) The effect of nationality on tourist behavior: Israeli tour guides' perceptions. *Journal of Hospitality and Leisure Marketing* 4 (1), 23–49.

Pizam, A. and Sussman, S. (1995) Does nationality affect tourist behavior? *Annals of Tourism Research* 22 (4), 901–917.

Pizam, A., Jansen-Verbeke, M. and Steel, L. (1997) Are all tourists alike regardless of nationality? The perceptions of Dutch tour-guides. *Journal of International Hospitality, Leisure & Tourism Management* 1 (1), 19–40.

Platt, B. (2002) Commercial sexual exploitation of children: A global problem requiring global action. *Sexual Health Exchange* 2002 (3), 10(2). On WWW at http:/ /80-web6.infotrac.galegroup.com.elibrary.jcu.edu.au/itw/infomark/499/737/ 49309634w6/purl=rc1_EAIM_0_A95555010&dyn=29!xrn_2_0_A95555010?sw_aep= james_cook. Accessed 17.03.04.

Plog, S. (1987) Understanding psychographics in tourism research. In J.R.B. Ritchie and C. Goeldner (eds) *Travel Tourism and Hospitality Research* (pp. 203–214). New York: Wiley.

Plog, S. (1991) *Leisure Travel: Making It a Growth Market .. Again!* New York: Wiley.

Plog, S.C. (1974) Why destination rise and fall in popularity. *Cornell Hotel and Restaurant Quarterly* 14 (4), 55–58.

Pocock, D. and Hudson, R. (1978) *Images of the Urban Environment*. London: The MacMillan Press.

Pors, N.O. (2000) Information retrieval, experimental models and statistical analyses. *Journal of Documentation* 56 (1), 55–70.

Potter, J. and Wetherell, M. (1987) *Discourse and Social Psychology: Beyond Attitudes and Behaviour*. London: Sage.

Powers, T. (1997) *Marketing Hospitality* (2nd edn). New York: John Wiley & Sons.

Prakash, V. (1984) Validity and reliability of the confirmation of expectations paradigm as a determinant of consumer satisfaction. *Journal of the Academy of Marketing Science* 12 (4), 63–76.

Preitz, T. (2000) Cruising the Internet: A qualitative analysis of cruise experience reviews posted on the Internet: Recommendations for Australia. Unpublished thesis, James Cook University, Townsville.

Prentice, R. (2003) Revisiting 'Heritage: A key sector of the (then) "New" tourism': Out with the 'new' and out with 'heritage'? In C. Cooper (ed.) *Classic Reviews in Tourism* (pp. 164–191). Clevedon: Channel View Publications.

Prentice, R.C., Witt, S.F. and Hamer, C. (1998) Tourism as experience: The case of heritage parks. *Annals of Tourism Research* 25 (1), 1–24.

Prideaux, B. and Carson, B. (2003) A framework for increasing understanding of self-drive tourism markets. *Journal of Vacation Marketing* 9 (4), 307–313.

Prince, D.R. (1982) Countryside interpretation: A cognitive evaluation. *Museums Journal* 28 (3), 165–170.

Pruitt, D. and Lafont, S. (1995) Love and money: Romance tourism in Jamaica. *Annals of Tourism Research* 22, 422–440.

Pyo, S., Mihalik, B.J. and Uysal, M. (1989) Attraction attributes and motivations: A canonical correlation analysis. *Annals of Tourism Research* 16, 277–282.

Queensland Government (2001) *2000–2001 Annual Report*. Brisbane: Tourism Queensland.

Rathmun, R. (1995) Factors in user group conflict between hikers and mountain bikers. *Leisure Sciences* 17, 159–169.

Ray, N.M. and Ryder, M.E. (2003) 'Ebilities' tourism: An exploratory discussion of the travel needs and motivations of the mobility-disabled. *Tourism Management* 24 (1), 57–72.

Redfoot, D. (1984) Tourist authenticity, tourist angst and modern reality. *Qualitative Sociology* 7, 291–309.

Reisinger, Y. and Turner, L. (1999) A cultural analysis of Japanese tourists: Challenges for tourism marketers. *European Journal of Marketing* 33 (11/12), 1203–1227.

Reisinger, Y. and Turner, L. (2003) *Cross-Cultural Behaviour in Tourism*. Oxford: Butterworth Heinemann.

Richards, G. and Richards, B. (1998) A globalised theme park market? The case of Disney in Europe. In E. Laws, B. Faulkner and G. Moscardo (eds) *Embracing and Managing Change in Tourism* (pp. 379–397). London: Routledge.

Richardson, S.L. and Crompton, J. (1998) Vacation patterns of French and English Canadians. *Annals of Tourism Research* 15 (3), 430–435.

Richter, L. (2000) Political science. In J. Jafari (ed.) *Encyclopedia of Tourism* (pp. 450–452). London: Routledge.

Riley, P. (1988) Road culture of international long term budget travellers. *Annals of Tourism Research* 15, 313–328.

Riley, R. and Love, L. (2000) The state of qualitative tourism research. *Annals of Tourism Research* 27 (1), 164–187.

Riley, R., Baker, U. and Doren, C. (1998) Movie induced tourism. *Annals of Tourism Research* 25 (4), 919–935.

Ritchie, B.W. with Carr, N. and Cooper, C. (2003) *Managing Educational Tourism*. Clevedon: Channel View Publications.

Ritchie, J.R.B. (1994) Roles of research in tourism management. In J.R.B. Ritchie and C. Goeldner (eds) *Travel, Tourism and Hospitality Research* (2nd edn; pp.13–22). New York: John Wiley & Sons.

Ritchie, J.R.B., Crouch, G.I. and Hudson, S. (2000) Developing operational measures for the components of a destination competitiveness/sustainability model: Consumer versus managerial perspectives. In J.A. Mazanec, G.I. Crouch, J.R.B. Ritchie and A.G. Woodside (eds) *Consumer Psychology of Tourism, Hospitality and Leisure* (pp. 1–17). Wallingford: CABI.

Robie, C., Bateson, A.G., Ellison, P. and Figler, M. (1993) An analysis of the tourist motivation construct. *Annals of Tourism Research* 20 (4), 773–776.

Rojek, C. (1997) Indexing, dragging and the social construction of tourist sights. In C. Rojek and J. Urry (eds) (1997) *Touring Cultures: Transformations of Travel and Theory* (pp. 52–74). London: Routledge.

Rojek, C. and Urry, J. (1997) Transformations of travel and theory. In C. Rojek and J. Urry (eds) *Touring Cultures: Transformations of Travel and Theory* (pp. 1–19) London: Routledge.

Rojek, C. and Urry, J. (eds) (1997) *Touring Cultures: Transformations of Travel and Theory.* London: Routledge.

Roper, A. (2000a) Business format. In J. Jafari (ed.) *Encyclopedia of Tourism* (p. 63). London: Routledge.

Roper, A. (2000b) Management contract. In J. Jafari (ed.) *Encyclopedia of Tourism* (pp. 370–371). London: Routledge.

Rosenow, J. and Pulsipher, G. (1978) *Tourism: The Good, The Bad and The Ugly.* Lincoln, NE: Media Productions.

Rosnow, R. (1981) *Paradigms in Transition: The Methodology of Social Inquiry.* New York: Oxford University Press.

Ross, G. (1994) *The Psychology of Tourism.* Melbourne: Hospitality Press.

Rowan, J. (1998) Maslow amended. *Journal of Humanistic Psychology* 38 (1), 81–93.

Ruddell, E.J. and Gramman, J.H. (1994) Goal orientation, norms, and noise-induced conflict among recreation area users. *Leisure Sciences* 16, 93–104.

Russell, J.A., Lewicka, M., and Niit, T. (1989) A cross-cultural study of a circumplex model of affect. *Journal of Personality and Social Psychology* 57 (5), 848–856.

Ryan, C. (1992) The child as a visitor. *World Travel and Tourism Review* 2, 135–139.

Ryan, C. (1995a) *Researching Tourist Satisfaction: Issues, Concepts, Problems.* New York: Routledge.

Ryan, C. (1995b) Learning about tourists from conversations: The over-55s in Majorca. *Tourism Management* 16 (3), 207–215.

Ryan, C. (1997a) *The Tourist Experience. A New Introduction.* New York: Cassell.

Ryan, C. (1997b) Tourism: A mature discipline. *Pacific Tourism Review* 1 (1), 3–5.

Ryan, C. (1998) The Travel Career Ladder: An appraisal. *Annals of Tourism Research* 25 (1), 936–57.

Ryan, C. (1999) Sex tourism: Paradigms of confusion? In S. Clift and S. Carter (eds) *Tourism and Sex: Culture, Commerce and Coercion* (pp. 23–40). London: Cassell.

Ryan, C. (2002a) Stages, gazes and constructions of tourism. In C. Ryan (ed.) *The Tourist Experience* (2nd edn; pp. 1–26). London: Continuum.

Ryan, C. (2002b) Motives, behaviours, body and mind. In C. Ryan (ed.) *The Tourist Experience* (2nd edn; pp. 27–57). London: Continuum.

Ryan, C. (2003) *Recreational Tourism: Demand and Impacts.* Clevedon: Channel View Publications.

Ryan, C. and Kinder, R. (1996) Sex, tourism and sex tourism: Fulfilling similar needs? *Tourism Management* 17 (7), 507–518.

Saarinen, J. (1998) The social construction of tourist destinations: The process of transformation of the Saariselka tourism region in Finnish Lapland. In G. Ringer (ed.) *Destinations* (pp. 154–173). London: Routledge.

Sacks, O. (1987) *The Man Who Mistook His Wife for a Hat*. London: Dockworth.

Salamone, F.A. (1997) Authenticity in tourism: The San Angel Inns. *Annals of Tourism Research* 24 (2), 305–321.

Saltzer, R. (2002) Understanding visitor–wildlife interactions Kangaroo Island: Data summary report. Townsville: Tourism Program, James Cook University.

Scarinci, J.L. (1997) The bed & breakfast sector: Market trends and distribution channels. Unpublished doctoral dissertation, James Cook University, Townsville.

Schneider, I.E. and Hammitt, W.E. (1995) Visitor response to outdoor recreation conflict: A conceptual approach. *Leisure Sciences* 17, 223–234.

Schofield, P. (2000) Deciphering day-trip destination choice using a tourist expectation/satisfaction construct. In A. Woodside, G. Crouch, J. Mazanec, M. Oppermann and M. Sakai (eds) *Consumer Psychology of Tourism, Hospitality and Leisure* (pp. 269–294). Wallingford: CABI.

Schon, D.A. (1987) *Educating the Reflective Practitioner*. London: Jossey-Bass.

Schonland, A. and William, P.W. (1996) Using the Internet for travel and tourism survey research: Experiences from the Net Traveler Survey. *Journal of Travel Research* 35 (2), 81–87.

Schutte, H. and Carlante, D. (1998) *Consumer Behaviour in Asia*. London: MacMillan.

Seaton, A.V. (1994) Are relatives friends? Re-assessing the VFR category in segmenting tourism markets. In A.V. Seaton (ed.) *Tourism: The State of The Art* (pp. 316–321). Chichester: John Wiley & Sons.

Seaton, A.V. (1996) Blowing the whistle on tourism referees. *Tourism Management* 17, 397–399.

Seaton, A.V. (1997) Unobtrusive observational measurements as a qualitative extension of visitor surveys at festivals and events: Mass observation revisited. *Journal of Travel Research* 3 (4), 25–30.

Seaton, A.V. and Tagg, S. (1995) Disaggregating friends and relatives in VFR tourism research: The Northern Ireland evidence 1991–1993. *Journal of Tourism Studies* 6 (1), 6–18.

Secord, P. and Backman, C. (1964) *Social Psychology*. New York: McGraw-Hill.

Selanniemi, T. (2003) On holiday in the liminoid playground: Place time and self in tourism. In T. Bauer and R. McKercher (eds) *Sex and Tourism: Journeys of Romance, Love and Lust* (pp. 19–34). Binghampton, Haworth.

Selwyn, T. (2000) Host and guest. In J. Jafari (ed.) *Encyclopedia of Tourism* (pp. 286–288). London: Routledge.

Shackley, M. (1996) *Wildlife Tourism*. London: International Thompson Business Press.

Sharma, P., Carson, D. and Delacy, T. (2000) National online tourism policy initiatives for Australia. *Journal of Travel Research* 39 (2), 157–162.

Shelby, B. (1981) Encounter norms in back country settings: Studies of three rivers. *Journal of Leisure Research* 13 (2), 129–138.

Sheridan, G. (1999) *Asian Values, Western Dreams*. Sydney: Allen and Unwin.

Shoemaker, S. (1989) Segmenting the US travel market according to benefits realized. *Journal of Travel Research* 28 (Winter), 8–21.

Shoham, A. and Dalakas, V. (2003) Family consumer decision making in Israel: The role of teens and parents. *Journal of Consumer Marketing* 20 (3), 238–252.

Silver, A. (1993) Marketing authenticity in Third World countries. *Annals of Tourism Research* 20 (2) 302–318.

Simmel, G. (1950) *The Sociology of Georg Simmel* (H. Woolf, trans.). New York: Free Press of Glencoe.

Simmel, G. (1971) *On Individuality and Social Forms* (D. Levine, ed.). Chicago: University of Chicago Press (first published 1908).

Simmons, D. (2000) Recreation. In J. Jafari (ed.) *Encyclopedia of Tourism* (pp. 488–490). London: Routledge.

Singh, S., Timothy, D. and Dowling, R.K. (eds) (2003) *Tourism in Destination Communities*. Wallingford: CABI Publishing.

Small, J. (2002) Good and bad holiday experiences: Women's and girl's perspectives. In M.B. Swain and J.H. Momsen (eds) *Gender/Tourism/Fun(?)* (pp. 24–38). New York: Cognizant Communication Corporation.

Small, J. (2003) Voices of older women tourists. *Tourism Recreation Research* 28 (2), 31–39.

Smith, S. and Godbey, G. (1991) Leisure, recreation and tourism. *Annals of Tourism Research* 18 (1), 85–100.

Smith, S. and Mannell, R. (2000) Leisure. In J. Jafari (ed.) *Encyclopedia of Tourism* (pp. 354–356). London: Routledge.

Smith, S.L.J. (1995) *Tourism Analysis: A Handbook*. Harlow Essex: Longman.

Smith, V. (1992) Introduction: The quest in guest. *Annals of Tourism Research* 19, 1–17.

Smith, V.L. (ed.) (1978) *Hosts and Guests*. Oxford: Blackwell.

Sommer, R. (1978) *The Mind's Eye: Imagery in Everyday Life*. New York: Delacorte Press.

Son, A. (2004) International students and their destination images and travel behaviours. Unpublished doctoral dissertation, James Cook University, Townsville.

Son, A. and Pearce, P.L. (2003) Overseas students' image of Australian cities: Applying a sketch map methodology. In Jae-Kyoon Jun (ed.) *Second Asia Pacific Forum for Graduate Students Research in Tourism* (pp. 154–169). Conference proceedings 2–4 October, Busan, Korea. Korea: The Korea Academic Society of Tourism & Leisure.

Sorensen, A. (2003) Backpacker ethnography. *Annals of Tourism Research* 30 (4), 847–867.

South Australian Department of Tourism (1984) tourism development and management on Kangaroo Island. Working party report. Adelaide: South Australian Department of Tourism.

Southworth, M. (1969) The sonic environment of cities. *Environment and Behavior* 1 (1), 49–70.

Spotts, D.M. and Mahoney, E.M. (1991) Segmenting visitors to a destination region based on the volume of their expenditures. *Journal of Travel Research* 29 (4), 24–31.

SPSS Inc. (1999) *SPSS 10.0 User's Guide*. New York: SPSS Inc.

Stebbins, R.A. (1982) Serious leisure: A conceptual statement. *Pacific Sociological Review* 25, 251–272.

Stebbins, R.A. (1992) *Amateurs, Professionals and Serious Leisure*. Montreal: McGill-Queens University Press.

Stephenson, M.L. and Hughes, H.L. (1995) Holidays and the UK Afro-Caribbean community. *Tourism Management* 16 (6), 429–436.

Stewart, E.J., Hayward, S.M. and Devlin, P.J. (1998) The 'place' of interpretation: A new approach to the evaluation of interpretation. *Tourism Management* 19 (3), 257–266.

Stewart, S.I. and Vogt, C.A. (1997) Multi-destination trip patterns. *Annals of Tourism Research* 24 (2), 458–460.

Stewart, W.P. and Hull IV, R.B. (1996) Capturing the moment: Concerns of the in situ leisure research. *Journal of Travel and Tourism Marketing* 5 (1/2), 3–20.

Strauss, A. and Corbin, J. (1990) Basics of Qualitative Research: Grounded Theory and Procedures and Techniques. Newbury Park, CA: Sage.

Stringer, P. (1984) Social psychology and tourism. *Annals of Tourism Research* 11 (1), whole issue.

Swain, M.B. (1995) Gender and tourism. *Annals of Tourism Research* 22 (2), 247–266.

Swain, M.B. (2002) Gender/Tourism/Fun(?): An introduction. In M.B. Swain and J. H. Momsen (eds) *Gender/Tourism/Fun(?)* (pp. 15–23). New York: Cognizant Communication Corporation.

Swain, M.B. and Momsen, J.H. (eds) (2002) *Gender/Tourism/Fun(?)*. New York: Cognizant Communication Corporation.

Swan, J.E. and Combs, L.J. (1976) Product performance and consumer satisfaction: A new concept. *Journal of Marketing* 40, 25–33.

Swarbrooke, J. (1999a) *Sustainable Tourism*. Wallingford. CABI.

Swarbrooke, J. (1999b) *Development and Management of Visitor Attractions* (2nd edn). Oxford: Butterworth Heinemann.

Sykes, B. (2001) *The Seven Daughters of Eve*. London: Bantam Press.

Tajfel, H. (1981) *Human Groups and Social Categories*. Cambridge: Cambridge University Press.

Tapachai, N. and Waryszak, R. (2000) An examination of the role of beneficial image in tourist destination selection. *Journal of Travel Research* 39 (1), 37-44.

Tan, C.E., McLaughlin, W.J. and Grussing, L. (1992) Using an agency-outfitter partnership to provide information services: An evaluation on the Lower Salmon River in Idaho. *Journal of Environmental Management* 36, 55–68.

Taylor, J.P. (2001) Authenticity and sincerity in tourism. *Annals of Tourism Research* 28 (1), 7–26.

Teas, R.K. (1993) Consumer expectations and the measurement of perceived service quality. *Journal of Professional Services Marketing* 8 (2), 33–53.

Teye, V. and Leclerc, D. (2003) The white Caucasian and ethnic minority cruise markets: Some motivational perspectives. *Journal of Vacation Marketing* 9 (3), 227–242.

Thornton, P., Shaw, G. and Williams, A. (1997) Tourist group holiday decision-making and behaviour: The influence of children. *Tourism Management* 18 (5), 287–297.

Tierney, P. (2000) Internet-based evaluation of tourism web site effectiveness: Methodological issues and survey results. *Journal of Travel Research* 39 (2), 212–219.

Tilden, F. (1977) *Interpreting Our Heritage* (3rd edn). Chapel Hill: University of North Carolina Press.

Tinsley, H.E.A. and R.A. Kass (1978) Leisure activities and need satisfaction: A replication and extension. *Journal of Leisure Research* 10, 191–202.

Tinsley, H.E.A. and R.A. Kass (1979) The latent structure of the need satisfying properties of leisure activities. *Journal of Leisure Research* 11, 278–291.

Todd, S. (1999) Examining tourist motivation methodologies. *Annals of Tourism Research* 26 (4), 1022–24.

Toft, K. (2002) *The Navigators*. Potts Point, Sydney: Duffy and Snellgrove.

Tourism Queensland (2002) *Tourism Queensland News 10. Tourism Research*. Brisbane: Tourism Queensland.

Tourism South Australia (1991a) *Kangaroo Island Tourism Policy.* Adelaide: Tourism South Australia.

Tourism South Australia (1991b) *Kangaroo Island Tourism Road Evaluation.* Adelaide: Tourism South Australia.

Towner, J. (2000) History. In J. Jafari (ed.) *Encyclopedia of Tourism* (pp. 278–280). London: Routledge.

Towner, J. and Wall, G. (1991) History and tourism. *Annals of Tourism Research* 18 (1), 71–84.

Triandis, H. (1972) *The Analysis of Subjective Culture.* New York: John Wiley.

Triandis, H. (1990) Cross-cultural studies of individualism and collectivism. In J.J. Berman (ed.) *Cross Cultural Perspectives* (pp. 42–133). Lincoln, NE: University of Nebraska Press.

Triandis, H. (1994) *Culture and Social Behavior.* New York: McGraw Hill.

Triandis, H.C., Chen, X.P. and Chan, D.K-S. (1998) Scenarios for the measurement of collectivism and individualism. *Journal of Cross-Cultural Psychology* 29 (2), 275–90.

Tribe, J. (1997) The indiscipline of tourism. *Annals of Tourism Research* 24, 638–657.

Tribe, J. (2004) Knowing about tourism: Epistemological issues. In J. Phillimore and L. Goodson (eds) *Qualitative Research in Tourism* (pp. 46–62). London: Routledge.

Trompenaars, F. and Hampden-Turner, C. (1997) *Riding the Waves of Culture: Understanding Cultural Diversity in Business.* London: Brealey.

Truong, T. (1990) *Sex, Money and Morality: Prostitution and Tourism in Southeast Asia.* London: Zed Books.

Tunnell, G.B. (1977) Three dimensions of naturalness: An expanded definition of field research. *Psychological Bulletin* 84 (3), 426–437.

Turley, S.K. (2001) Children and the demand for recreational experiences: The case of zoos. *Leisure Studies* 20, 1–18.

Turner, L. and Reisinger, Y. (1999) Importance and expectations of destination attributes for Japanese tourists to Hawaii and the Gold Coast compared. *Asia Pacific Journal of Tourism Research* 4 (2), 1–18.

Turner, U. and Turner, E. (1978) *Image and Pilgrimage in Christian Culture.* New York: Columbia University Press.

Um, S. and Crompton, J.L. (1990) Attitude determinants in tourism destination choice. *Annals of Tourism Research* 17, 432–448.

Urry, J. (1990) *The Tourist Gaze: Leisure and Travel in Contemporary Societies.* London: Sage.

Uysal, M. and Jurowski, C. (1994) Testing the push and pull factors. *Annals of Tourism Research* 21, 844–846.

van Gennep, A. (1960) *The Rites of Passage.* Chicago: The University of Chicago Press (first published 1906).

van Raaij, W.F. (1986) Consumer research in tourism. *Annals of Tourism Research* 13 (1), whole issue.

Vaske, J.J., Donnelly, M.P.L., Wittmann, K. and Laidlaw, S. (1995) Interpersonal versus social conflict. *Leisure Sciences* 17, 205–222.

Veal, A.J. (1997) *Research Methods for Leisure and Tourism* (2nd edn). London: Financial Times, Prentice Hall.

Veijola, S. and Jokinen, E. (1994) The body in tourism. *Theory, Culture and Society* 11 (1), 125–151.

Verkuyten, M., Rood-Pijpers, E., Elffers, H. and Hessing, D. (1994) Rules for breaking formal rules: Social representations and everyday rule-governed behaviour. *The Journal of Psychology* 128 (5), 485–498.

Wagner, W., Kronberger, N. and Seifert, F. (2002) Collective symbolic images coping with new technology: Knowledge, images and public discourse. *British Journal of Social Psychology* 41 (3), 323–336.

Wahab, S. (2000a) Law. In J. Jafari (ed.) *Encyclopedia of Tourism* (pp. 349–350). London: Routledge.

Wahab, S. (2000b) Legal aspects. In J. Jafari (ed.) *Encyclopedia of Tourism* (pp. 352–353). London: Routledge.

Wahab, S.E. (1975) *Tourism Management*. London: Tourism International Press.

Walker, P., Greiner, R., McDonald, D. and Lyne, V. (1999) The Tourism Futures Simulator: A systems thinking approach. *Environmental Modeling and Software* 14, 59–67.

Wall, G. (2000a) Geography. In J. Jafari (ed.) *Encyclopedia of Tourism* (pp. 248–251). London: Routledge.

Wall, G. (2000b) Planning. In J. Jafari (ed.) *Encyclopedia of Tourism* (p. 438–440). London: Routledge.

Walle, A. (1997) Quantitative versus qualitative tourism research. *Annals of Tourism Research* 24 (3), 123–137.

Waller, J. and Lea, S.E.G. (1999) Seeking the real Spain? Authenticity in motivation. *Annals of Tourism Research* 26 (1), 110–129.

Walmsley, D.J. and Jenkins, J.M. (1991) Mental maps, locus of control, and activity: A study of business tourists in Coffs Harbour. *Journal of Tourism Studies* 2 (2), 36–42.

Walmsley, D.J. and Jenkins, J.M. (1992) Tourism cognitive mapping of unfamiliar environments. *Annals of Tourism Research* 19, 268–286.

Wan, C.S. (2002) The web sites of international tourist hotels and tour wholesalers in Taiwan. *Tourism Management* 23 (2), 155–160.

Wang, N. (2000) Authenticity. In J. Jafari (ed.) *Encyclopedia of Tourism* (pp. 43–45). London: Routledge.

Want, P. (2002) Trouble in Paradise: Homophobia and resistance to gay tourism. In S. Clift, M. Luongo and C. Callister (eds) *Gay Tourism: Culture Identity and Sex* (pp. 191–209). London: Continuum.

Ward C., Bochner, S., and Furnham, A. (2001) *The Psychology of Culture Shock* (2nd edn). East Sussex: Routledge.

Ward, L.M. and Russell, J.A. (1981) The psychological representation of molar physical environments. *Journal of Experimental Psychology: General* 110, 121–152.

Watson, A.E., Niccolucci, M.J. and Williams, D.R. (1994) The nature of conflict between hikers and recreational stock users in the John Muir Wilderness. *Journal of Leisure Research* 26 (4), 372–385.

Waugh, A. (1999) *Time*. London: Headline Book Publishing.

Wearing, B. (1995) Leisure and resistance in an ageing society. *Leisure Studies* 14 (4), 263–280.

Wearing, S. (2001) *Volunteer Tourism: Experiences That Make a Difference*. New York: CABI Publications.

Weber, K. (2001) Outdoor adventure tourism: A review of research approaches. *Annals of Tourism Research* 28 (2), 360–377.

Weiler, B. and Richins, H. (1995) Extreme, extravagant and elite: A profile of ecotourists on Earthwatch expeditions. *Tourism Recreation Research* 20 (1), 29–36.

West, R. (1991) *Computing for Psychologists: Statistical Analysis Using SPSS and Minitab*. Chur: Harwood Academic Publishers.

Westwood, S., Pritchard, A. and Morgan, N.J. (2000) Gender-blind marketing: Businesswomen's perceptions of airline services. *Tourism Management* 21 (4), 353–362.

Wight, P. (1996) North American ecotourism markets: Motivations, preferences and destinations. *Journal of Travel Research* 35 (1), 3–10.

Williams, J. and Lawson, R. (2001) Community issues and resident opinions of tourism. *Annals of Tourism Research* 28 (2), 269–290.

Wilson, E. (1998) *Consilience: The Unity of Knowledge.* New York: Alfred A. Knoff.

Wober, K.W. (2003) Information supply in tourism management by marketing decision support systems. *Tourism Management* 24, 241–255.

Woods, B. (1998) Animals on display: Principles for interpreting captive wildlife. *Journal of Tourism Studies* 9 (1), 28–39.

Woods, B. (2000) Beauty and the beast: Preferences for animals in Australia. *Journal of Tourism Studies* 11 (2), 25–35.

Woods, B. (2001) Wildlife tourism and the visitor experience: Flinders Chase National Park Kangaroo Island. In C. Pforr and B. Janeczko (eds) *Cauthe 2001 Capitalising on Research* (pp. 377–394). Proceedings of the Eleventh Australian Tourism and Hospitality Research Conference, 7–10 February. Canberra: University of Canberra.

Woods, B. and Moscardo, G. (1998) Researching interpretive techniques in tourism: An evaluation of the effectiveness of pictorial symbols in reef tourist education. In B. Faulkner, C. Tideswell and D. Weaver (eds) *Progress in Tourism and Hospitality Research* (pp. 320–333). Canberra: Bureau of Tourism Research.

Woods, B., Moscardo, G. and Greenwood, T. (1998) A critical review of readability and comprehensibility tests. *Journal of Tourism Studies* 9 (2), 49–61.

Woods, B.A. (2003) Examining the characteristics of wildlife tourists and their responses to Australian wildlife tourism experiences. Unpublished doctoral dissertation. Townsville: James Cook University.

Woodside, A.J. and Jacobs, L.W. (1985) Step two in benefit segmentation: Learning the benefits realised by major travel markets. *Journal of Travel Research* 24 (Summer), 7–13.

Woodside, A.G. and Lysonski, S. (1989) A general model of traveler destination choice. *Journal of Travel Research* 27 (4), 8–14.

WTO (1999) *International Tourism: A Global Perspective.* Madrid: World Tourism Organisation.

Wurman, R.S. (1989) *Information Anxiety.* New York: Doubleday.

Wurman, R.S. (1991) *San Diego Access Including Tijuana.* San Francisco: Access Press.

Wurman, R.S. (1992) *Hawaii Access.* San Francisco: Access Press.

Yagi, C. (2001) How tourists see other tourists: Analysis of online travelogues. *Journal of Tourism Studies* 12 (2), 22–31.

Yagi, C. (2003) Tourist encounters with other tourists. Unpublished doctoral dissertation, James Cook University, Townsville.

Yagi, C. and Pearce, P.L. (2002) Tourists' preferences for seeing other tourists. In *Proceedings of First Asia Pacific Forum for Graduate Students Research in Tourism, 22 May 2002, Macao* (pp. 452–466). Hong Kong: The Hong Kong Polytechnic University.

Yamamoto, D. and Gill, A.M. (1999) Emerging trends in Japanese package tourism. *Journal of Travel Research* 38, 134–143.

Yang, B.E. and Brown, T.J. (1992) A cross-cultural comparison of preferences for landscape styles and landscape elements. *Environment and Behaviour* 24 (4), 471–507.

Yau, O.H.M. and Chan, C.F. (1990) Hong Kong as a travel destination in South-East Asia: A multidimensional approach. *Tourism Management* 11 (2), 123–132.

Yiannakis, A. and Gibson, H. (1992) Roles tourists play. *Annals of Tourism Research*, 19(2), 287–303.

You, X. and O'Leary, J.T. (1999) Destination behaviour of older UK travellers. *Tourism Recreation Research* 24 (1) 23–34.

You, X. and O'Leary, J.T. (2000) Age and cohort effects: An examination of older Japanese travellers. *Journal of Travel and Tourism Marketing* 9 (1/2), 21–42.

Young, M. (1999) Cognitive maps of nature based tourists. *Annals of Tourism Research* 26, 817–839.

Yuan, S. and MacDonald, C. (1990) Motivational determinants of international pleasure time. *Journal of Travel Research* 29 (1), 42–44.

Yuan, Y., Gretze, U. and Fesenmaier, D.R. (2003) Internet technology use by American convention and visitors bureaus. *Journal of Travel Research* 41 (3), 240–255.

Zalatan, A. (1998) Wives' involvement in tourism decision processes. *Annals of Tourism Research* 25 (4), 890–904.

Zinovieff, S. (1991) Hunters and hunted: Kamaki and the ambiguities of sexual predation in a Greek town. In P. Loizos and E. Papataxiarchis (eds) *Contested Identities: Gender and Kinship in Modern Greece* (pp. 203–220). Princeton: Princeton University Press

Index

Authors

Subjects